METROPOLITAN TRANSPORT PROBLEMS AND POLICY

- Gwangju, Republic of Korea -

Metropolitan Transport Problems and Policy

- Gwangju, Republic of Korea -

First published June 2015
Written by Bonghyun Jeong (Ph.d), Chonnam National University
Publisher: Byung-Moon Jee

Cataloging-in-Publication Data
Sustainable Transport, Land Use and Information: Urban Transport Planning and Policy for Gwangju Metropolitan City, Republic of Korea
Gwangju: Chonnam National University, 1981, Korea
includes bibliographic
ISBN 978-89-6849-213-6 (93320)
Price: 20,000 Won

Published by Chonnam National University Press, 77 Yongbong-ro, Bukgu, Gwangju, Republic of Korea, 500-757
Tel: 82-62-530-0571/3, Fax: 82-62-530-0579

Printed and bound in the Republic of Korea

CIP No : CIP2015016573

METROPOLITAN TRANSPORT PROBLEMS AND POLICY

- Gwangju, Republic of Korea -

Bonghyun Jeong(Ph.D.)

CHONNAM NATIONAL UNIVERSITY PRESS

Preface

Transportation is the movement of people and goods from one location to another. Transport is important because it enables trade between people, which is essential for the development of civilizations. Transportation is arguably the backbone of urban life; without it, activities in metropolitan cities grind to a halt. Transportation is also the source of many seemingly intractable urban problems, namely, congestion, pollution, in-equality, accidents, and reliance on fossil fuels. This first edition of **Metropolitan Transport Problems and Policy** sustains the fundamental content of argument that informed the book's previous core subjects: how citizens and policy-makers conceptualize a problem informs how they go about studying and analyzing it, and analysis, in turn, informs policy formulation, decision making, and ultimately the shape of the urban transportation system itself.

The metropolitan transportation problem is no longer conceived of simply as congestion; questions of environmental management and citizen participation, among others, have been placed firmly on the mainstream transportation agenda. In this first edition, I trace out how this shift in thinking has altered the nature of urban transport planning process, changed the policy context, and enlarged the scope for citizen input.

This book is aimed at advanced undergraduates and beginning graduate students. This edition retains a basic three-part structure. The first part sets the scene by explaining basic concepts, providing overviews of passenger movements in the urban context. The second part introduces students to the public transportation systems and provides an overview of transport demand management in the urban context. In the final part, each chapter takes up a pressing policy issue-parking, safety, environment, greenway and high-speed rail. This book has a sharper focus on policy. I have achieved this altered emphasis by refocusing the contents of each chapter.

Metropolitan Transport Problems and Policy encourages students to see the links among problem formulation, research design, analytical approach and planning decisions. I hope that students can appreciate how the current metropolitan transport planning and policy can be understood in a large part as the outcome of policy choices, themselves a result of how planners, citizens, business, and elected officials have conceptualized problems, envisioned solutions, and taken action. And I hope that understanding will enable students to imagine-and actively work as-new transportation planners.

Thanks are due to many. First and foremost I thank the persons concerned of Chonnam National University (CNU), who provided me with a wonderful chance to publish this book. I am also grateful to Alan Brown, who edited the first two rounds of **Metropolitan Transport Problems and Policy**. Finally I would like to express my thanks to graduates under my supervision and fellow professors in CNU. I would like to dedicate this book to my wife, J. Han and to my son, E. Jeong.

I will give thanks to the Lord because of His righteousness and will sing praise to the name of the Lord Most High.

Bonghyun Jeong

List of Abbreviations

CBD	Central Business District
CNU	Chonnam National University
GDI	Gwangju Development Institute
GMC	Gwangju Metropolitan City
GMG	Gwangju Metropolitan Government
GMRTC	Gwangju Metropolitan Rapid Transit Corporation
HSR	High Speed Rail
Korail	Korea Railroad
KOTI	Korea Transport Institute
KR	Korea Rail Network Authority
KTX	Korean Train Express
MLTM	Ministry of Land, Transport and Maritime Affairs
MOLIT	Ministry of Land, Infrastructure and Transport
PBS	Public Bike-sharing System
SCG	Seoul City Government
SUTP	Sustainable Urban Transport Policy
TDM	Transport Demand Management
TIF	Transportation Impact Fee
TSM	Transportation System Management

Contents

Chapter 02 Development and Transport Problems of Gwangju

Chapter 03 Bus Transit Problems and Policy

Chapter 05 Transport Demand Management Policy

Chapter 06 Urban Parking Problems and Policy

Chapter 07 Road Traffic Accidents and Safety Policy

Chapter 09 Sustainable Transport Problems and Policy

Chapter 10 Greenway Planning and Policy

Chapter 11 High Speed Rail and Transport Policy

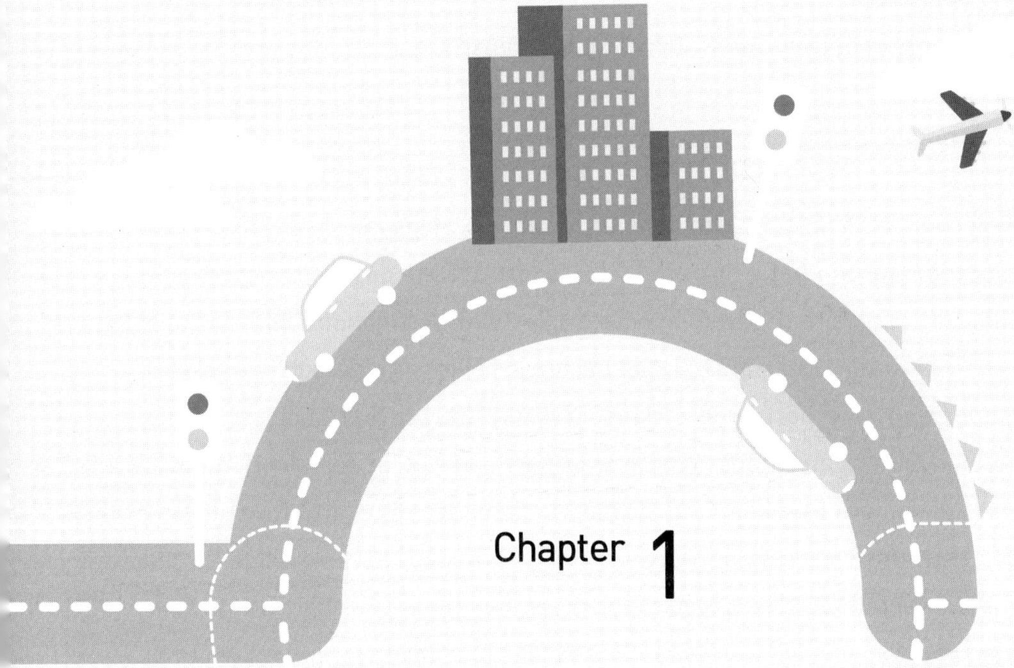

Chapter 1

The Context of Urban Transport

1. Transportation and Transport Mode

1.1. Concept of Urban Transportation

Transport or transportation is the movement of people and goods from one location to another. The urban transport system provides access and mobility for people and goods, linking origins and destinations both internal and external to the urban area. It has many elements, such as public transport, non-motorized transport (pedestrians, cyclists), freight and business traffic, and motorized private traffic.[1] These transport services in combination cover a range of important social and economic activities. The activities include leisure trips, business journeys, commuting, shopping, trips to schools, and freight transportation. The targeted objectives for urban transport are to fulfil the demand for accessibility with an efficient and quality service, while at the same time promoting sustainable patterns and levels of traffic that take account of economic, social, environmental and safety concerns.

Modes of urban transport include urban rail, road and space. The field can be divided into infrastructure, vehicles and operation.[2] Transport is important since it enables trade between peoples, which is in turn essential for the development of civilizations. Infrastructure is basic physical and organizational structures needed for the operation of a society or enterprise, or the services and facilities necessary for an economy to function. Urban transportation infrastructure include road and highway networks, mass transit systems, railways, bicycle paths and pedestrian walkways. Urban transport infrastructure consists of the fixed installations necessary for transport, and may be roads, railways, terminals (railway stations, bus stations, trucking terminals), bicycle paths, and pedestrian walkways. Terminals can be used both for the interchange of passengers and cargo and for maintenance.

---

[1] EU(2001), pp.11-12.

[2] Source: http://en.wikipedia.org/wiki/Transport

A vehicle is a device that is designed and used to transport people or cargo. Vehicles travelling on these networks are manufactured, and may include automobiles, bicycles, buses, trains, and trucks. Operations deal with the way the vehicles are operated, and the procedures set for this purpose including financing, legalities and policies. In the urban transport industry, operations and ownership of infrastructure can be either public or private, depending the country and mode.

Passenger transport may be public, where operators provide scheduled services, or private. Freight transport has become focused on containerization, although bulk transport is used for large volumes of durable items. Transport plays an important part in economic growth and globalization, but most types cause air pollution and use large amounts of land. While it is heavily subsidized by governments, good planning of transport is essential to make traffic flow, and restrain urban sprawl.

Table 1.1. Elements of Urban Transportation

Elements	Detailed contents
Infrastructure	■ Road and highway networks, mass transit systems ■ Railways, bicycle paths, pedestrian walkways
Vehicles	■ Automobiles, bicycles, buses, trains, trucks
Operations	■ Way, financing, legalities, policies

Source: http://en.wikipedia.org/wiki/Transport

1.2. Urban Transport Mode

A mode of transport is a solution that makes use of a particular type of vehicle, infrastructure and operation. The transport of a person or of cargo may involve one mode, or several modes, with the latter case being called intermodal or multimodal transport. Each mode has its advantages and disadvantages, and will be chosen on the basis of cost, capability, route, and speed.

Major urban transport modes consist of road transport and rail transport. A road is an identifiable route, way, or path between two or more places. Roads are typically smoothed, paved, or otherwise prepared to allow easy travel. In urban areas, roads may pass through a city or village and be named as streets, serving a dual function as urban space easement and route. The most common road vehicle is the automobile; a wheeled passenger vehicle that carries its own motor. Other users of roads include buses, trucks, motorcycles, bicycles and pedestrians.

Automobiles offer high flexibility and with low capacity, but are high energy and area users, and are the main source of noise and air pollution in cities; buses allow for more efficient travel at the cost of reduced flexibility. Road transport by truck is often the initial and final stage of freight transport.

Rail transport is where a train runs along a set of two parallel steel rails, known as a railway or railroad. Alternative methods include monorail and maglev. A train consists of one or more connected vehicles that run on the rails. Some or all the cars can be powered, known as a multiple unit. Railed vehicles move with much less friction than rubber tires on paved roads, making trains more energy efficient, though not as efficient as ships. Intercity trains are long-haul services connecting cities; modern high-speed rail is capable of speeds up to 350 km/h (220 mph), but this requires specially built track. Regional and commuter trains feed cities from suburbs and surrounding areas, while intra-urban transport is performed by high-capacity tramways and rapid transits, often making up the backbone of a city's public transport. Freight trains traditionally used box cars, requiring manual loading and unloading of the cargo.

2. Function of Urban Transport

2.1. Passenger Transport

Passenger transport, or travel, is divided into public and private transport.

Public is scheduled services on fixed routes, while private is vehicles that provide ad hoc services at the riders' desire. The latter offers better flexibility, but has lower capacity, and a higher environmental impact. Travel may be as part of daily commuting, for business, leisure or migration.

Short-haul transport is dominated by the automobile and mass transit. The latter consists of buses in rural areas and small cities, supplemented with commuter rail, trams and rapid transit in larger cities. Long-haul transport involves the use of the automobile, trains, coaches and aircraft, the last of which have become predominantly used for the longest, including intercontinental, travel. Intermodal passenger transport is where a journey is performed through the use of several modes of transport; since all human transport normally starts and ends with walking, all passenger transport can be considered intermodal. Public transport may also involve the intermediate change of vehicle, within or across modes, at a transport hub, such as a bus or railway station. Taxis and buses can be found on opposite ends of the Public Transport spectrum. Whereas buses remain the cheaper mode of transport but are not necessarily flexible, taxis are very flexible but more expensive.

2.2. Freight Transport

Freight transport or shipping is a key in the value chain in manufacturing. With increased specialization and globalization, production is being located further away from consumption, rapidly increasing the demand for transport. While all modes of transport are used for cargo transport, there is high differentiation between the nature of the cargo transport, in which mode is chosen. Logistics refers to the entire process of transferring products from producer to consumer, including storage, transport, transshipment, warehousing, material-handling and packaging, with associated exchange of information. In deals with the handling of payment and responsibility of risk during transport. Traditionally, all cargo had to be manually loaded and unloaded into the haul of any ship or car; containerization allows for automated handling and transfer between modes, and standardized sizes allow for gains in economy of scale in vehicle operation. This has been one of the key driving factors in international trade and globalization since the 1950s.

Bulk transport is common with cargo that can be handled roughly without deterioration; typical examples are ore, coal, cereals and petroleum. Because of the uniformity of the product, mechanical handling can allow enormous quantities to be handled quickly and efficiently. The low value of the cargo combined with high volume also means that economies of scale become essential in transport, and gigantic ships and whole trains are commonly used to transport bulk.

Air freight has become more common for products of high value; while less than one percent of world transport by volume is by airline, it amounts to forty % of the value. Time has become especially important in regards to principles such as postponement and just-in-time within the value chain, resulting in a high willingness to pay for quick delivery of key components or items of high value-to-weight ratio.

Table 1.2. Function of Urban Transportation

Functions	Detailed contents
Passenger transport	■ Public transport - scheduled service on fixed routes; private transport - provide ad hoc services at ride desire. ■ Short-haul transport - dominated by automobile and mass transit (buses, commuter rail, trams and rapid transit) ■ Long-haul transport - automobile, trains, coaches and aircraft ■ Intermodal passenger transport - performed through the use of several modes of transport
Freight transport	■ A key in the value chain in manufacturing ■ Containerization - automated handling and transfer between modes; standardized sizes - gains in economy of scale ■ Bulk transport - handled roughly without deterioration, mechanical handling, economies of scale ■ Air freight - common for products of high value, postponement and just-in-time

3. Impact of Urban Transport

3.1. Economic

Transport is a key component of growth and globalization, such as in Gwangju or Seoul, Republic of Korea. Transport is a key necessity for specialization — allowing production and consumption of products to occur at different locations. Transport has, throughout history, spurred to expansion; better transport allows more trade and a greater spread of people. Economic growth has always been dependent on increasing the capacity and rationality of transport. But the infrastructure and operation of transport has a great impact on the land and is the largest drainer of energy, making transport sustainability a major issue.

Modern society dictates a physical distinction between home and work, forcing people to transport themselves to places of work or study, as well as to temporarily relocate for other daily activities. Passenger transport is also the essence of tourism, a major part of recreational transport. Commerce requires the transport of people to conduct business, either to allow face-to-face communication for important decisions or to move specialists from their regular place of work to sites where they are needed.

3.2. Planning

Transport planning allows for high utilization and less impact regarding new infrastructure. Using models of transport forecasting, planners are able to predict future transport patterns. On the operative level, logistics allows owners of cargo to plan transport as part of the supply chain. Transport as a field is studied through transport economics, the backbone for the creation of regulation policy by authorities. Transport engineering and a sub-discipline of civil engineering must take into account trip generation, trip distribution, mode choice and route assignment, while the operative level is handled through traffic engineering.

The engineering of roundabout in the United Kingdom attempts to make traffic flow free-moving. Because of the negative impacts made, transport often becomes the subject of controversy, related to choice of mode, as well as increased capacity. Automotive transport can be seen as a tragedy of the commons, where the flexibility and comfort for the individual deteriorate the natural and urban environment for all. Density of development depends on mode of transport, with public transport allowing for better spacial utilization. Good land use keeps common activities close to peoples homes and places higher-density development closer to transport routes and hubs; minimizing the need for transport. There are economies of agglomeration. Beyond transportation some land uses are more efficient when clustered. Transportation facilities consume land, and in cities, pavement (devoted to streets and parking) can easily exceed 20 % of the total land use. An efficient transport system can reduce land waste.

Too much infrastructure and too much smoothing for maximum vehicle throughput means that in many cities, there is too much traffic and many—if not all—of the negative impacts that come with it. It is only in recent years that traditional practices have started to be questioned in many places, and as a result of new types of analysis which bring in a much broader range of skills than those traditionally relied on—spanning such areas as environmental impact analysis and public health, sociologists as well as economists, are increasingly questioning the viability of the old mobility solutions. European cities are leading this transition.

3.3. Environment

Traffic congestion persists in São Paulo, Brazil despite the no-drive days based on license numbers. Transport is a major use of energy, and burns most of the world's petroleum. This creates air pollution, including nitrous oxides and particulate, and is a significant contributor to global warming through emission of carbon dioxide, for which transport is the fastest-growing emission sector. By sub-sector, road transport is the largest contributor to global warming. Environmental regulations in developed countries have reduced the emissions of individual vehicles; however, this has been offset by an increase in the number of vehicles, and more use of each vehicle. Some pathways to the considerable reduction of carbon emissions of road vehicles have been studied. Energy use and emissions vary largely between modes, causing environmentalists to call for a transition from air and road to rail and human-powered transport, and increased transport electrification and energy efficiency.

Other environmental impacts of transport systems include traffic congestion and automobile-oriented urban sprawl, which can consume natural habitat and agricultural lands. By reducing transportation emissions globally, it is predicted that there will be significant positive effects on the Earth's air quality, acid rain, smog and climate change.

Table 1.3. Impact of Urban Transportation

Impact	Detailed contents
Economic	▪ Transport - a key component of growth, a key necessity for specialization, and a spur to expansion ▪ Economic growth - dependent on increasing the capacity and rationality of transport ▪ Passenger transport - a essence of tourism and a major part of recreational transport
Planning	▪ Transport planning - allows for high utilization and less impact of new infrastructure, ▪ Transport engineering, density of development, efficient transport system, transport demand forecasting ▪ Considering environments, public health, and economics, etc.
Environment	▪ Transport - a major use of energy, a significant contributor to global warming, and creating air pollution ▪ Traffic congestion and automobile-oriented urban sprawl

4. Urban Transport Problems[3]

4.1. Challenges Facing Urban Transportation

Cities are locations which have a high level of accumulation and concentration of economic activities and are complex spatial structures that are supported by transport systems. The most important transport problems are often related to urban areas and take place when transport systems, for a variety of reasons, cannot satisfy the numerous requirements of urban mobility. Urban productivity is highly dependent on the efficiency of its transport system to move labor, consumers and freight between multiple origins and destinations. Additionally, important transport terminals such as ports, airports, and railyards are located within urban areas, contributing to a specific array of problems. Some problems are ancient, like congestion, while others are new like urban freight distribution or environmental impacts. Among the most notable urban transport problems are:

Traffic Congestion and Parking Difficulties

Congestion is one of the most prevalent transport problems in large urban agglomerations, usually above a threshold of about 1 million inhabitants. It is particularly linked with motorization and the diffusion of the automobile, which has increased the demand for transport infrastructures. However, the supply of infrastructures has often not been able to keep up with the growth of mobility. Since vehicles spend the majority of the time parked, motorization has expanded the demand for parking space, which has created space consumption problems, particularly in central areas; the spatial imprint of parked vehicles is significant.

[3] http://people.hofstra.edu/geotrans/eng/ch6en/conc6en/ch6c4en.html

Longer Commuting

On par with congestion, people are spending an increasing amount of time commuting between their residence and workplace. An important factor behind this trend is related to residential affordability as housing located further away from central areas (where most of the employment remains) is more affordable. Therefore, commuters are trading time for housing affordability. However, long commuting is linked with several social problems, such as isolation, as well as poorer health (obesity).

Public Transport Inadequacy

Many public transit systems, or parts of them, are either over or under used. During peak hours, crowdedness creates discomfort for users as the system copes with a temporary surge in demand. Low ridership makes many services financially unsustainable, particularly in suburban areas. In spite of significant subsidies and cross-financing (e.g. tolls) almost every public transit system cannot generate sufficient income to cover its operating and capital costs. While in the past deficits were deemed acceptable because of the essential service public transit was providing for urban mobility, its financial burden is increasingly controversial.

Difficulties for Non-motorized Transport

These difficulties are either the outcome of intense traffic, where the mobility of pedestrians, bicycles and vehicles is impaired, or because of a blatant lack of consideration for pedestrians and bicycles in the physical design of infrastructures and facilities.

Loss of Public Space

The majority of roads are publicly owned and free of access. Increased traffic has adverse impacts on public activities which once crowded the streets such as markets, agoras, parades and processions, games, and community interactions. These have gradually disappeared to be replaced by automobiles. In many cases, these activities have shifted to shopping malls while in other cases, they have been abandoned altogether. Traffic flows influence the life and interactions of residents and their usage of street space. More traffic impedes social interactions and street activities. People tend to walk and cycle less when traffic is high.

Environmental Impacts and Energy Consumption

Pollution, including noise, generated by circulation has become a serious impediment to the quality of life and even the health of urban populations. Furthermore, energy consumption by urban transportation has dramatically increased and so has the dependency on petroleum. Yet, peak oil considerations are increasingly linked with peak mobility expectations where high energy prices incite a shift towards more efficient and sustainable forms of urban transportation, namely public transit

Accidents and Land Consumption

Growing traffic in urban areas is linked with a growing number of accidents and fatalities, especially in developing countries. Accidents account for a significant share of recurring delays. As traffic increases, people feel less safe to use the streets.

The territorial imprint of transportation is significant, particularly for the automobile. Between 30% and 60% of a metropolitan area may be devoted to transportation, an outcome of the over-reliance on some forms of urban transportation. Yet, this land consumption also underlines the strategic importance of transportation in the economic and social welfare of cities.

Freight distribution

Globalization and the materialization of the economy have resulted in growing quantities of freight moving within cities. As freight traffic commonly shares infrastructures with the circulation of passengers, the mobility of freight in urban areas has become increasingly problematic. City logistics strategies can be established to mitigate the variety of challenges faced by urban freight distribution.

Many dimensions to the urban transport problem are linked with the dominance of the automobile.

Table 1.4. Challenges Facing Urban Transportation

Challenges	Detailed contents
Traffic congestion / Parking difficulties	■ Linked with motorization and the diffusion of the automobile. ■ The supply of infrastructures doesn't keep up with the growth of mobility.
Longer commuting	■ Related to residential affordability ■ Housing located further away from central areas
Public transport inadequacy	■ Crowdedness during peak hours, low ridership in suburban areas ■ Insufficient income, deficits increase
Difficulties for non-motorized transport	■ Blatant lack of consideration for pedestrains and bicycles ■ Outcome of intense traffic in urban areas
Loss of public space	■ Increased traffic has adverse impacts on public activities. ■ Disappeared to be replaced by automobiles.
Environmental impacts	■ Pollution and noise become a serious impediment to the quality of life and the health of urban populations.
Accidents / Land consumption	■ Growing traffic in urban areas is linked with a growing number of accidents and fatalities ■ Between 30 and 60% of a metropolitan area may be devoted to transportation
Freight distribution	■ The mobility of freight in urban areas becomes increasingly problematic.

4.2. Automobile Dependency

Major Factors

Automobile use is obviously related to a variety of advantages such as on demand mobility, comfort, status, speed, and convenience. These advantages jointly illustrate why automobile ownership continues to grow in urban areas. When given the choice and the opportunity, most individuals will prefer using an automobile. Several factors influence the growth of the total vehicle fleet, such as sustained economic growth (increase in income and quality of life), complex individual urban movement patterns (many households have more than one automobile), more leisure time and suburbanization. Therefore, rising automobile mobility can be perceived as a positive consequence of economic development. The acute growth in the total number of vehicles also gives rise to congestion at peak traffic hours on major thoroughfares, in business districts, and often throughout the metropolitan area.

Metropolitan cities are important generators and attractors of movements, which have created a set of geographical paradoxes that are self-reinforcing. For instance, specialization leads to additional transport demands while agglomeration leads to congestion. Over time, a state of automobile dependency has emerged which results in a diminution in the role of other modes, thereby limiting still further alternatives to urban mobility. In addition to the factors contributing to the growth of driving, two major factors contributing to automobile dependency are:

Underpricing and Consumer Choices

Most road infrastructures are subsidized as they are considered a public service. Consequently, drivers do not bear the full cost of automobile use. When a resource is free of access (road), it tends to be overused and abused (congestion). This is reflected in consumer choice, where automobile ownership is a symbol of status, freedom and prestige, especially in developing countries. Single home ownership also reinforces automobile dependency.

Planning and Investment Practices

Planning and the ensuing allocation of public funds aim towards improving road and parking facilities in an ongoing attempt to avoid congestion. Other transportation alternatives tend to be disregarded. In many cases, zoning regulations impose minimum standards of road and parking services and de facto impose a regulated automobile dependency.

Levels of Automobile Dependency

There are several levels of automobile dependency, ranging from low to acute, with their corresponding land use patterns and alternatives to mobility. Among the most relevant indicators of automobile dependency are the level of vehicle ownership, per capita motor vehicle mileage and the proportion of total commuting trips made using an automobile. A situation of high automobile dependency is reached when more than three quarters of commuting trips are done using the automobile. Automobile dependency is served by a cultural and commercial system promoting the automobile as a symbol of status and personal freedom, namely through intense advertising and enticements to purchase new automobiles. Not surprisingly, Korea has perceived motorization as a condition for development. Even though the term automobile dependency is often negatively perceived and favored by market distortions such as the provision of roads, its outcome reflects the choice of individuals who see the automobile more as an advantage than an inconvenience.

The second half of the 20th century saw the adaptation of many cities in North America and Europe to automobile circulation. Motorized transportation was seen as a powerful symbol of modernity and development.

Highways were constructed, streets were enlarged, and parking lots were set often disrupting the existing urban fabric with the creation of motorized cities. However, from the 1980s, motorization started to be seen more negatively and several cities implemented policies to limit automobile circulation, at least in specific areas, by a set of strategies including:

Dissuasion

Although automobile circulation is permitted, it is impeded by regulations and physical planning. For instance, parking space can be severely limited and speed bumps placed to force speed reduction.

Prohibition of Downtown Circulation

During most of the day the downtown area is closed to automobile circulation but deliveries are permitted during the night. Such strategies are often undertaken to protect the character and the physical infrastructures of an historical city. They do however, like most policies, have unintended consequences. If mobility is restrained in certain locations or during certain time periods, people will simply go elsewhere (longer movements) or defer their mobility for another time (more movements).

Tolls

Imposing tolls for parking and entry (congestion pricing) to some parts of the city has been a strategy being considered seriously in many areas it confers the potential advantage of congestion mitigation and revenue generation. Most evidence underlines however that drivers are willing to bear additional toll costs, especially for commuting since it is linked with their main income.

Tentative solutions have been put forth such as transport planning measures (synchronized traffic lights, regulated parking), limited vehicle traffic in selected areas, the promotion of bicycle paths, and public transit. In Mexico City, vehicle use is prohibited according to license plate numbers and the date (even-uneven). Affluent families have solved this issue by purchasing a second vehicle, thus worsening the existing situation. Singapore is the only country in the world which has successfully controlled the amount and growth rate of its vehicle fleet by imposing a heavy tax burden and purchasing permits on automobile owners. Such a command-based approach is unlikely to be possible on other contexts.

There is a growing body of evidence underlining that a peak level of car mobility is unfolding, at least in developed countries. Higher energy prices, congestion and the general aging of the population are all countervailing forces to car dependency. There are many alternatives to automobile dependency such as inter-modality (combining the advantages of individual and collective transport), car-pooling or non-motorized transportation (walking and cycling). These alternatives can only be partially implemented as the automobile remains in the short and medium terms the prime choice for providing urban mobility.

4.3. Congestion

Introduction

Congestion occurs when transport demand exceeds transport supply at a specific point in time and in a specific section of the transport system. Under such circumstances, each vehicle impairs the mobility of others. Congestion can be perceived as an unavoidable consequence of the usage of scarce transport resources, particularly if they are not priced. The last decades have seen the extension of roads in rural but particularly in urban areas, most of them free of access. Those infrastructures were designed for speed and high capacity, but the growth of urban circulation occurred at a rate higher than often expected. Investments came from diverse levels of government with a view to provide accessibility to cities and regions. There were strong incentives for the expansion of road transportation by providing high levels of transport supply. This has created a vicious circle of congestion which supports the construction of additional road capacity and automobile dependency. Urban congestion mainly concerns two domains of circulation, often sharing the same infrastructures:

Domains of Circulation

Passengers

In many regions of the world incomes have significantly increased to the point that one automobile per household or more is common. Access to an automobile conveys flexibility in terms of the choice of origin, destination and travel time. The automobile is favored at the expense of other modes for most trips, including commuting. For instance, automobiles account for the bulk of commuting trips in Korea.

Freight

Several industries have shifted their transport needs to trucking, thereby increasing the usage of road infrastructure. Since cities are the main destinations for freight flows (either for consumption or for transfer to other locations) trucking adds to further congestion in urban areas. The "last mile" problem remains particularly prevalent for freight distribution in urban areas. Congestion is commonly linked with a drop in the frequency of deliveries tying additional capacity to ensure a similar level of service.

It is important to underline that congestion in urban areas is dominantly caused by commuting patterns and little by truck movements. On average, infrastructure provision was not able to keep up with the growth in the number of vehicles, even more with the total number of vehicle-km. During infrastructure improvement and construction, capacity impairment (fewer available lanes, closed sections, etc.) favors congestion. Important travel delays occur when the capacity limit is reached or exceeded, which is the case of almost all metropolitan areas. Once a population threshold of about

1 million is reached, cities start to experience recurring congestion problems. This observation must be nuanced by numerous factors related to the urban setting, modal preferences and the quality of existing urban transport infrastructures. Still, large cities have become congested most of the day, and congestion is getting more acute. Another important consideration concerns parking, which consumes large amounts of space and provides limited economic benefit. In automobile dependent cities, this can be very constraining as each economic activity has to provide an amount of parking space proportional to their level of activity. Parking has become a land use that greatly inflates the demand for urban land.

Congestion Patterns

Urban mobility also reveals congestion patterns. Daily trips can be either "mandatory" (workplace-home) or "voluntary" (shopping, leisure, visits). The former is often performed within fixed schedules while the latter complies with variable and discretionary schedules.

Recurrent Congestion

Recurrent congestion is the consequence of factors that cause regular demand surges on the transportation system, such as commuting, shopping or weekend trips. However, even recurrent congestion can have unforeseen impacts in terms of its duration and severity. Mandatory trips are mainly responsible for the peaks in circulation flows, implying that about half the congestion in urban areas is recurring at specific times of the day and on specific segments of the transport system.

Non-recurrent Congestion

The other half of congestion is caused by random events such as accidents and unusual weather conditions (rain, snowstorms, etc.), which are unexpected and unplanned. Non-recurrent congestion is linked to the presence and effectiveness of incident response strategies. As far as accidents are concerned, their randomness is influenced by the level of traffic as the higher the traffic on specific road segments the higher the probability of accidents.

Behavioral and response time effects are also important as in a system running close to capacity, simply braking suddenly may trigger what can be known as a backward traveling wave. It implies that as vehicles are forced to stop, the bottleneck moves up the location it initially took place at, often leaving drivers puzzled about its cause. The spatial convergence of traffic causes a surcharge on transport infrastructures up to the point where congestion can lead to the total immobilization of traffic. Not only does the massive use of the automobile have an impact on traffic circulation and congestion, but it also leads to a decline in public transit efficiency when both are sharing the same roads.

Mitigating Congestion

In some areas, the automobile is the only mode for which infrastructures are provided. This implies less capacity for using alternative modes such transit, walking and cycling. At some levels of density, no public infrastructure investment can be justified in terms of economic returns. Longer commuting trips in terms of average travel time, the result of fragmented land uses, and congestion levels are a significant trend. Convergence of traffic occurs at major highways that serve vast low density areas with high levels of automobile ownership and low levels of automobile occupancy. The result is energy (fuel) wasted during congestion (additional time) and supplementary commuting distances. In automobile dependent cities, a few measures for alleviating congestion consist of ramp metering, traffic signal synchronization, incident management, carpooling, High Occupancy Vehicle (HOV) lanes, congestion pricing, better public transit services and non-motorized transportation, etc.

5. Development of and Future Changes in Korea's Urban Transport

5.1. Development of Korea's Urban Transport[4]

Advent of Modern Transport Modes

Before the 1960s, tram functioned as the most important mode of urban transport in Seoul, Korea. Entering into the 1960s, city buses ran on the streets and the use of trams decreased gradually. The tram service caused traffic congestion due to low operating speed, spoilt the beauty of the streets, and had an ever-present danger of accidents. A freeze in tram fare left little room for its improvement. Increases in labor costs and charges for exclusive use of streets resulted in the aggravation of deficits in the tram business. In 1966, Seoul City Government (SCG) had an new idea to establish a subway system in the long term to alleviate traffic congestion, then removed the trams from the streets in November 1968. Until the subway line started to operate in 1974, buses replaced trams as the main mode of public transport in Seoul. However, the increasing car traffic volume aggravated street congestion, which adversely affected the punctuality of the bus services. Air pollution, caused by the use of diesel-powered buses, emerged as a growing social concern.

City buses: Axis of Urban Transport

As the bus service in Seoul was doing brisk business before the 1960s, related laws, regulations, and institutions were established for bus service. Along with the legal arrangements, the enterprization of bus business was promoted. Its purpose was to make its size bigger, and bring business under the direct control of company management. In 1966, SCG issued a municipal

---

[4] KOTI(2012), pp.178-186.

ordinance for setting up a transport office and operated buses directly in the remote areas where private companies were reluctant to serve for fear of deficit in revenue. The total of 17 municipal buses run by Seoul city was then increased to 200.

Because of an open license policy of the Ministry of Transportation in 1968, the number of operating buses almost doubled. This created fierce competition in bus routes, and led to the operation of high-yielding routes. As the increase in passenger cars exacerbated the traffic congestion, buses ran for longer times than before and were not punctual any more. Bus users thus shifted their mode of transport to subway to be punctual. The increase of private cars resulted in a decrease of public transport demand, and also the subway-centered policy was another factor to lower the share of bus use.

Financial problems of bus operating companies came from the increase in operation costs and the decrease in revenue. Continuous cost increases in labor and fuel, and institutional regulations to prevent fare hikes pushed bus companies into financial difficulties. Under these conditions, the companies had a huge accumulated deficit and kept losing their competitiveness over the subway in terms of punctuality and speed of service. The chronic traffic congestion on main roads worsened the bus operating environment. Seoul's bus service had several problems in operation such as irregular intervals, low operating speeds, long travel times, overlapped routes, etc.

In an effort to resolve such problems, the government introduced an exclusive bus lane system, which still had limitations in improving bus speed on curb-side bus lanes. Enormous financial burdens on extending subway lines forced government officials to inevitably introduce public transport reforms centering on the bus transport system. In 2004, a quasi-public operating system for buses was introduced to make city buses play a more important role as a public service. The major contents of the reforms included the following: introduction of a quasi-public operating system for buses;

redesign of bus routes viz. hub-and-spokes network; an integrated fare structure including transfer discount; improvements of bus management systems. The evaluation of the quasi-public operating system showed that, in Seoul, Daejeon, and Daegu, subsidies for bus companies increased from two-fold to fivefold, and the increasing trend of government's financial support was expected to continue. The government's financial burden was an obstacle to the application of this system in other cities. In light of its effectiveness, survey results showed that declining bus passenger volume swung to an increase, and route efficiency and customers' satisfaction started to improve.

In Seoul, the public transport reforms boosted the number of bus passengers. The continuously declining bus transport volume from 1990 started to rise in 2004 when the reforms were implemented. The quasi-public operating system helped redesign the bus network reasonably by giving the government much more flexibility on route coordination. According to the agreements signed at the time of the introduction of the system, the bus companies were granted a revenue guarantee when they offered over a certain quality level of service. Other benefits of the bus reforms were shown by a decline in bus-related accidents and improvements of customer service.

Subway: A Major Public Transport Mode

Seoul's population has continued to increase during the past 30 years. Seoul city faced limitations in increasing transport capacity. Subway construction commenced to solve this problem in Seoul. The first subway line with a 9 km length was operated from Seoul Station to Jongno and Cheongyangni. The construction cost was jointly borne by the central government and Seoul city, and financing loans were also acquired. In 1970, SCG established the "Seoul Metropolitan Government Office of Subway Construction" then drew up a master plan of subway construction for the metropolitan and neighboring areas.

In March 1971, subway line 1 received approval from the Ministry of Construction, and the construction started on 15 sections step-by-step, and began to operate in 1974. The daily frequency of service was only 210 runs in 1974, and then increased to 526 in 1978. Even after the opening of subway line 1, the population density of Seoul was growing, naturally causing an increase in traffic demand and heavy congestion. It was thus necessary to construct more facilities. So subway lines 2, 3 and 4 were built to relieve these problems. SCG shifted its development direction for urban structure from single-nucleus to multi-nuclei. Based on the new direction, it established a "Seoul Master Plan," under which subway line 2 was revised to have a circular line connecting three nuclei including the center of northern Seoul, Youngdeungpo, and Youngdong.

The subway construction had problems such as the capacity to build underground railways, the supply of required materials, and the security of financial resources. Based on the experiences from the operation and construction of railways, the most difficult issue was to look for investment funding for the construction. In the case of subway line 2, the project cost was funded by only domestic capital. As the subway line circulated the northern and southern parts of Seoul, there were technical difficulties in crossing the Han River. This served as a motivation to develop a variety of techniques for subway construction. The networks of subway lines 3 and 4 formed an "X" shape, criss-crossing the center of Seoul, because the existing line 1 and circular line 2 were not enough to solve traffic congestion in Seoul. Also, SCG aimed to seek balanced development along the north-south and west-east axes, and to establish the backbone of public transport with subway lines. In August 1981, the Seoul Metro Subway Corporation was established and assumed responsibility for building subway lines 3 and 4.

The introduction of subways is essential to solve the traffic problems in a metropolitan city. However, it causes local governments to suffer from the deterioration of their overall financial situations. When the subway has fewer passengers than estimated, the operating deficit could exacerbate the financial situation. Recently, it was claimed that LRT (Light Rail Transit) and BRT (Bus Rapid Transit) are more reasonable, because they require less investment. Currently, LRT are operating in Seoul's neighboring cities and the Busan area, and also BRT is implemented on major arterial roads and is tending to expand its routes. Before the public transport reforms, the fare systems of bus and subway offered transfer discounts. As a part of the 2004 reforms, the Seoul government implemented an integrated fare system with free transfers permitted between bus lines and as well as subway and bus. There is no additional payment on transfer within 10 km travel distance, which encourages public transport use as a result. The fare payment, which was made possible by using wireless communications and a stored-value smartcard, allowed the introduction of such an integrated fare collection system.

Taxi: A Mode of Public Transport

Small-sized taxi operating companies had incessantly developed in the 1960s. The "Automobile Transport Service Act," enacted in 1961, promoted the development of taxi businesses into corporations and the introduction of a taxi license system. Taxi companies were developed into bigger and more organized ones, and good drivers with long experience in taxi companies were granted rights to operate private taxis as an incentive. However, private taxi licenses could be inherited, and this later became a stumbling block to reforming taxi services. In particular, while taxi license holders increased in number, the issued licenses have remained in the market permanently.

This caused the problem of an oversupply of taxi licenses. As of 2008, taxis accounted for over 9% of total traffic volume, serving as a public transport mode. Taxis still have various problems, but as a high-quality public transport mode, they play an important role in urban transport.

Motorization: Popularization of Private Passenger Cars

After the mid-1980s, the increase of national income led to the popularization of private car ownership. In 1985, the number of registered cars exceeded one million, and hit two million in 1988. Thereafter, the number of cars increased by one million every year, and recorded five million in 1992, and finally ten million at the end of 1997. The annual average growth in the number of cars from 1980 to 1990 was 20.5%, an unprecedented record in the world. In 2008, the number of registered cars amounted to 16.8 million, 74% of which, or 12.5 million, were private passenger cars.

The skyrocketing increase in the number of cars was attributed to the successful implementation of six five-year economic development plans from 1962 to 1991. Other factors contributing to the increased car numbers were the development of the domestic automobile manufacturing industry and the government's policy to promote car sales to boost the domestic market.

Driving subsidies were a typical promotion policy of the government. Another example was the "Act on Special Cases Concerning the Settlement of Traffic Accidents," which stipulates that a driver shall not receive a criminal penalty for a traffic accident if the accident does not involve the violation of ten major regulations.

The increasing number of cars, along with the modernization of the transport system, stimulated the development of other industries. It also resulted in changes in the city such as broader one-day living zones and expanded urban space. The increase of cars and transport services produced severe traffic congestion on the roads not only in the Seoul metropolitan area but also in other cities. As of 2005, the cost of traffic congestion in the nation's seven major cities amounted to 14.5 billion USD, while that of Seoul alone was 6.2 billion USD. It is alarming that traffic jams occur so frequently.

Together with traffic congestion, parking problems are also acute because they occur in the residential areas as well as in the commercial areas. The lack of parking spaces leads to reckless parking in residential areas, which lowers road capacity, blocks streets used for firefighting purposes, and creates inconvenience and friction among residents. In that sense, parking issues are emerging as a growing social problem.

As car dependency increased, the use of public transport decreased, and investment in public transport was relatively low. Also, the mobility-centered transport policy showed limitations in securing a safe environment for walking and bicycling. Even people who had short-distance trips tended to use private cars, and it was a widespread habit to use cars for shopping trips. Due to high car dependency and the unsafe transport environment, as of 2008, Korea had the highest number of traffic accidents among OECD nations. The total number of accidents in 2008 amounted to 215,822 cases, causing 5,870 deaths and 338,962 injuries. In 2008 the comprehensive cost of traffic accidents, considering human casualty cost, property damages, administrative expenses, and social costs such as pain, grief and suffering (PGS), reached 9.1 billion USD, or 1.1% of GDP. Although cars provide fast and comfortable travel, socio-economic costs are incurred in various aspects. In the coming days, the continuous increase in income level will obviously result in an increase in traffic demand of private cars. Therefore, it is expected that, without restraint on traffic demand, the quality of life and national competitiveness will not improve.

5.2. Future Changes in Urban Transport Systems

The urban transport system is likely to change in the future. The change will not be absolute or quick. There are some likely directions for change over the next 20 years.[5] First, the demand for urban transportation will grow and change. Most analysts expect the population and economies of cities to grow in the long run. In-migration will continue to cause growth in

---

[5] NLC(2013), pp.11-13.

metropolitan areas, even as some current metropolitan residents exit for smaller cities, which will also grow. Some metropolitan areas will grow geographically (suburbanize); others already have such large boundaries that their development will have a larger component of infill (urbanize). All will become more polycentric (the central city downtown will still be important, but its share of metropolitan employment will probably decrease). In that context, there will certainly be a public voice for more transportation facilities in urban areas. But, for several reasons, the composition of those facilities may change. Highways and urban railways will continue to receive the largest share of total transportation funding (though a greater share of highway money will go to maintenance), but their relative share will probably decrease as more money goes to transit, bicycle and pedestrian facilities. More attention will be given to surface-transportation connections (commuter rail) between metropolitan cities in "mega-regions."

Second, transportation demand will change with advances in telecommunications and logistics. People will be more able to do work from home. Internet purchase will consolidate shopping trips by individual consumers into deliveries to multiple consumers by service trucks. Those and related communications advances will reduce the need for travel. But many other factors (e.g., growth of population, incomes and economic activity) will encourage more travel. The net effect is likely to be growth in all measures of transportation usage unless there are big changes in market conditions (e.g., the price of fuel) or public policy (e.g., larger gas taxes, more tolling).

Third, urban transportation policy and investment will continue to become more diversified. Though roads will continue to have the biggest budget, there will be changes in the way governments spend transportation money, which will change how local governments set goals and plan their communities to meet these goals. Local governments should place increased attention on the following issues; funding, maintenance; demand management; access and connectivity; alternative modes; effect on public objectives; and performance measurement.

Securing funding for urban transportation projects will continue to be a challenge, probably an increasing one, because of the increasing backlog of maintenance, the inadequacy of central government's funds, slower economic growth, and weakened reliance on public-private partnerships. The funding pinch will hit new projects the hardest. Cities will be pressed by the public and interest groups to make do with less revenue. Local leaders must place more attention on pricing and other types of policies that change the incentives people have to be traveling in a certain place at a certain time, because of diminishing returns to new capacity. Most transportation planners now stress that transportation decision-making is more about what travelers can get to (access) than about how fast they can move (mobility). Alternative modes will be a growing share of all trips in most urban areas, but they will remain a relatively small share of all trips in all but the biggest metropolitan areas. Performance measures will increasingly address the effects of transportation facilities and programs on other non-transportation objectives. Good transportation can contribute to that quality of life, of course, but so can economic prosperity, health, education, urban design, a clean environment and so on.

A self-portrait in the newspaper

The joy of travel by train

What is the most familiar transportation method to you? Cars, planes or subways? How about trains?

When I was a child, I used to ride a train to visit my parents' hometown and I usually walked to middle school alongside the tracks with my friends. Even though I never thought I'd be working for the railroad industry, the train has unconsciously stayed in my mind.

Until the late 2000s, our country had spent a large portion of its budget on improving and building roads. During the last political administration, our government aimed to grow our economy by investing on eco-friendly technology so we could construct more railroads to increase the speed of trains.

Though the paradigm has changed into a creative economy, hopefully we can still expect some huge investments in the railroad industry. But from an economic perspective, the train is the most efficient kind of transportation in the world. So I think our government should nudge people to use the train more.

If we could make people ride trains more frequently, we could get some important benefits. We could reduce air pollution because most of our trains don't use fossil fuels. And we could reduce the social cost caused by car accidents and traffic jams. Furthermore, we could liberate people from driving in the hell of horrible traffic jams.

The problem is everyone does not share my love for railroads. People prefer driving their own cars than riding trains because the car is more convenient to directly access specific locations. Even if a train ticket is cheaper than the price of gas, people don't want to transfer several times. But if we could remedy this inconvenient situation by developing more direct routes, people would be more willing to ride the train. Then we would hand over a cleaner environment to our descendents.

According to recent statistics, Korea is ranked first in road accident fatalities among the OECD nations. On the other hand, the UIC (Union Internationale des Chemins de Fer), the international union of railways, announced that the Korean railroad was the safest railway in the world in 2012. Our country spent more than 28.5 billion won to relieve the problems caused by traffic congestion in 2010, according to 2013 statistics from the Ministry of Land, Transport and Construction.

What if we could have used that money to upgrade our railroad systems? Those funds would have made a big difference in improving the convenience and comfort of trains. There are a few improvements that could attract more passengers.

First, we should construct more railroad lines to help people get to any city. Second, we should continue developing much safer, faster and more comfortable trains like ITX (Intercity Train eXpress) and TTX (Tilting Train eXpress). Third, we should set up the terminals where people can transfer from the train to the bus or taxi in every big city — Busan, Gwangju and Daejeon. Finally, our government should subsidize train operators to give some discounts to families of four.

If we put these policies and efforts into practice, we could encourage more people to return to trains. People should be free from the wheels of stress and don't need to worry about being late again. And you could save money by travelling with your families. Most of all, you could be on the safest vehicle in the world. You can be happy, sit back, relax and enjoy the view. Train travel is the model transportation of an eco-friendly society. Koreans have to look toward the future.

There's no need to force people to use the train. Once people notice that it is more convenient, cost-effective and safer than cars, they will be willing to get on board. Koreans should realize that train travel is one of the ways to contribute to our society's development.

*** Source: The Korea Times (2014.2.25)**

References

Dickey, John W et al., Metropolitan Transportation Planning, Scripta Book Company, 1975.

European Commission (EU), Urban Transport, Thematic Synthesis of Transport Research Results, Paper 5, Transport RTD Programme, July 2001.

Edwards, John D., Jr., Transportation Planning Handbook, Second edition, Washington, DC: Institute of Transportation Engineers, 1999.

Hanson, Susan Hanson and Giuliano, Genevieve edit., The Geography of Urban Transportation, Third Edition, New York: The Guilford Press, 2004.

Homburger, Wolfgang S., Transportation and Traffic Engineering Handbook, Institute of Traffic Engineers, Washington DC., 1981.

Jeong, Bonghyun, New Transportation Policy in Regional Metropolitan City: Gwangju, Korea, CNU Press, 2005 (in Korean).

Jeong, Bonghyun, SOC and Regional Development: Standing Transportation Problems and Solutions in the Jeonlla Provinces, Korea, CNU Press, 2010 (in Korean).

Kim, Daewoong, Urban Transportation Planning, Hyungseol Publishing Co., 2006 (in Korean).

National League of Cities (NLC), Understanding Urban Transportation Systems: An Action Guide for City Leaders, Washington: Center for Research and Innovation, 2013.

OECD, Cities and Transport, Paris, 1980.

The Korea Transport Institute (KOTI), Economic Growth and Transport Models in Korea, KOTI Knowledge Sharing Report: Korea's Best Practices in the Transport Sector Issue 2, 2012.

Paddison, Ronan, Handbook of Urban Studies, SAGE Publication Ltd., 2001.

Won, Jaemu, Urban Transportation Theory, Parkyoung Publishing Co., 2009 (in Korean).

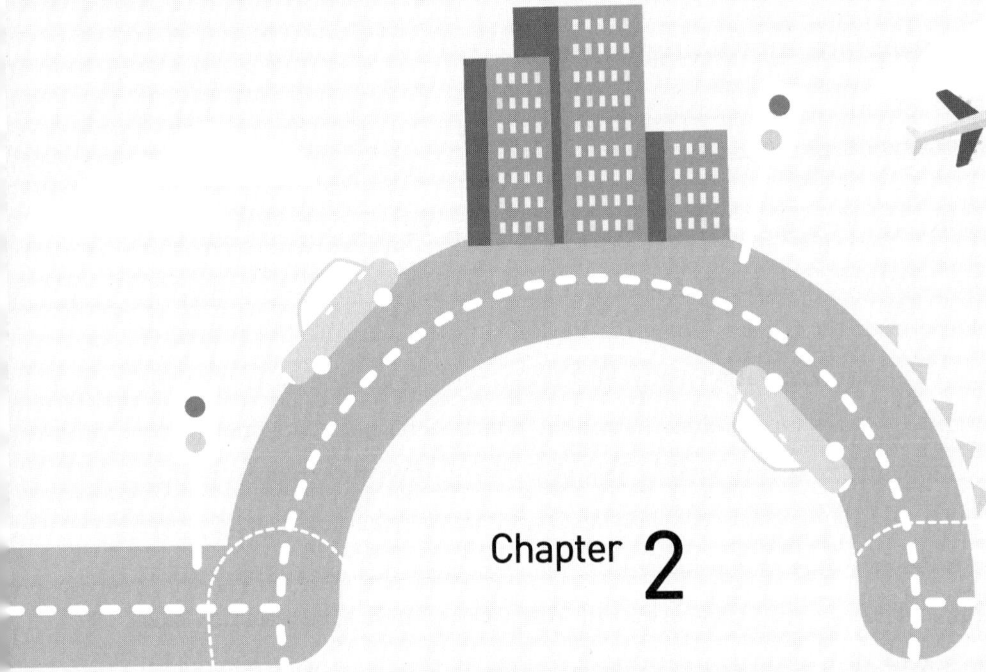

Chapter 2

Development and Transport Problems of Gwangju

1. Introduction to Gwangju City

1.1. History of Gwangju[1]

The city was established in 57 BC, and has been a major political and economic centre of Korea ever since. It was one of the administrative centres of Baekje during the Three Kingdoms Period. In 1929, during the period of Japanese rule, a confrontation between Korean and Japanese students in the city turned into a regional demonstration, which culminated in one of the major nationwide uprisings against Japanese rule during the colonial period.

Modern industry was established in Gwangju with the construction of a railway to Seoul. Some of the industries that took hold include cotton textiles, rice mills and breweries. Construction of a designated industrial zone in 1967 encouraged marked growth in industry, especially in the sectors linked to the automobile industry.

In 1986, Gwangju separated from Jeollanam-do to become a Directly Governed City (Jikhalsi), and then became a Metropolitan City (Gwangyeoksi) in 1995. It was a designated metropolitan city under the direct control of the central government's Home Minister. The city was also the capital of South Jeollanam-do until the provincial office moved to the southern village of Namak in Muan County in 2005. Gwangju (Gwangju Metropolitan City) is located in the south-western part of the Korean peninsula.

1.2. Location and Natural Environment[2]

Gwangju Metropolitan City (GMC) is located in central Honam, which is in the southwest of the Korean peninsula. Gwangju extends from Nam-gu Seungchon-dong (35°03'13" north latitude) in the south to Sanpo-myeon, and

---

1 http://en.wikipedia.org/wiki/Gwangju#History

2 http://eng.gwangju.go.kr/

Youngsan River to Buk-gu Yongkang-dong (35°15'22" north latitude) in the north. On the east side of Biseonggul, Buk-gu Chunghyo-dong forms the eastern boundary (127°00'34" east longitude) of the city. The city extends 34.3 km from east to west and 23.1 km from north to south. Gwangju borders Damyang-gun on the northeast, Jangseong-gun on the north, Hampyeong on the west, Naju city on the south, and Hwasun on the southeast. After Seoul, Busan, Daegu, Incheon, and Daejeon, it is the sixth largest city in Korea, and is the metropolitan city that represents the southwestern region. Cities located on a similar latitude are Busan and Jinhae in Korea, Tokyo in Japan, Jungsen in China, Algiers in Algeria, and Oklahoma City in the US. Seoul is located on a similar longitude.

Geographically, Gwangju is situated in the north of Jeollanam-do, centered in Jeolla-do, serving as a hub of economy, administration, education, and culture including some parts of Jeollabuk-do. Surrounding Gwangju, there has been development toward Mokpo going through agricultural areas and toward Wando in terms of the bounty of agricultural products, toward Yeosu extending to Gwangyang international container port, and toward Namwon connecting Yeongnam. Likewise, Gwangju is located in the center of the 6 directions of the Jeolla-do, providing the chance to geographically develop into the hub of Jeolla-do.

The city is located in the median latitude maritime temperate climate zone. Its climate is somewhere in between the west coast climate and the continental climate but more similar to the west coast climate which means that the city is warm and has enough rainfall. Winter is freezing and dry and summer is hot and humid. It has 4 distinct seasons. Recently, due to climate change, spring and fall have been shorter, causing characteristics of a semi-tropical climate.

Figure 2.1. Location of Gwangju City

Figure 2.2. Overall Map of Gwangju City

Map

Name	Hangul	Hanja
Gu (Districts)		
Buk-gu	북구	北區
Dong-gu	동구	東區
Gwangsan-gu	광산구	光山區
Nam-gu	남구	南區
Seo-gu	서구	西區

1.3. Origin and Symbol

Origin and Meaning

Gwang (광, hanja 光) means "light" and Ju (주, hanja 州) means "province." Areas of exquisite scenery along the outskirts of the city gave birth to gasa, a form of Korean classical poetry. Located in the center of the agricultural Jeolla region, the city is also famous for its rich and diverse cuisine. Gwangju is the 'city of light'. Light means a bright glimmer. The idea of light is our traditional faith, original spirit and basic philosophy. Gwangju is the city of the sun and light. Its citizens look to the sun and live toward the light. This spirit has been the driving force by which Gwangju citizens have overcome each difficult time and have become a leading power in history. It has been inherited as a symbol of our spirit across society.

Gwangju is regarded as a city rich in culture and art, and there are always ongoing exhibitions and performances which make the city vibrant and colorful. Every two years, the Gwangju Biennale features a two-month long contemporary art exhibition that invites international artists to display their theme based work. The Gwangju Design Biennale is staged in alternate years, when the main Biennale is not held. Gwangju continues to host the annual Gwangju Kimchi Festival, held in late fall, which promotes the varieties of delicious Korean kimchi and traditional Korean culture.

Symbol and Logo

The symbol of Gwangju takes the form of the sun and humans, the source of light and life. It represents aspirations for the world and the future. The circular shape represents the sun while the lively curves symbolize the free human spirit. The logo is in perfect harmony with the symbol of Gwangju, and serves as an important element in symbolizing the city of Gwangju. The logo was designed to make it easy to understand and convey the dependability, friendliness, warmth and security of the city government administration to viewers.

The characters of Gwangju are based on the concept of Gwangju as "the city of light." The three fairies of light, Areumi, Euiromi and Masi, who were born on January 1, personify the virtues of art, righteousness and refinement, respectively. When united, they produce a shining beam of life that represents eternal life and reflects the desire of Gwangju's citizens to light up the world in the 21st century.

Figure 2.3. Symbol and Character of Gwangju

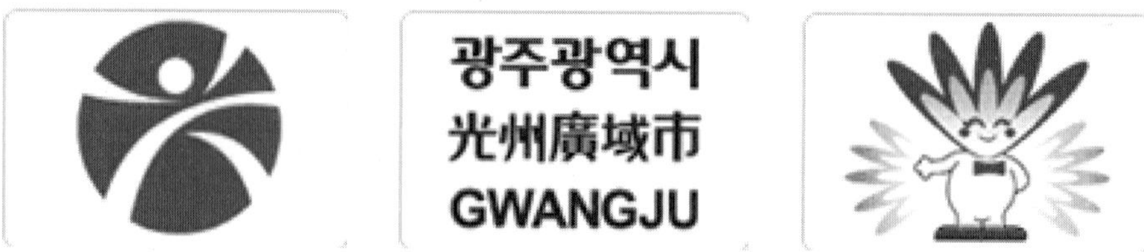

Symbol | Logo Type | Character

1.4. Characteristics of Gwangju[3]

Key City of SouthWest Region

Gwangju is the leading city of the Jeolla-do, with the entire nation within a day's reach. The emerging importance of Korea's western coastline and the government's effort to balance growth across the nation have triggered large-scale urban development projects such as the construction of the Gwangju hi-tech industrial complex, transformation of Gwangju into a center of production, and improvement of housing and leisure facilities. Such support will boost Gwangju's status as the hub of Korea's southwest region.

---

[3] http://eng.gwangju.go.kr

Historic City of Patriotism

Gwangju successfully defended itself during the seven-year-long Japanese invasion into Korea beginning in 1592 and, since then, has always been at the forefront of the movement against invaders. This tradition, in which citizens fought bravely in times of crisis in the nation has continued throughout history. Citizens sacrificed their lives during the Japanese invasion in 1592, fought against the colonialist Japanese rule in the early 1900s, and again, lost many lives during the democratic movement in May 1980 in defense of justice, democracy, human rights and freedom.

City of Culture and the Arts

Gwangju has long been regarded as a city rich in culture and art. It has given birth to renowned and respected scholars, poets, and artists. Gwangju is also the place where the Southern School of Chinese Painting, or Namjonghwa, as well as Pansori (a form of Korean performance art), a traditional Korean singing genre, originated.

The level of artistic sophistication is higher than any other region in Korea, with a large proportion of the population involved in the arts field. The humble nature of the people, who do not pursue worldly gain, has enabled legions of people to enjoy art, dance and music over the years. The Gwangju Biennale, an international arts festival first held in 1995 and now taking place every two years, has further enhanced Gwangju's worldwide reputation as a city of art.

Traditional City of Education

The hometown of numerous renowned scholars, Gwangju has 662 schools, consisting of 295 kindergartens, 151 elementary schools, 87 middle schools, 67 high schools, 6 junior colleges, 11 universities, 37 graduate schools, and 8 others (as of 2013) with a total of 367,721 students, or 24.8% of the total city population. The average number of students per household (0.7) reflects the city's characteristic as the home of education.

2. Development of Gwangju

2.1. Socio-economic Growth

In 2012, Gwangju's population numbered 1,484,000, which accounted for 2.9% of the national total. It increased at an annual average growth rate of 0.8% during the 2000-2012 period. The total number of households in 2012 increased by 1.3 times from the 430,000 households in 2000. The average growth rate over the last 10 years in car ownership has been 4.2% per annum. It was the most reliable determinant of travel demand in Gwangju. To conclude, the unsustainable situation has been heavily affected by the dramatic increase in the city's socio-economic condition.

Table 2.1. Trends of Socio-economic Growth

Division	Unit	2000	2005	2012	AAGR ('00-'12)
Population	1,000 persons	1,351	1,444	1,484	0.8%
Household	1,000 hou.	430	482	556	2.2%
Car registration (Private car's ratio)	1,000 vehicle (%)	337 (67.5)	436 (73.5)	551 (79.3)	4.2% **(+11.8)**

Note: AAGR refers to average annual growth rate.
Source: GMC (each year)

2.2. Evolution of Urban Structure

Urban structure is the arrangement of land use in urban areas. Gwangju Metropolitan City (GMC) has experienced rapid growth since it became the metropolitan city of the southern part of the divided Jeollanam-do in 1986. The growth of GMC has been closely connected with national land development, and has taken over as a centre of residential and commercial areas.

GMC was given only limited autonomy to execute urban planning projects within the boundary authorized by the central government. This was an area 744.2 km^2 in size, within a radius of about 40 km from the city center of Gwangju. Although the transport problem is now viewed as a common problem facing GMC, it has surfaced as a result of the growing population and an increase in car ownership, and has changed with urban development and spatial structure, which are of vital importance for urban transport. This is why urban transport policy has also developed out of changes which have already happened in urban development.

The most used methods for urban development in GMC were Land Readjustment Projects (LRP) and Residential Land Development Projects (RDP). During the 1980s, main arterial roads were formed under residential land development projects to providc thc ncccssary land for massive housing projects in Gwangju. The urban structure was formulated as a line shape structure developed around the main arterial roads radiating in all directions, and was very similar to sector concepts formulated by Hoyt. With progress, a "⊃" shaped urban spatial structure was formed centered around the Gwangju stream.

In the 1990s, urban development projects mainly focused upon residential land development, and little emphasis was given to the land use plan. This resulted in a scattered settlement of housing and an urban development pattern in the outskirts, forming a scattered clustering of housing and a multiple nuclei urban structure of GMC. Due to the wide-spreading urbanized area and the enlarged housing development projects, GMC experienced the increasing multi-centric process of urban structure in the 2000s. Two CBDs and nine sub-CBDs were established in two areas, respectively. The CBD is the commercial and often geographic heart of GMC, and has performed the central-place function of Gwangju Metropolitan Area. In addition, a sub-CBD is the center of wide-area community and accepted part of the commercial and business functions in the CBD. Community centers were established in 9 sites, and became the center of urban life zones by district in GMC.

Figure 2.4. Evolution of Urban Structure in Gwangju

【1980s】	【1990s】	【2000s】
■ LRP-5 sites, RDP-4 sites ■ Line shape structure ■ Sector concepts ■ ⊃ shaped structure	■ LRP-3 sites, RDP-12 sites ■ Scatted clustering of housing ■ Multi-nuclei structure ■ Strong ⊃ shaped structure	■ CBD-2 sites, SubCBD-2 sites ■ Wide-area community-9 sites ■ Enlarged multi-nuclei structure
	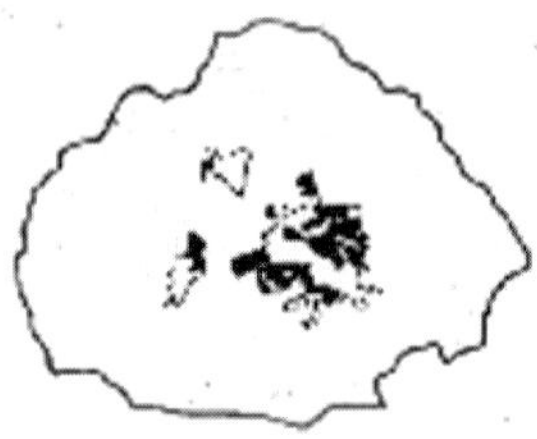	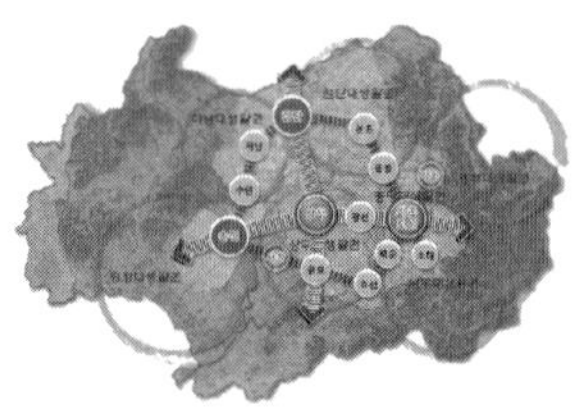

Notes: LRP-Land Readjustment Project; RDP-Residential Land Development projects; CBD-Central Business District

Sources: Jeong(2001); GMC(2011)

2.3. Existing Condition

Gwangju is the most central city of the south western coastal area of Korea and a hub in the national transportation system. Gwangju is composed of administrative districts called "Gu". Gwangju city is divided into 5 districts ("Gu"). As of 2012, Gwangju covered an area of 501.2 m^2 and had a population of 1.48 million persons. The population density of Gwangju was 2,960 persons / km^2, and average family size per household was 2.67 persons. The total length of roads was 2,335 km, and the total number of registered vehicles was 371 per thousand persons and 0.99 per household.

In terms of traffic access, it has a well-established transportation environment ranging from air, railway and express bus within one day's drive to major cities including Seoul, Incheon, and Busan. It takes 55 minutes to travel the 290.9 km from Gwangju to Seoul by air, 1.6 hours by the KTX (Korean Train Express), and 3.5 hours by car. Incheon, which serves as the gate to Korea, is 311.4 km from Gwangju and it takes about 2 hours and 50 minutes to get from Incheon to Gwangju. The distance between Gwangju and Busan is 286.8 km and it takes 3 hours and 50 minutes by car.

Table 2.2. Existing Condition of Gwangju (2012)

General status		Vehicle condition (1,000 vehicles)		Road facility (km)	
Area(km^2)	501.2	Total vehicle population	551	Total road length	2,335
Household (thousand)	556	Passenger car	437	Expressway	28
Population (thousand)	1,484	Van	26	National road	87
Person/ household	2.67	Truck	85	City road	2,198
Population density (person/km^2)	2,960	Others	1.7	Constructed road	1,634
		Vehicle ownership/ household	0.99	Construction ratio	70.4%

Source: GMC(2013)

3. Urban Transport Conditions

3.1. Trends of Transport Indicators

The growth in road traffic volumes in Gwangju closely parallels the increase in socio-economic indicators. The total traffic population increased at the average annual growth rate of 0.92% during the 2000-2012 period.

The total length of constructed road grew from 1,151 km in 2000 to 1,634 km in 2012. This was mainly due to the road construction-oriented policy of GMC. The number of cars per road-km increased from 292 cars in 2000 to 337 cars in 2012. This indicates the increasing intensity of the road network problem in Gwangju.

Table 2.3. Trends of Transport Indicators in Gwangju

Division	Unit	2000	2005	2012	AAGR (2000-'12)
Traffic population	Thousand	1,252	1,322	1,397	0.92%
Road length	Km	1,151	1,363	1,634	2.96%
Road ratio	%	18.5	20.5	23.1	+4.6
Cars per road	Cars/km	292	319	337	1.20%
Cars per person	Cars/1000	247	300	371	3.44%

Note: AAGR refers to average annual growth rate.
Source: GMC(each year)

3.2. Share of Modal Split

The taxi share as a proportion of the total daily trips by traffic mode decreased from 23.8% in 2000 to 15.2% in 2012. This was primarily caused by travelers being diverted from taxi to other modes. As a result of the drastic increase in the number of private cars in Gwangju, the share of private cars by traffic mode grew rapidly from 13.9% in 2000 to 36.4% in 2012. This resulted in heavy traffic congestion and air pollution in the built-up area of the city.

Table 2.4. Share of Modal Split (%)

Mode	2000	2005	2012	Changes ('00-12)
Bus	49.4	37.5	36.3	−13.1
Taxi	23.8	20.2	15.2	−8.6
Private car	13.9	27.3	36.4	+22.5
Subway	-	1.7	2.7	+1.0
Walking, others	12.9	13.3	9.4	+3.5

Note: AAGR refers to average annual growth rate.
Source: GMC(each year)

3.3. Transport Networks

Road Network

Gwangju's basic road network is determined by two main ring-roads encircling the gridiron-network of both the downtown and area-wide community's streets. The first ring road was built in the built-up area and has played a key role in dispersing old city-center functions. The second ring road, which crosses the radial lines, has contributed much to dispersing otherwise unnecessary city-center bounded traffic to outlying areas. In Gwangju, the roads created or set to be created under the city's land use plan extended 2,335 km in a combined length as of 2012. The planned ratio of roads to the city stands at 33.5%, but the ratio was no more than 23.1% in 2012. Of these roads, those already opened reached about 1,634 km. As streets and roads need to be expanded continuously in parallel with urban development, road expansion is projected in mid and long-term road programs in the future.

Figure 2.5. Road Network of Gwangju City

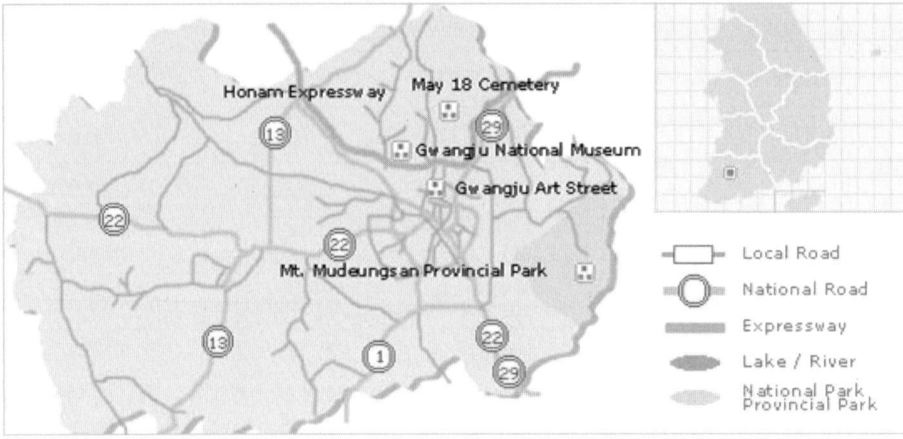

Urban Metro Route

Gwangju Metro Line 1 is a rapid transit line in Gwangju, South Korea, operated by the Gwangju Metropolitan Rapid Transit Corporation (GMRTC, or Gwangju Metro). It connects Nokdong Station in Dong-gu at its eastern terminus to Pyeongdong Station in Gwangsan-gu in the west, via the old central business district and Gwangju Airport. On maps, it is designated by dark green. The line began operations in 2004, making Gwangju the fifth South Korean city with a rapid transit system.

Gwangju's Metro was constructed by the city government and is operated by the city metro transit corporation. It forms a reliable and comfortable mass transit system within Gwangju's transport policy. The construction of Metro Line 1 began in 1996 and was completed in twelve years. Although Gwangju Metro has only a short history dating from 2008, it is a key transport mode, but occupied 1.3% of the total passenger trips in 2004. When phase 2 of the Metro Line 1 was completed in 2008, the total route length was 20.1 km and about 3% of all passenger trips were transported by Metro. Previously, an additional line in the city was proposed to achieve a target share of 15%. However, the GMC replaced the plan with a new Metro Line based on new metro projects. The network plan consists of two lines providing a light rail system.

Figure 2.6. Gwangju Metro Route

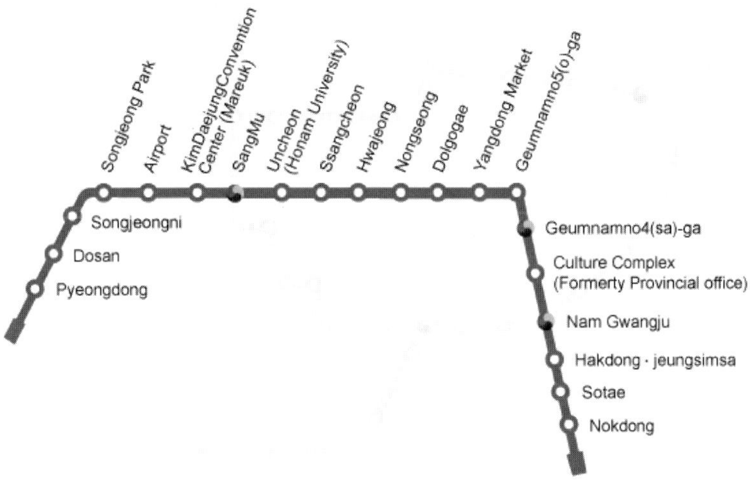

Bus Route Network

Services of bus transit in Gwangju are classified into three types by color codes. The services include red bus (express bus), yellow bus (standard bus), and green bus (village bus). Purple buses are district circulator buses. In Gwangju City, there were 10 private companies operating 94 bus routes in 2012. The total bus routes in Gwangju increased from 84 routes in 2000 to 94 routes in 2012. Each bus travelled 23.3km in a route-day on average, and carried about 433 passengers in a day in 2012. Daly service frequencies per bus showed 10.3 times as of 2012.

Figure 2.7. Overlay of Bus Routes in Gwangju

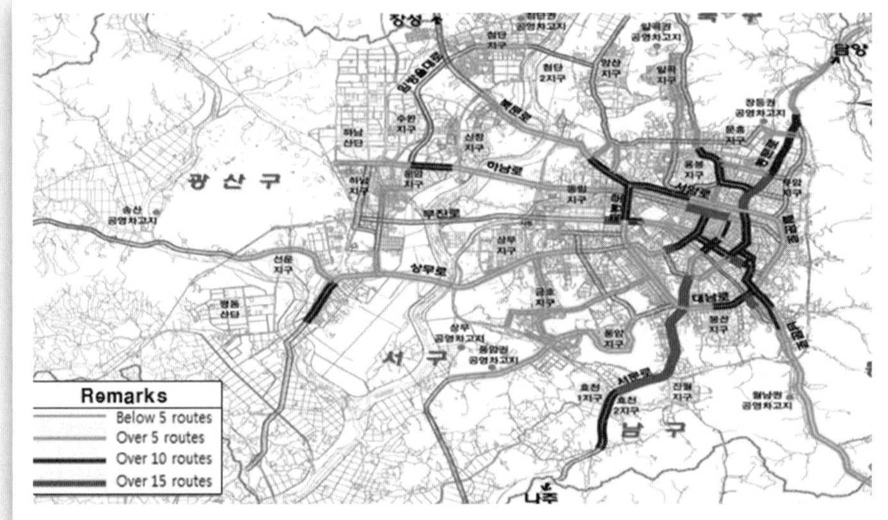

4. Urban Transport Problems

4.1. Traffic Congestion

Congestion is a problem in Gwangju, with relatively high levels of car ownership and poor road infrastructures. The degree of severity of congestion rose with the size of the city, and it extends as far as the suburbs. In considering congestion, it is helpful to compare average travel speeds. For instance, there was a rapid increase in average travel time in the outskirts of the city between 2005 and 2012. It is very difficult to estimate the true costs of congestion as it depends very much on the definition chosen. The total congestion costs in Gwangju grew at an average rate of 2.6% annum during the 2000-2012 period.

Table 2.5. Changes in Congestion Costs

Division	Unit	2000	2005	2012	Changes('00-'12)
Travel speed (Outskirts)	km/hour	40.2	45.8	42.4	+2.2
Congestion cost	Billion Won	711.0	788.3	965.5	AAGR: 2.6%

Note: AAGR refers to average annual growth rate.
Source: GMC(each year)

4.2. Air Pollution

The transport emissions which cause the greatest concern include carbon dioxide (CO_2), carbon monoxide (CO), nitrogen oxides (NOx), sulphur dioxide (SO_2), volatile organic compounds (Voids), lead, particulate and smoke. Most vehicles also emit very fine particles of carbon (from diesel engines), inorganic lead compounds (from gasoline engines using leaded gasoline) and other metals used in oils to enhance engine performance. These particles cause dust, damage to health, and soil buildings.

Total emissions in Gwangju decreased slightly during the 2000-2010 period, while total emissions from Gwangju's road traffic also decreased slightly during the same period. Road transport is still the largest source of air pollution, accounting for 51.0% of Gwangju's total emissions in 2010.

Table 2.6. Emissions of Transport-related Pollutants

Items / Year	Unit	2000	2010	AAGR('00-12)
Emissions	1,000 kg/ year	52,371	45,186	-1.46%
Emissions from road traffic		28,243	23,045	-2.01%
Transport's share	%	53.9	51.0	-2.9

Note: AAGR refers to average annual growth rate.
Source: GMC (each year)

4.3. Traffic Accidents

Traffic accidents are, on the whole, the most dramatic and terrifying of Gwangju's transport problems. The total number of traffic accidents increased at an annual average rate of 0.76% during the 2000-2012 period. There were 114 people killed, and 13,886 people injured on the roads in 2012. In addition, an increasing number of cars still leads to a great many traffic accidents in Gwangju. Apart from the suffering caused by road causalities, the economic and social costs are high, both in Gwangju and throughout Korea.

Table 2.7. Trends of Road Traffic Accidents in Gwangju

Year	Accidents(cases)	Deaths(person)	Injuries(person)
2000	7,853	154	10,528
2005	7,797	103	12,361
2012	8,600	114	13,886
AAGR	0.76%	-2.48%	2.33%

Source: GMC(2001-2011)
Note: AAGR refers to average annual growth rate.

4.4. Imbalance of Economic Activity

There has been a tendency for Gwangju to take the lion's share of Jeollanam-do's economic growth. Too much growth has resulted in too much traffic; undue congestion; overcrowding of the public transport system; longer trip lengths; an expansion of the urban sprawl, giving limited access to open countryside; and to high land and property prices. In addition, Gwangju's area takes the bulk of the new employment growth at the expense of Jeonnam's other centers: and the area which attracts higher growth frequently suffers from traffic congestion, and many other problems as a result. In Gwangju, the use of public transport is of course more concentrated in the morning and evening rush hours. The majority of buses in Gwangju are subject to considerable traffic congestion, as well as to chronic overcrowding at these times.

4.5. Problems of Land Use-Transport System

Urban development did not occur adjacent to the transportation network where it could most easily be served. Many grid systems in Gwangju provided an almost infinite number of paths between various points. The spacing of network elements was not dependent upon the density of the development they served. Furthermore, the hierarchy of streets was not functionally classified and well established. The early inhabitants were not offered the necessary infrastructures for supply, education, leisure, and public transport connection in order to give them the immediate possibility to reduce their need to travel by car.

Metro Line 1 was not built in corridors with very large traffic demand in Gwangju. Most of the bus routes didn't follow major streets of new housing development sites. Public transport companies were not included in early stages of the policy planning process of new housing development sites. Bus routes did not fit well with recent urban developments. The capacity of radial road networks was not large enough to accommodate the inbound and outbound traffic volumes, so that eventually they came to be heavily congested. Since land-use planning did not coordinate with transport planning, the behaviour patterns of housing development sites were never taken into consideration.

A self-portrait in the newspaper

Gwangju court rules against Macquarie Infrastructure

Court decision sends message that public infrastructure is for public good, not private profit.

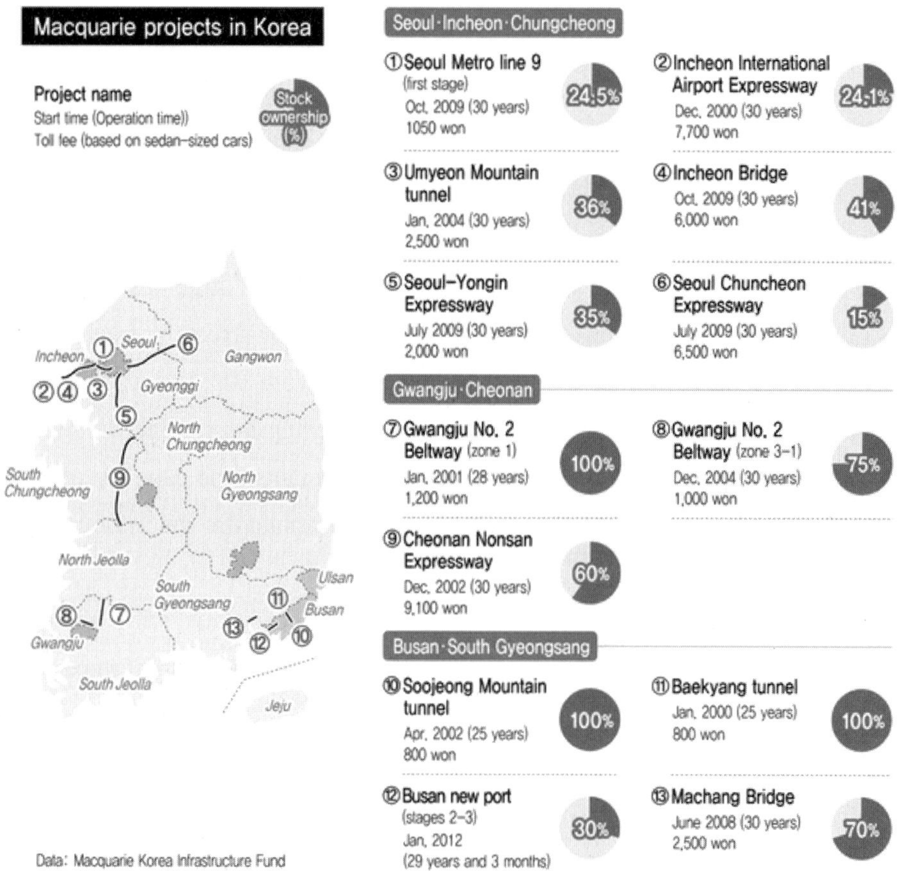

On Feb. 20, the administrative division of the Gwangju District Court sided with the city of Gwangju in the administrative suit filed by the Gwangju Beltway Investors (Gwangju Investors) against the city government. The

Gwangju Investors are the private operator of the Gwangju No. 2 Beltway, which has been criticized as a huge waste of tax money. It appears that the decision will have a considerable effect on other negotiations and litigation between private operators and cities, which have been ailing because of the snowballing cost of the financial compensation it has had to provide the operators.

The court found that the administrative organization was justified in exercising its right of oversight over the private operator, which had aggravated its operating deficit by arbitrarily worsening the capital structure to increase the profits of Macquarie Korea Infrastructure Fund (Macquarie Infrastructure), its majority shareholder. The effect of the court's decision is to underscore the fact that social infrastructure is to be operated for the public good.

The city of Gwangju has long maintained that one of the obstacles to normal operation of the Beltway is that the Gwangju Investors have aggravated the fiscal situation by raising interest rates through reducing its own capital rate to 6.93% and arbitrarily adjusting external capital loans.

The Gwangju Investors switched the location of 142 billion won (US$ 131.64 million) in loans from the central city bank of Gwangju, which keeps its interest rate around 7%, to Macquarie Infrastructure, whose interest rate ranges from 7% to 20%, making it both main stockholder and creditor. In addition to the fact that the predicted amount of traffic on the road had been exaggerated to begin with, changing the interest rate on the loan to a higher rate resulted in a worse financial structure.

The Gwangju Investors contend that they were not obliged to keep their rate of capital above 25%, and that since the road is operating normally, it was a deviation from and an abuse of the city's discretionary power to give administrative orders.

If the private operator fails to restore the capital to its original state despite the decision of the court, the city of Gwangju is planning to cancel the agreement that gives the Gwangju Investors the right to operate and manage the road. In the event that the private operator does not implement the city of Gwangju's directive to restore the capital to its original condition, this provides the city with sufficient cause to purchase the right to operate and manage the Beltway at 80% of the amount paid.

If the city of Gwangju repurchases the operation and management rights from Macquarie, it will likely result in a budget reduction of around 55.1 billion won (US$ 51.08 million) and fiscal losses in excess of 500 billion won (US$ 463.52 million) through 2028, the year when free use will start.

The first section of the Gwangju No. 2 Beltway (the 5.67 km stretch from the Duam neighborhood to the Sotae neighborhood in North district) was completed in 2001 by the private investor Daewoo Engineering and Construction Consortium, which put 181.6 billion won (US$ 168.34 million) into the project. In 2003, Daewoo handed the project over to Macquarie Infrastructure.

After this, Gwangju Investors, in which Macquarie International Infrastructure Fund (MIIF) holds a 100% share, lowered the ratio of its own capital from 29.91% to 6.93% and changed part of the borrowed amount (142 billion won) to money borrowed from Macquarie Infrastructure and other stockholders. The next year, the interest rate climbed from 7.25% to 10%, and during the 6-year period from 2003 to 2008, the city of Gwangju paid 194.7 billion won (US$ 180.44 million) just in interest payments to Macquarie Infrastructure, which was both stockholder and creditor.

Trapped by a minimum revenue guarantee (MRG) agreement that guaranteed the city of Gwangju would cover revenue corresponding to 85% of predicted traffic, Gwangju was forced to pay 119 billion won (US$ 110.28 million) in compensation from the opening of the road through 2012.

Gwangju used its supervisory authority to order the operator to restore the 2011 capital structure to what existed at the time that the agreement was made in Dec. 2000. In response to this, Gwangju Investors requested an administrative judgment from the Central Administrative Judgment Board, and when this was dismissed, they filed a lawsuit. "Once the decision in our favor is confirmed, we are planning to invalidate the agreement and restore its operation and management rights," said Moon Pyeong-seop, chief of roads for Gwangju city government.

Seoul, Busan, Daegu, and other city governments are showing a great deal of interest in the court's decision. These city governments brought in private capital for the construction of roads and tunnels only to see the compensation payments for operating deficit balloon. They would like to buy back operation rights to the facilities and renegotiate the rate of profit, but they are frustrated by the refusal of Macquarie Infrastructure, the main investor in the private operators of these projects.

Interest is now focusing on upcoming negotiations concerning Seoul Metro Line 9 and the Umyeon Mountain tunnel. Macquarie Infrastructure has invested in both projects in a manner similar to the first section of the Gwangju second ring road. Macquarie Infrastructure is the second largest stockholder (24.5%) in Seoul Metro Line 9, the operator of the subway line, following Hyundai Rotem (25%), and it is the majority stockholder (36%) in Woomyunsan Infraway, the operator of Umyeon Mountain Tunnel.

In both of these projects, as with Gwangju Investors, a minimum revenue guarantee agreement is in effect, guaranteeing subway line 9 8.9% profits after taxes and Umyeon Mountain tunnel 8.03%. The financial structure is also the same, with the main stockholders procuring the loan from companies and profiting from the high interest rates.

For subway line 9, the interest rate was 7.2% on the earlier loan and 15% on the later loan, while for the Umyeon Mountain tunnel, the earlier interest rate was 5.5%-7.7% while the later interest rate was 20%. Inasmuch as the court's decision is intended to justify Gwangju's administrative directions to Gwangju Investors to replace the usurious loan, the decision is expected to be used to advantage by the city of Seoul in its negotiations with Macquarie Infrastructure over the right to determine fares.

*** Source: The Hankyoreh Newspaper (2013.2.21)**

References

Gwangju Metropolitan City (GMC), City Administration White Paper, 2000-2011 (Each Year) (in Korean).

GMC, GMC Statistical Yearbook, 2000-2011 (Each Year) (in Korean).

GMC, Gwangju Urban Master Plan, Final Draft, August 2007 (in Korean).

GMC, Gwangju Metropolitan Transportation Master Plan, Final Draft, August 2007 (in Korean).

GMC, Gwangju Metropolitan Public Transportation Plan, 1st Draft, December 2011 (in Korean).

Edwards, John D., Jr., Transportation Planning Handbook, Second edition, Washington, DC: Institute of Transportation Engineers, 1999.

Hanson, Susan and Giuliano, Genevieve edit., The Geography of Urban Transportation, Third Edition, New York: The Guilford Press, 2004.

Lee, In-keun, Experiences in Seoul Subway Developments, ITA 2004, 2004.

Jeong, Bonghyun, New Transportation Policy in Regional Metropolitan City: Gwangju, Korea, CNU Press, 2005 (in Korean).

Jeong, Bonghyun, SOC and Regional Development: Standing Transportation Problems and Solutions in the Jeonlla Provinces, Korea, CNU Press, 2010 (in Korean).

Manns, Jonathan, Park-and-ride - politics, policy and planning", Town and Country Planning, Vol 79, No. 3, London: Town and Country Planning Association. March 2010.

State of Montana (SOM), Public Transportation / Policy Paper, Tranplan 21, Department of Transportation, State of Montana, 2007.

White, Peter, Public Transport: Its Planning, Management and Operation, Third edition, London: UCL Press, 1995.

Gwangju Metropolitan Government http://www.gwangju.go.kr/

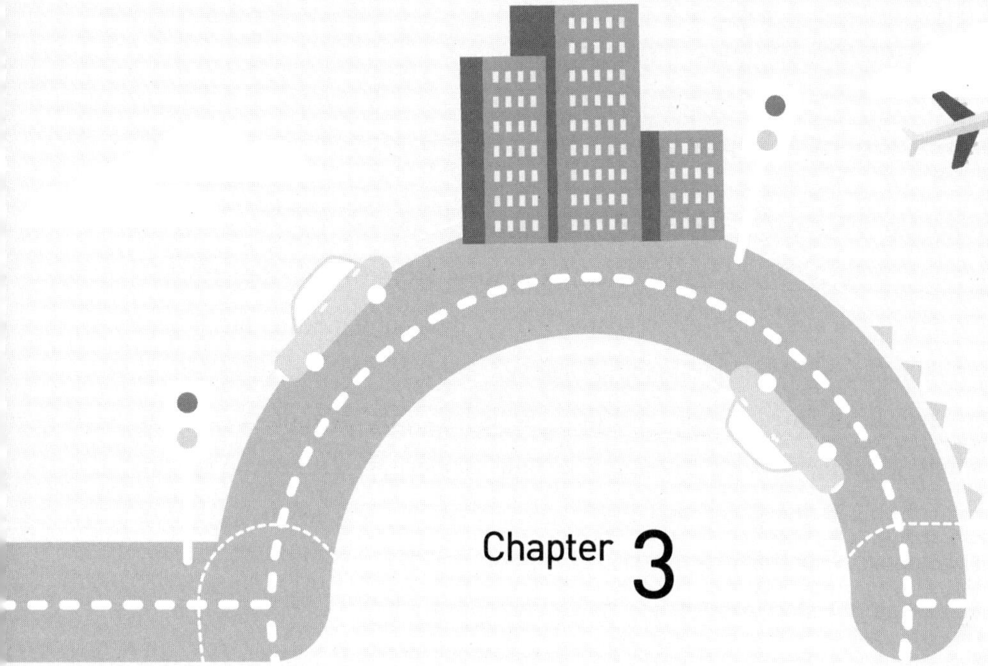

Chapter 3

Bus Transit Problems and Policy

1. Introduction to Bus Transit

1.1. Definition and Types of Bus

A bus is a road vehicle designed to carry passengers. Buses can have a capacity as high as 300 passengers. The most common type of bus is the single-decker rigid bus, with larger loads carried by double-decker buses and articulated buses, and smaller loads carried by midi buses and mini buses; coaches are used for longer distance services. Bus manufacturing is increasingly globalized, with the same design appearing around the world. Buses may be used for scheduled bus transport, scheduled coach transport, school transport, private hire, tourism; promotional buses may be used for political campaigns and others are privately operated for a wide range of purposes.

Formats include single-decker bus, double-decker bus (both usually with a rigid chassis) and articulated bus (or 'bendy-bus'), the prevalence of which varies from country to country. Bi-articulated buses are also manufactured, and passenger-carrying trailers - either towed behind a rigid bus (a bus trailer), or hauled as a trailer by a truck (a trailer bus). Smaller minibuses have a lower capacity and open-top buses are typically used for leisure purposes. In many new fleets, particularly in local transit systems, there is an increasing shift to low-floor buses primarily for easier accessibility.

1.2. Importance of Bus Transit

City buses are the most common means of transportation in Gwangju. They are frequent, reliable and probably the most inexpensive way of getting around. Gwangju's bus network is quite extensive. They were approximately 94 bus routes with 973 city buses in 2012. An exclusive lane for buses (marked with a blue line painted on the road) is enforced on several major roads during the daytime, which makes it possible to spend less time on bus rides than in private cars. Local buses are often crowded, so passengers should be prepared to stand and be jostled. The drivers often seem unware that they are not driving a car and so tend to stop rather abruptly, which can be a strain on standing riders. May of them also tend to ride the brake rather than change gears, so the ride can be pretty rough at times.

Public transport in metropolitan cities is used extensively for trips to and from the city center, and for school and work trips to other destinations. Bus transit is the dominant form of public transport in Gwangju. Buses in Gwangju city carried about 36.3% of the daily passenger trips in 2012. Bus services operate in mixed traffic over streets. Bus priority lanes are operated on downtown streets and are also provided along radial arterial roads in Gwangju. As car ownership has grown in Gwangju, it has had a direct effect on bus transport use. The percentage share of city buses has decreased, while the percentage share of private cars continued to increase rapidly between 2000 and 2012.

2. Condition of Gwangju Bus Transit

2.1. Trends of Transport Condition

Trends of Transport Condition

Gwangju, ranking among the 6 largest cities in Korea, is a bustling regional metropolitan city. There were 1.484 million people living in an area of 501 km^2 in 2012. The population of Gwangju increased 0.8% annually on average, while the car ownership increased by 4.2% on average annually during the period 2000-2012. The drastic increase in cars exacerbated the transportation problems in Gwangju.

Table 3.1. Trends of Socio-economic Condition

Division	Unit	2000	2005	2012	AAGR ('00-'12)
Population	1,000 persons	1,351	1,444	1,484	0.8%
Household	1,000 household	430	482	556	2.2%
Car registration (Private car's ratio)	1,000 vehicle (%)	337 (67.5)	436 (73.5)	551 (79.3)	4.2% **(+11.8)**

Note: AAGR refers to average annual growth rate.
Source: GMC (each year)

The bus share as a proportion of the total daily trips by traffic mode decreased from 49.4% in 2000 to 36.3% in 2012. This was primarily caused by travelers being diverted from bus among other factors. As a result of the drastic increase in the number of private cars in Gwangju, the share of taxi by traffic mode decreased rapidly from 23.8% in 2000 to 15.2% in 2012. Rapid automobile increase has led to heavy traffic congestion and air pollution in the built-up area of the city.

Table 3.2. Trends of Modal Split (%)

Mode	2000	2005	2012	Changes ('00-12)
Bus	49.4	37.5	36.3	−13.1
Taxi	23.8	20.2	15.2	−8.6
Private car	13.9	27.3	36.4	+22.5
Subway	-	1.7	2.7	+1.0
Walking, others	12.9	13.3	9.4	+3.5

Note: AAGR refers to average annual growth rate.
Source: GMC (each year)

Trends of Bus Transit Condition

Services of bus transit in Gwangju are classified into three types by color codes. The services include red bus (express bus), yellow bus (standard bus), and green bus (village bus). Purple buses are district circulator buses. In Gwangju City, there were 10 private companies operating 94 bus routes in 2012. The total bus routes in Gwangju increased from 84 routes to 94 routes in 2012. The total number of registered buses grew from 932 buses in 2000 to 973 buses in 2012. It led to a decline in average bus route length during the 2000-2012 period. Each bus travelled 23.3 km in a route-day on average, and carried about 433 passengers in a day in 2012. Daily service frequencies per bus showed 10.3 times as of 2012.

Table 3.3. Trends of Bus Transit Characteristics

Items	Unit	2000	2012	Variation
No. of bus routes	Route	84	94	+10
No. of registered buses	Vehicle	932	973	+41
Average operating bus per route	Vehicle	11.1	10.3	−0.8
Average bus route length	Km	23.5	23.3	-0.2
Daily service frequency per bus	Times	5.9	10.3	+4.4
Daily carried passengers per bus	Person	542	433	−109

Source: GMC (each year)

2.2. Bus Transit Systems in Gwangju

Types of City Bus

Gwangju has three main bus color codes: red, yellow and green. That is, buses are arranged by colors. The red buses are the fastest buses and stop at the three most popular districts, Dong-gu (Downtown area of Gwangju), Seo-gu (West District, Sangmu residential area), and Gwangsan-gu (Gwangsan

District and Cheomdan area). Red buses are express buses, running often, making very few stops, and covering large parts of the city. Bus number 1 connects Sangmu area to the train station to Chosun University. Buses 6, 7, and 9 cover the rest of the city making large squares that intersect in important locations.

The yellow and green buses travel throughout Gwangju and have longer bus routes than the red buses. Yellow buses are standard buses that run every 10-20 minutes. Green buses are village buses that connect smaller communities and rural areas to transfer points. Purple buses are district circulator buses, generally going to the outskirts of the city. Most bus stops in Gwangju have electronic display boards informing when the next bus arrives.

Currently, all bus stop announcements are made in Korean. Only bus #1000 with a route covering Gwangju City Hall, the Gwangju International Airport, U-Square – Express Bus Terminal, and downtown provides announcements in both English and Korean. The Gwangju Bus Information website is only available in Korean, shown at http://bus.gjcity.net.

Figure 3.1. Types of City Buses in Gwangju

Bus Fare Structures

Buses in Gwangju cost 1,200 won cash for each ride. When you enter the bus you put the money into the machine. Many people use a transit card. The fare is 1,100 won for an adult. The Gwangju public transit system has expanded to the nearest counties: Naju, Damyang, Hwasun, Hampyeong, Jangseong. Passengers who transit from Gwangju buses to county buses only have to pay 50% of the transit bus fare when transferring. Within Gwangju buses, free transfers must be made within the first 30 mins after getting off the first bus and the number of transit time is unlimited. Before, free transit was only applicable when taking the second bus within 1 hour after getting on the first bus. To get a free transfer for the next buses, transit passengers must touch their transportation card to the card reader near the exit door when getting off the first bus.

Table 3.4. Bus Fare Structure

Division	Adult	Youth	Child
Cash	1,200 won	900 won	400 won
Transit card	1,100 won	750 won	350 won

Source: GMC's homepage http://www.gwangju.go.kr

Transit Card Use

Adults, youths and children can purchase transit card to use on the bus, subway, and in other areas of Gwangju. College students are offered a discount when they use this card to take the subway. Middle and High school students must present their student ID card. Children must present a health insurance card and a certificate of residence when they purchase this card at authorized places, such as newsstands, supermarkets and subway stations. A mini card costs 4,000 won while an accessory card costs 6,000~7,000 won. Refill amounts range from 5,000 won (min.)~500,000 won (max.) Card refill is available at any authorized Bitgoeul card refill stations such as convenience stores, newsstands, supermarkets and subway stations.

2.3. Bus Transit Facilities and Routes

Gwangju Bus Terminal[1]

There is one major bus terminal, U-Square Bus Terminal (also known as Gwangcheon Bus Terminal), in Gwangju. From here one can take buses to the surrounding regions, or indeed almost any major town and city throughout Korea. There are several intercity bus stops throughout the city handling suburban buses. In Korean terminology regarding bus connections, 'Go-Sok-Buh-Su' means long-haul, non-stop, intercity express bus/coach, and 'Shi-Wae-Buh-Su' indicates buses going beyond the city boundary, mostly unnumbered. Routes of suburban buses connecting Gwangju and its satellite cities are titled as 'Shi-Wae-Buh-Su' or 'Nong-Chon-Buh-Su', even if they run far beyond the city's boundary. A complication is, though, that sometimes a 'Shi-Wae-Buh-Su' goes as far away as a 'Go-Sok-Buh-Su' hence there's no difference in real terms. Often times, the former also calls at small counties and towns along the way, while the latter serves between major cities throughout the country.

Buses from major cities throughout the country arrive and depart from U-Square Bus Terminal, a large, fancy and recently renovated bus terminal near the geographic center of the city. The terminal is the largest and most lavish in the country. Every taxi driver in Gwangju knows the bus terminal as "U-Square Bus Terminal". Seoul Gangnam to Gwangju prices are either 17,600 or 26,100 for the standard bus or the limousine bus respectively. Prices to other cities are comparable. This bus terminal operated 101 intercity bus routes and 29 express bus routes in 2012.

---

1 http://www.usquare.co.kr

Bus Stops and Garages

There were a total number of 2,532 bus stops, including 2012 stops in the city and 425 stops outside the city, as of 2012. By district, the total 703 stops in Gwangsan District shared 28.8% of the city total, and 172 stops in Seo District, 6.8%, respectively. The total length of bus exclusive lanes in Gwangju is 47.2 km and is operating on 8 sections of the road networks in 2013. The operation hours of bus lanes are between 7-9 a.m. and 5:30-7:30 p.m.

Most turning places of the private bus companies are located along arterial roads of the city center in Gwangju. The GMC has constructed seven public bus garages at the outskirts of the city. Most of the bus turning places were forced to relocate from downtown to outside the city. It resulted in improving the environment of public transport and the operation condition of buses in Gwangju. Nine public bus garages have been built in three stages since the year 1997. Seven of them were completed, and two are under construction until 2016.

Bus Stops are easily identified by the 'B' inside their round signs. The stop signs are colour-coded – green for green buses, etc. There is a bus stop outside every subway station. Some stops have benches inside a shelter while others are in the open. Next to the bus stop is a list of the buses that stop there as well as a map of the route each bus takes. Some drivers don't always stop at the scheduled bus stops so you have to watch for them and signal them to stop. These and some others don't always stop at the curb and riders have to walk out into the street to get on the bus. Also, since median bus lanes are in the middle of the road, the bus stop may be on an island rather than on the curb.

Bus Route Networks

The total number of bus routes is 106 routes, which included 4 rapid main bus routes, 21 main bus routes, 67 feeder bus routes and 14 rural area bus routes as of 2011. The average service frequency of a rapid main bus was 7.9 minutes, the shortest, and that of a feeder bus, 52.4 minutes, which is the longest. The service intervals of the buses through the center area are similar to that of main buses in Gwangju. However, the service intervals of the buses; running in the suburban area are long. Thus, the average service interval is longer than the other types of buses. It is important to know bus routes by road. This is because it is otherwise impossible to grasp the spatial distribution of the bus lines. More than 15 bus routes are mainly concentrated on Seomun-Ro, Dongmun-Ro, and Gia-ro.

Table 3.5. Characteristics of Bus Routes by Route Type in Gwangju(2011)

Route type	No. of service	No. of Routes	Service frequency	Average length	No. of services per route
Rapid main bus	103	4	7.9min.	24 km	25.8veh.
Main bus	480	21	13.2min.	24.6 km	17.1veh.
Feeder bus	347	67	52.4min.	21.4 km	5.6veh.
Rural area bus	29	14	25.2min.	23.6 km	5.8veh.
Remarks	Total: 959	Total: 106	Average: 39.4min.	Average: 23.4	Average: 13.6veh.

Source: GMC(2012)

To stop the bus at your destination, you must push one of the stop buttons located along the length of the bus. Before boarding the bus, you may call out the name of your destination, or show the driver the written name of your destination and he will indicate whether his bus goes there by waving you on or off. By swiping your transit card on the reader by the back door, you will be able to transfer to another bus at no charge (within 30 minutes) or at a lower fare on the subway.

3. Problems of Gwangju Bus Transit

3.1. Problem of Bus Route Networks

In Gwangju, the pattern of bus routes has changed little for years. Most of the bus route networks are very long, irregular, and indirect in Gwangju. They are also very concentrated in the city center and are more complex. Bus routes in Gwangju city normally include a few radial lines that meet in the city center. The bus routes do not fit well with recent urban developments, and don't resemble any simple pattern. The new activity centers in housing development sites are not served. Most routes follow major streets, so the network apes the street pattern. There are chronic traffic congestion and overcrowding on the majority of the Gwangju city buses providing trunk-type services during the rush hours. The speed and reliability of city bus travel is also impaired. In Gwangju city, which has prominent radial streets, the busiest street are radials.

In the past, the overall bus routes were mainly concentrated in the city's old downtown. This was because GMC carried about the public transit administration easily. Residents living in densely populated areas of new towns experience difficulty catching buses to their destinations[2]. The population of new towns, such as Suwan district, Cheomdan district, Hyocheon, and Jinwol districts is rapidly increasing. Because there have been few new bus routes that go by there for several years, the residents have trouble functioning in everyday life. For instance, Suwan and Cheomdan districts have a total population of 383,000 persons, and are serviced by 37 bus routes in 2013. The average number of passengers per bus route is calculated at about 14,000 persons. Only one bus route, No. 40, passes through the districts of Cheomdan-Suwan-Shinga-Unnam-Usan-Songjeong, and its total service time is approximately 1 hour and 19 minutes.

---

2 Gwangju Ilbo(2013.11.29.)

On the other hand, many bus routes are duplicated in the old city center, and this produces various side effects such as deficit operation, traffic inconvenience, and road traffic congestion etc. The Dong-gu has a total population of 108,000 people and a total of 53 bus routes, so the average population per bus route is about 2,000 persons. The city government received a total number of 152 civil complaints on city bus services in 2012, and the complaints about bus routes accounted for 77.0% of the total complaints.

Despite the poor bus transit services, the city government indicated that it was difficult to reform and expand bus routes for a little while, owing to its limited budget. An additional bus route reform plan also was not reflected in the following year's budget. Even if the city is fully aware of the civil complaints about bus routes, it seems to neglect the traffic inconveniences of citizens, on the plea of budget deficit. GMC is responsible for providing better bus transit services with the citizens. As long as buses offer faster and more comfortable service, more and more people will patronize these relatively inexpensive public bus transits. Therefore, the city government should expand bus routes servicing new towns, and the buses need to come by there frequently. It is also necessary to aviod excessive overlapping of bus routes in the old city center. It would result in traffic congestion relief and the saving of operation cost.

3.2. Problem of Bus Transit Operation

An individual bus company services one or two bus routes in Gwangju. If the bus company is operating at a deficit, the city government makes up for the deficit. Operational deficit is a serious problem to the city, and is becoming social issues in Gwangju. The city should establish the entire bus route plan, and is responsible for managing and supervising bus companies. Because private companies are in charge of the operation of buses, there is less of an increase in passengers carried by bus companies, and the operation efficiency of bus routes is generally at a low level[3].

Bus Quasi-public Operation System (BQOS) was designed to intervene in the bus operation system, and to improve the publicity of bus operation in general. BQOS is depicted as an informal hippo which wastes the tax-payer's precious money in Korea's metropolitan cities. The GMC implemented the BQOS in December, 2006. Gwangju is also not an exception to it. The GMC has already spent about 269 million won per annum to keep the buses running during the 2007-2011 period. The Gwangju government spent more than 301 billion won to keep the buses running as of 2011.

Although the city government has provided more financial support to bus companies, their financial bases are worsening. The yearly financial aid increase has become a great burden to the financial condition of the city government. This was mainly caused by the improper management of the local autonomous body and the careless operation of bus companies. Citizen satisfaction with the bus service has declined slightly. The citizens in Gwangju are still dissatisfied with bus transit services.

Especially, the directors of bus companies make hundreds of millions of won a year. They have managed their companies carelessly, and embezzled the profits of scrapped vehicles. Their ethical standards were terribly lax. It has been suggested that the city government must claw back some of the support fund from the bus companies and the bus companies should be excluded from the further funding of the city. For instance, the city government conducted a special inspection of the suspected bus companies, and exposed cases of unreasonable remuneration. It is very important to secure transparency in the financial accounting of the bus companies, and to supervise the company operation strictly.

3 Segyeilbo(2011.11.25.) http://local.segye.com/

Table 3.6. Trends of Gwangju's Financial Support to Bus Co.

Year	Unit	2007	2008	2009	2011	AAGR ('07-10)
Financial support	100 million	196	293	288	301	22.01%

Note: AAGR refers to annual average growth rate.
Source: GMC (2012); GDI(2013)

3.3. Problem of Bus Transit Services

Citizens hope for easy and quick to travel around Gwangju and the surrounding areas by bus. Bus transit services are generally based on regular operation of transit buses along a route calling at agreed bus stops according to a published bus transit timetable.[4] Buses usually run to a fixed route and schedule, serving specified bus stops or bus stations.

Many public bus services are run to a specific timetable giving specific times of departure and arrival at way-points along the route. These are often difficult to maintain in the event of traffic congestion, breakdowns, on/off bus incidents, road blockages or bad weather. Predictable effects such as morning and evening rush hour traffic are often accounted for in timetables using past experience of the effects, although this then prevents the opportunity for drafting a 'clock face' timetable where the time of a bus is predictable at any time through the day. Predictable short term increases in passenger numbers may be dealt with by providing "duplicate" buses, where two or more buses operate the same slot in the timetable. Unpredictable problems resulting in delays and gaps in the timetabled service may be dealt with by 'turning' a bus early before it reaches it terminus, so that it can fill a gap in the opposite direction, meaning any passengers on the turned bus need to disembark and continue on a following bus. Also, depending on the location of the bus depot, replacement buses may be

[4] http://en.wikipedia.org/wiki/Public_transport_bus_service

dispatched from the depot to fill in other gaps, starting the timetable part of the way along the route.

The level and reliability of bus services is often dependant on the quality of the local road network and levels of traffic congestion, and the population density. Services may be organised on tightly regulated networks with restrictions on when and where services operate, while other services are operated on an ad hoc basis in the model of share taxis.

3.4. Problem of Bus Transfer System

It was found that U-Square bus terminal had 12,866 daily passengers, the largest number in Gwangju. The overall average transfer time between buses was found to be 8 minutes and 4 seconds. Average transfer time between city buses was found to be 8 minutes and 5 seconds, and that between red buses, 13 minutes and 28 seconds, respectively. According to a GDI's report(2013), the bus stops with more than 5,000 daily passengers are inclusive of bus stops such as Asia Culture Center (9,536 persons), Gyungshin high school (6,028 persons), Chungjang police box, Malbau Traditional Market, and Unam 3rd Site. The total number of daily adult passengers in Gwangju numbered 261,694 persons, which accounted for 67% of the total daily passengers. Following were 12.0% for students and 1.1% for children respectively. The total number of passenger transferred from bus to bus was calculated at 75,473 people. It shared approximately 19.3% of the total bus passengers transferring. The total number of passengers between red buses was found to be 2,285 persons, and it accounted for 0.6 % of the total daily passengers in Gwangju. Most of the bus stops with over 5,000 transfer passengers were not designed for convenient transfer between buses. There were insufficient bus bays at bus stops. This has brought about severe road traffic congestions and traffic accident increase. The city government should establish more crosswalks and sidewalks to provide better access to transfer bus stops.

4. Gwangju Bus Transit Policy

4.1. Integrated Public Transport Systems

Korean metropolitan cities particularly require a transportation system which is integrated across all modes of public transport. The main aim of system integration should be to offer an attractive and easier to use urban transport system, leading to a better use of existing resources and consequently, reduced congestion. The various modes of public transport have to work in tandem. They should complement one another rather than involve themselves in unhealthy competition. At the same time, a single ticket system, where commuters can buy a transport ticket that is valid throughout the public transport network, should also be developed and promoted. This will improve efficiency of service delivery and comfort for commuters.

4.2. Promotion of Bus Transport

Passenger mobility in Gwangju city relies heavily on its roads. Although a metro transit service is available in the city, this hardly plays any role in meeting the transport demand in the rest of the cities with populations of greater than a million. Considering the financial health of various levels of governments (central, and city governments) and investment requirement to improve the rail-based mass transport system, it is evident that bus transport will have to play a major role in providing passenger transport services in Korean metropolitan cities in the future. It is amply clear that among various modes of road based passenger transport, bus occupies less road space and causes less pollution per passenger-km than personalized modes.

Therefore, a transport policy should especially emphasize and promote the bus transport system. Fiscal policy of government can play an important role in this regard. Most of the bus transport operators in Korea face high operational deficit which badly affects their financial performance. Due to this, along with other reasons, they are unable to manage and augment fleets which, in the long-run, affects their operational performance. The private bus companies in Gwangju can't use the additional investment to expand transit services to meet the growing traffic demand in GMC. This will increase the operational cost of bus companies, which may be passed on to the passengers in the form of either increased fare or poor quality of service. Revenue loss to the government may be compensated by municipal budget.

4.3. Various Bus Transit Services

Currently, it is increasingly difficult to achieve good market acceptance with a single type of product. Bus transport operators in Korea still believe that the vast majority of their users make the same type of commuting trips every day, and so promotes package that essentially assume this regularity. It may be possible that current users of bus transport have such regular patterns of use, but certainly many of those that have left it had varying mobility needs that they felt were poorly satisfied either by the services themselves or by the price deals available. Therefore, it is required to segment the supply of bus transport system to provide different services for different people, and even to the same person at different occasions.

4.4. Improving Efficiency

A serious effort should be made to improve the productive efficiency of private bus companies since they are the main provider of public transport services in Korean cities. The system requires a huge subsidy since revenues cover less than half of the costs. These buses are operated mainly by small companies. Private operators are unable to survive financially without any subsidy. Their success is attributed to a high level of productivity, which is reflected in their low staffing ratios. The private bus operators play a major role in meeting the demand.

It is recognized that some form of competitive pressure is needed to ensure that a serious effort is made towards productive efficiency. This competitive pressure may be obtained either through direct competition for the market or through some form of systematic comparison with similar undertakings. Direct competition for the market, for example through periodic tenders for the right to supply the service in a partly or totally protected environment, is more appropriate for cities where presently there is no bus transport operation. In this case, private operators may be encouraged to provide the service where a negative result will mean loss of business for the incumbent operator. This will impose a competitive pressure on the operator to improve productive efficiency.

As cost of operation rises, for example, a transport undertaking comes under financial pressure to raise fares, but politicians are under contrary pressure to keep fares at existing levels. Unless the undertaking is subsidized, it will have to eliminate some of its less profitable services. However, politicians will face pressure from those whose services are threatened and may insist on maintaining money-losing operations. Due to this, transport undertakings find it difficult to raise their revenue enough to meet the cost of operation. It is increasingly becoming very difficult for loss making urban transport undertakings to augment and manage their fleet, which in turn leads to poor operational performance and deterioration in quality of services.

4.5. Adoption of Optimal Pricing Strategies

Pricing of transport services is another key issue which should be addressed properly. The price of transport services must be seen not only as an instrument for cost recovery but also for driving consumers' behavior. Although there is no such thing as the 'right' price, there are rather optimal pricing strategies, which facilitate attainment of specific goals. The optimum price to achieve profit maximization may differ from the one needed to maximize welfare or to ensure the highest traffic revenue.

Many economists recommend adoption of prices based on marginal costs, particularly in case of public enterprises. The driving force behind the argument in favor of marginal cost pricing for public enterprises is the assertion that they ought to maximize welfare rather than profits. The adoption of marginal cost pricing may, however, in certain circumstances, result in an undertaking making a financial loss. The classic example of this is the decreasing cost industry where, because of high initial capital costs, the setting of charges equal to marginal cost will result in a financial deficit. This deficit may not be necessarily indicative of mismanagement.

Most of the urban transport undertakings in the city appear to operate on increasing returns to scale and consequently marginal cost pricing will result in a financial deficit. When they are restricted to meet a revenue-cost constraint, it is required to find the second-best set of prices which could be based on inverse elasticity rule. The price and output combinations that it computes minimize the deadweight loss due to unavoidable deviation of price from marginal cost. Since this pricing rule takes into account price elasticity of demand, it is superior to the average-cost pricing rule that most urban transport undertakings tend to adopt.

Apart from this one could also envisage a differential pricing mechanism such as peak period, off-peak period, peak-direction, off-peak direction etc. based pricing strategy. The problem of the peak is peculiar to the transport sector. The problem here arises from systematic variation in demand, frequently over a relatively short period. The problem is further aggravated due to the fact that transport can not be stored to reconcile the systematic changes in demand with smooth, even production. Reconciliation can only be through price. Justification of differential pricing for peak and off-peak passengers stems from the fact that marginal cost of production during peak exceeds that during off-peak.

Charging peak and off-peak passengers prices equal to their respective marginal costs not only maximizes social welfare but also has the potential to augment traffic revenue. Even after adopting such a pricing strategy, if traffic revenue is not sufficient to cover costs, then one may have to adopt the second best pricing, where price charged to a particular group of passengers equals marginal cost plus mark-up. The mark-up over marginal cost would be inversely proportional to the price elasticity of demand. For example, peak travelers whose demand is relatively inelastic could be charged a price substantially higher than the marginal cost as compared to off-peak passengers.

4.6. Reorganization of Bus Networks

A bus system has to provide the best possible service to the greatest number of people within the governing economic constraints. Bus services should be concentrated in heavy travel corridors, with the greatest service frequency and route coverage usually provided on approaches to the city centre. Representative guidelines for bus route reform can be presented in terms of bus routes and services, its service area and route coverage, and bus route structure, etc.

More than 90% of the residents of Gwangju city should live in within a 500m radius of bus stops. Bus systems must serve major employment concentrations, schools and hospitals. The bus routes are needed to be fitted to major streets and land use patterns. Dispersed routing patterns are suited for downtown Gwangju because of its dispersed outlying development areas or with the limited capacity of side bus lanes. It will result in promoting the accessibility of residents in outlying areas. More than 80% of total bus passengers should get to their destinations in the city center in a single transfer, but one transfer is inevitable in GMC when getting around using public transit. Bus routes should also be direct and simple. But, irregular routes emerge due to topographic barriers or irregular street networks. Bus routes should be as short as possible to serve their markets; excessively long routes need to be avoided.

The bus route reformation plan in Gwangju aims to improve efficiency in bus services and to provide the best bus service to the greatest number of people. This planning is a short-range process that is usually done on a route-by-route basis. It is important to establish clearly the steps to be addressed.

Publicly owned urban transport undertakings can think of charging different (optimal) prices for different quality of services. Assuming that the shift of consumers between different quality of services is negligible, the availability of the range of services means that total potential consumer surplus will exceed that generated if only a single price and service package were available. The operator stands to gain as a result of this pricing strategy since costs of servicing each customer group are not drastically different.

4.7. Demand-Supply Side Management Measures

Improving the city bus transport system in isolation may not be a very effective tool to reduce air pollution and congestion in a metropolitan city. Besides taking measures to improve the bus transport system, city government should also use market based instruments to restrain the usage of private vehicles. Congestion pricing, parking fees, fuel taxes etc. could be used effectively to restrain the usage of all personalized modes.

At the same time, it is equally important to improve the infrastructure facilities in a metropolitan city. Measures such as new road alignments, hierarchy of roads, provision of service roads, bye passes, bus priority lanes, construction and repair of footpaths, removal of encroachments, improvement of signals etc. should be taken in the metropolitan city. These low cost short-and medium-term measures have the potential to reduce congestion significantly. Since congestion and air pollution in the city are positively correlated, these measures could reduce air pollution as well. Besides short-and medium-term measures, there is a need to have long-term measures as well, involving technology upgradation and the introduction of a high speed, high capacity public transport system particularly along high-density traffic corridors.

4.8. Encouraging Green Transport

An urban transport strategy should also encourage green (non-motorized) transport modes like bicycles and pedestrians. First of all, the safety concerns of cyclists and pedestrians have to be addressed adequately. For this purpose, there has to be a segregated right of way for bicycles and pedestrians. Apart from improving safety, this will help improve traffic flow, increase the average speed of traffic, and reduce emissions resulting from low speeds. In order to enable longer trip lengths to be undertaken on bicycles, there is a need to improve bicycle technology. Lighter bicycles with gears and tubeless tires would be handy for longer trip. GMC may promote the development and commercialization of lighter and more efficient bicycles.

Among various factors affecting the quality of life and safety in the city, the transport system is among the most important. The urban transport situation in Gwangju is deteriorating. The deterioration is faster in the metropolitan city where there is an excessive concentration of vehicles. Commuters in the city are faced with acute road congestion and rising air pollution. These problems cannot be solved without focusing on public transport in general and bus transport in particular.

A metropolitan city cannot afford to cater only to the private cars and two-wheelers and there has to be a general recognition that policy should be designed in such a way which reduces the need to travel by personalized modes and boosts the bus transport system. This could be achieved by enhancing the quantity as well as introducing a variety of bus transport services.

At the same time, there is a need to integrate different modes of public transport, segment supply of the bus transport system to provide different services for different groups of people, enhance productive efficiency of the bus transport system, and adopt optimal pricing strategies. Since bus transport services in Korean metropolitan cities are mainly provided by private companies, there should be an effort to restructure the functioning of these companies. Currently, it is increasingly becoming very difficult for these loss making undertakings to augment and manage their fleet, which in turn leads to poor operational performance and deterioration in quality of services. Improving the urban bus transport system in isolation may not be a very effective tool to reduce air pollution and congestion in large Korean cities. City government should use market based instruments to promote cleaner technology and fuel and encourage people to use non-motorized transport.

A self-portrait in the newspaper

Seoul expats happy with public transit

Foreigners living in Seoul were most satisfied with transport when rating a range of services last year, according to a survey released Monday by the Seoul Metropolitan Government. But satisfaction with their residential environment was rated lowest in the survey of 900 expatriates in Seoul.

The city began conducting the research in 2008 as part of its globalization efforts. It commissioned the local pollster Korea Society Opinion Institute to conduct the survey which took place between December last year and February this year. Respondents scored their satisfaction with transport at 4.03 out of 5 points. The rating was down slightly from 4.05 in the previous year, but was still higher than their ratings for other services.

Those questioned were generally happy with translation services for public transport and with public transit fares, officials explained. But they voiced complaints about taxi services, reporting that some drivers shun or overcharge foreigners. The respondents marked satisfaction with their living conditions at 3.55 points. The figure was slightly up from 3.52 points in 2009, but the lowest in all the categories surveyed. Some respondents complained of difficulties getting proper information on their rental houses, officials said.

Overall, foreigners living in Seoul gave an average of 3.81 points for all five categories which were: educational, living, medical and cultural environments as well as transport services. The overall satisfaction rating increased for the third consecutive year, with figures in 2008 and 2009 at 3.59 and 3.78, respectively. Foreigners' satisfaction with Seoul's educational environment rose to 3.78, from 2009's rating of 3.66.

The municipality is pushing ahead with a package of measures to help foreigners in the city. On Monday, the city announced 35 projects for foreign residents. Seoul plans to build a 15-story building in which foreign residents will be able to receive diverse municipal services. In September, the city will also open a global business center in the Seoul International Finance Center to help foreign financiers do business in Korea conveniently.

By 2015, the city plans to set up dormitory and educational facilities for foreign students in Seoul on a 29,000-square-meter site in the district of Mapo. The city also seeks to introduce special courses to three elementary schools to help foreigners and their children learn Korean. In Seoul, there are some 263,000 people of foreign nationality as of December last year, a remarkable jump from 130,000 in 2006. The current figure accounts for 2.5 % of the population in the capital.

*** Source: The Korea Herald (2011.5.2)**

References

Allen, Heather, Bus Reform in Seoul, Republic of Korea, Gobal Report on Human Settlement, 2013, pp.1-21.

Chung, Ha-wook, Bus Transit System Improvement Plan in Gwangju, Policy Research 2001-9, Gwangju Jeonnam Development Institute, 2002 (in Korean).

Edwards, John D., JR. (ed.), Transportation Planning Handbook, Institute of Transportation Engineers, New Jersey: Prentice Hall, 1999.

Glass, James J., Citizen Participation in Planning: the Relationship Between Objectives and Techniques, Journal of the American Planning Association Vol. 45, No. 2, 1979, pp.180-190.

Gwangju Development Institute, A Study on the Establishment of Public Transportation Policies through the Analysis of Big Date for Transit Card, Policy Research 2013-10, 2013 (in Korean).

Gwangju Metropolitan City (GMC), Reformation Plan of City Bus Route Networks, Seminar Papers, 1996.

GMC, Gwangju Transportation Improvement Midterm Plan, 1996.

GMC, Travel Pattern Survey and Analysis for the Bus Route Planning, 1997

Gwangju Metropolitan City (GMC), City Administration White Paper, 2000-2011 (Each Year) (in Korean).

GMC, GMC Statistical Yearbook, 2000-2011 (Each Year) (in Korean).

GMC, Gwangju Metropolitan Transportation Master Plan, Final Draft, August 2007 (in Korean).

GMC, Gwangju Metropolitan Public Transportation Plan, 1st Draft, December 2011 (in Korean).

GMC, Improvement Plan of the Bus Quasi-public Operation System (BQOS) in Gwangju City, June 2013 (in Korean).

Gundry, Kathleen G. and Heberlein, Thomas A., Do Public Meeting Represent the Public, Journal of the American Planning Association Vol. 50, No. 2, 1984, pp.175-182.

Gray, George E. Gray and Hoel, Lester A. (ed.), Public Transportation, New Jersey: Prentice Hall, 1992.

Hartgen, David T., Transportation Myths: Travel Behavior, System Condition, and

Land Use, ITE Journal, Vol. 61, No. 9, 1992, P 40-45.

Jeong, Bonghyun, New Transportation Policy in Regional Metropolitan City: Gwangju, Korea, CNU Press, 2005 (in Korean).

Jeong, Bonghyun, SOC and Regional Development: Standing Transportation Problems and Solutions in the Jeonlla Provinces, Korea, CNU Press, 2010 (in Korean).

Korea Institute of Science and Technology (KAIST), Urban Transportation Problems and Policy in korea, 1980

Lee, Sang-Min and Lim, Jung-Sil, Best Experiences from Public Transport Reform, Korea's Best Practices in the Transport Sector, KOTI knowledge Sharing Report Issue 09, The Korea Transport Institute, 2013.

Seoul Development Institute (SDI), Effective Reformation of Seoul's Bus Line System, 1995.

White, Peter, Public Transport: Its Planning, Management and Operation, London: UCL press, 1995.

Wickstorm, George V. and Grant, Alberta A., Planning for Implementation, Transportation, Vol.1 No.3, 1972, pp.419-453.

Yang, Cheol-Soo, A Study on the System of Exclusive Bus Lanes for Efficient Roads Operation, Basic Research 2011-15, Gwangju Development Institute, 2011 (in Korean).

Yang, Cheol-Soo, A Study on the Establishment of Public Transportation Policies through the Analysis of Big Data for Transit Card, Basic Research 2013-10, Gwangju Development Institute, 2013 (in Korean).

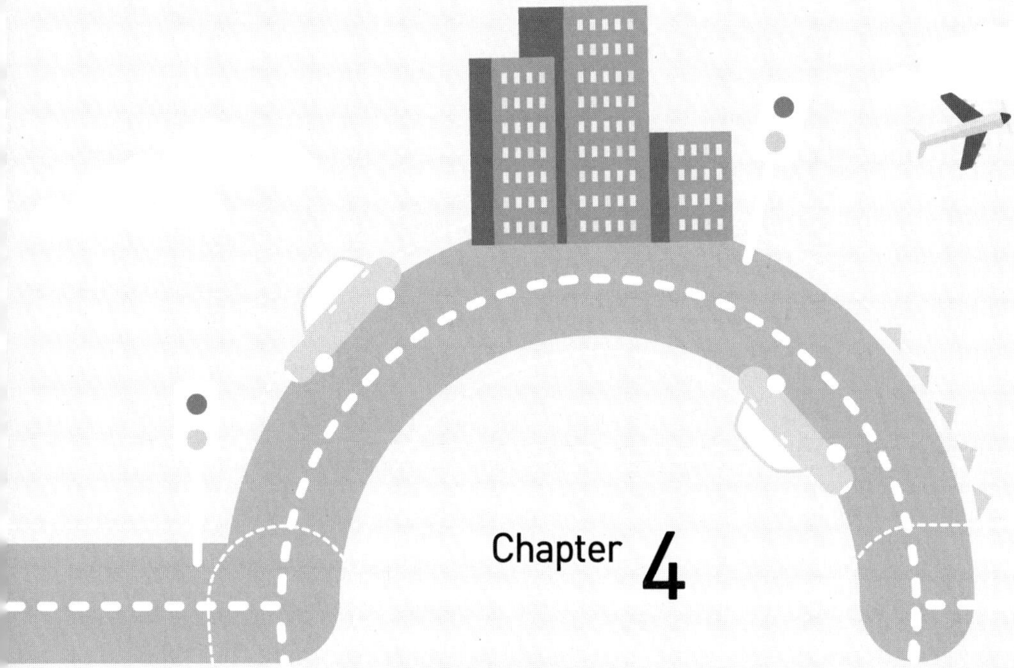

Chapter 4

Urban Metro Problems and Policy

1. Concept of Urban Metro

1.1. Concept and Type of Urban Metro

Metro is an all-encompassing term for various types of local rail systems providing passenger service within and around urban or suburban areas. The set of urban rail systems can be roughly subdivided into the following categories, which sometimes overlap because some systems or lines have aspects of each. Metro systems are commonly classified as heavy, medium or light systems. These terms refer to the type of construction; however, the weight of vehicle affects the acceleration, gradient and curvature of the track, which in turn affects the average speed and station spacing, and hence the carrying capacity, the headway, and the need for automatic signalling and segregated tracks. It is these latter qualities which determine the type of transport which a rail system provides.[1] Simpson(1988) classifies urban rail systems into subMetros, metros, light rail transit, and auto-guided transit.

Table 4.1. Types of Metro Systems

Type	Concept
Suburban railway	▪ Conventional heavy rail commuter services ▪ An electricity propelled vehicle usually operated in trains on exclusive right-of-way
Metros	▪ Traditional, mostly underground, medium weight railways ▪ A standard railroad passenger car with high-density seating
Light rail transit	▪ An electricity propelled vehicle usually operated signally or in trains on shared, semi-exclusive or exclusive right-of-way
Auto guided transit	▪ Small-and-medium sized vehicles that operate fully automatically on guideways

Source: Edwards(1999), p.430

[1] David Walmsley and Ken Perrett(1992), p.4.

1.2. Functions and Benefits of Urban Metro

Metro is an essential public service and a major public transport system in metropolitan cities. It is necessary for the metropolitan areas to function, and serves several primary purposes: it increases transportation capacity in heavily traveled corridors and reduces reliance on passenger car trips. It supports and fosters densely developed areas, especially city centers. It also provides mobility for the elderly, handicapped, and others who are unable to drive.

Metro provides important benefits to its riders, the adjacent land development, and the community. The benefits consist of social benefits, congestion relief benefits, environmental benefits, economic benefits, and energy benefits.[2] Metro acts a safety net for individuals who can't afford an automobile, who are handicapped, or too old to drive. It reduces the number of vehicles on streets and in high travel demand corridors. Metro makes contributions to reduction in air pollution. It is a significantly less-expensive alternative than using an automobile, and reduces oil consumption.

2. Developments and Operation of Gwangju Metro

2.1. Outline of the Gwangju Metro Line 1

Gwangju Metro Line 1 is a rapid transit line in Gwangju, South Korea, operated by the Gwangju Metropolitan Rapid Transit Corporation (GMRTC, or Gwangju Metro). It connects Nokdong Station in Dong-gu at its eastern terminus to Pyeongdong Station in Gwangsan-gu in the west, via the old central business district and Gwangju Airport. On maps, it is designated by dark green. The line began operations in 2004, making Gwangju the fifth South Korean city with a rapid transit system.

[2] Edwards, John D., Jr(1999), p.428.

Unlike the city bus services, Gwangju's Metro was constructed by the city government and operated by the city metro transit corporation. It forms a reliable and comfortable mass transit system within Gwangju's transport policy. The construction of Metro Line 1 began in 1996 and was completed in twelve years. Although Gwangju Metro has only a short history dating from 2008, it is a key transport mode, but occupied 1.3% of the total passenger trips in 2004. When phase 2 of the Metro Line 1 was completed in 2008, the total route length was 20.1 km and about 3% of all passenger trips were transported by metro. Previously, an additional line in the city was proposed to achieve a target share of 15%. However, the GMC replaced the plan with a new metro line based on the new metro projects. The network plan consists of two lines providing a light rail system. It is expected to satisfy demands and improve the efficiency of the rail system through the metropolitan area.

Table 4.2. Outline of the Gwangju Metro Line 1

Division	Detailed items
Route	■ East-west single line, Length: 20.1 km ■ Section: Yongsandong, Dong-Gu ↔ Okdong, Gwangsan-Gu
Station	■ 20 stations, 2 Subway base depots ■ Rolling stock formations: 52 cars 13 formations
Operation	■ Service hours: am 5:30 - pm 24:00 ■ Headway: Peak hour (5 - 7minutes), Off-peak (8 - 10minutes) ■ Travel time: 38-39 minutes, Frequency: Weekday (246 times / day)

Source: GMC(2011)

Figure 4.1. Gwangju Metro Route

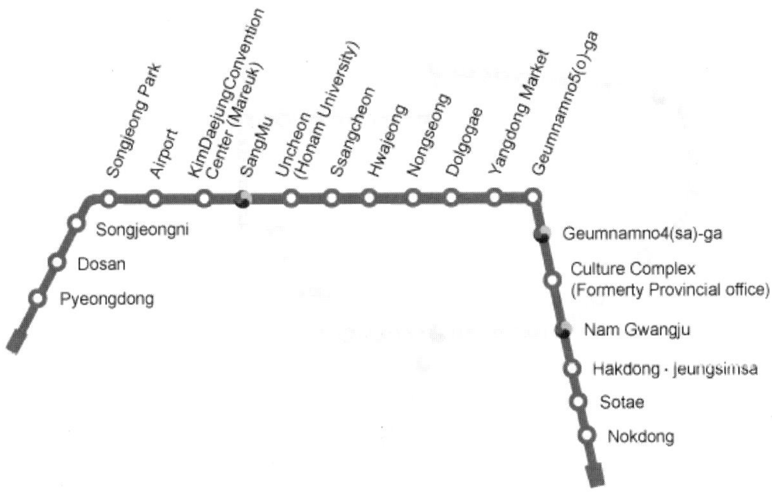

2.2. Facilities and Operation of Metro Systems

The metro network in Gwangju is an east-west single line operated by GMRTC. It totalled 20.1 km in length and carried about 49.4 thousand persons daily in 2012. To improve safety, the GMRTC has installed colour TV monitors and automatic alarms on every platform. Passenger are informed of all train arrivals and departures. Railway stations are furnished with air-conditioning, and barrier-free facilities for disabled people are installed in order to improve passenger comfort. In particular, wheelchair lifts have been installed in every station along with barrier-free toilets and tactile tiles. Parking-and-ride facilities are built at 4 stations for improving intermodal transfer in the metropolitan area. Six stations have both car and bicycle parking lots.

The average rail speed is about 35 km per hour, but the headways are different by the hour. The capacity is increased by making constant efforts to introduce new rolling stock and to shorten headways. The headway is 5 to 7 minutes during rush hours and 8 to 10 minutes at off-peak hours. Metro service starts at 05:30, and the last train is at 24:00. Ridership has increased a little over the last 4 years as the GMC reorganized the city bus routes for better connections between the metro lines and buses early in the operation. Interestingly, the new Metro Line 2 is proposed in order to increase ridership, suggesting that metro policy should focus more on increasing transport demand as a whole.

Table 4.3. Passenger Traffic Volumes of Gwangju Metro Line 1

Division	Unit	2005	2006	2007	2008	2010	2012	AAGR (%)
Total person trips	Thousand person	11,308	10,808	13,922	15,790	17,442	18,036	6.9
Total travel distance	Thousand km	1,038	1,031	998	1,490	1,632	1,632	12.0
Daily person trips	Thousand persons/day	31.0	29.6	38.1	43.3	47.8	49.4	6.9

Note: AAGR means average annual growth rate.
Source: GMCb(2013); GMRTC(each year)

2.3. Gwangju Metro Line 2 Master Plan

The Gwangju Metropolitan City embarked on the expansion of Gwangju Metro Line 2 as soon as the Ministry of Land, Transport and Marine Affairs (MLTM) approved the revised plan in 2013. Construction will begin after the 2015 Universiade. It will proceed in three phases, and is expected to be completed by 2023. Specifics on the second line haven't been finalized yet. The newly revised plan aims to expand Line 2 from the initial 22.1 km to 41.7 km, connecting Gwangju City Hall, Baegungwangjang, Gwangju Station, Jeonnam University and the Cheomdan area. The city will form a task force team as soon as it gets approval and collect opinions to be gathered at public hearings

Metro should be built to ease the traffic congestion and to accommodate the increasing traffic in Gwangju. MLTM announced the basic plan of Gwangju

Metro Line 2 on November, 2011. The overall route is characterized by an enlarged circular line which covers most of the city's new housing sites. There has been a change of the basic plan because of the construction method of Gwangju Metro line 2 in 2013. According to the plan, it is supposed to build a railroad low underground.

Table 4.4. Gwangju Metro Line 2 Master Plan

Division	Detailed items
Length	41.9 km (44 stations, 1 car depot)
Route of line	City hall - World cup stadium - Baegungwangjang - Gwangju station - Cheomdanjigu - Suwanjigu - City hall
Construction type	Low underground (Automatic Guided Transit)
Construction Period	2016 - 2024 year, 3 phases
Total cost	1,905.3 billion won (government 60%, local 30%, local bond 10%)

Source: GMC(2013)

Figure 4.2. Gwangju Metro Line 2 Route

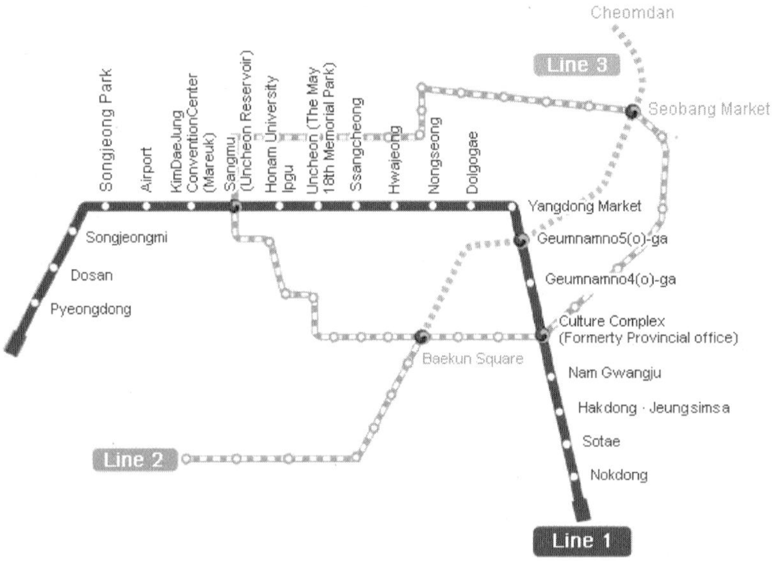

Figure 4.3. Aerial View of Urban Metro Station

3. Urban Metro Problems in Gwangju[3]

3.1. Irrational Metro Route 1

Metro routes have a decisive impact on land use pattern, urban developments and the city's profit performance in general. The construction of a metro route is very expensive. In fact, it is impossible to alternate and shut down a completed metro route. A scientific evaluation process and rational planning is essential to select a good metro route in the metropolitan area. Metro Line 1 was constructed along the existing arterial road linking Songjeong with Juwoldong and covers most of Gwangju's old city center. Line 1 has been clearly inconsistent with the city structural changes, development patterns, and urbanization trends. The multi-purposed facilities, such as the university, city hall and transit station are not near metro stops for quick travel anywhere in Gwangju. For example, traffic population has steadily decreased as a result of the relocation of the provincial government building and declining downtown. Accordingly, Metro Line 1 is a single east-west line which has a basic limitation to induce more metro travellers. The metro service area is limited to less than 3% of the whole city.

3.2. Low Modal Share of Metro

The city bus is a basic and major urban transit system, because it transported about 36.4% of daily travellers in the city in 2012. Private automobile carried about 36.3% of the city's daily passengers in 2012. It resulted in severe traffic congestion, parking difficulties and a rapid increase in transport costs as a whole.

Many Gwangju commuters don't use the mass transit railway for their daily rides to work and to home. It is because Gwangju Metro does not cover most parts of the Gwangju Metropolitan Area (GMA). GMC did not reorganize

---

3 Jeong, Bonghyun(2008), pp.69-71.

the city bus routes for better connections between the metro lines and bus early in the operation.

Table 4.5. Percentage Share of Daily Trips by Transport Mode

(Unit: %)

Mode / year	2004	2005	2008	2010	2012	증감(+,-)
Private car	24.6	27.3	31.3	31.7	36.3	+11.7
Taxi	20.0	20.2	17.6	15.6	15.2	-4.8
Bus	37.3	37.5	38.2	38.0	36.4	-0.9
Metro	1.8	1.7	2.1	2.5	2.7	+0.9
Others	16.3	13.3	10.8	12.2	9.4	-6.9
Total	100	100	100	100	100	-

Source: GMC(Each year)

3.3. Yearly Operational Deficit

Metro is a massive and major transport mode in a metropolitan city. Building a metro require huge sums of money and take a long time. Metro facilities have existed for a hundred years and have become permanent. Therefore, there are the basic limitations for the metro to make an operational profit after the construction work is completed. The operational profit of the metro is mainly dependent upon the increasing passengers and reducing operational expenses. In the case of Gwangju Metro Line 1, the operating deficit increased steadily, because the demand of the Metro Line 1 didn't increase in general. The operating deficit decreased by 2.89% annually from 42.0 billion won in 2005 to 34.2 billion won in 2012. In 2012, the average deficit of operation marked 2.85 billion won per month and 93.7 million won daily. GMRTC is operating at a heavy loss due to lack of sufficient travelling demand. The deficit at the moment is really a big financial problem to GMC. Reducing the operating deficit of Gwangju Metro is paramount. On the other hand, the total fare of free ride shared about 20.5% of the yearly operating deficit in 2012, which once again underlines the structural problem of operating deficit in Gwangju Metro.

Table 4.6. Operating Deficit of Gwangju Metro Line 1

Division	Unit	2005	2006	2007	2008	2010	2012
Operating deficit	Billion won/year	42.0	49.5	49.8	23.7	30.8	34.2
Monthly deficit	Billion won/month	3.5	4.13	4.15	1.98	2.57	2.85
Daily deficit	Million won/day	115.1	135.6	136.4	64.9	84.4	93.7

Notes: Operating deficit (current account deficit) = operating profit - operating expense

AAGR refers to average annual growth rate.

Source: GMC (2013)

3.4. Poor Connections between the Metro Routes and Bus Networks

GMRTC operates Metro Line 1, while private companies run city buses in the entire city of Gwangju. This has made it difficult to establish convenient transfer systems between the metro line and buses. The overall bus network in Gwangju was not reorganized in harmony with Metro Line 1 in advance. It basically caused a major element which lowers the transport efficiency between the metro and city buses. What is worse, the GMC didn't reorganized the entire routes of city buses before the opening of Gwangju Metro phase 1 Line in 2004. An electronic transportation card is valid on public transits (metro and city bus), and is easy and very convenient for transfer to other transport modes. Gwangju citizens experienced some difficulties in using public transits, because new transportation vehicles were not introduced as scheduled. It resulted in decreasing the total transport efficiency as well as poor public transit services in the city. The city's reorganization plan of bus route hasn't been confirmed due to civil complaints and a clash of bus operators' interests over the plan.

3.5. Huge Losses from Free Riding

The loss Korea's subway operators incurred due to the country's free ride program for the elderly and infirm has risen over the past five years. Senior citizens aged 65 or older, the disabled and people of "national merit" who have contributed to the country, such as war veterans, can ride the subway for free. The benefit is available in the capital city of Seoul and five major metropolitan cities — Busan, Daegu, Incheon, Gwangju and Daejeon. The basic fair for a trip is 900 won ($0.78).

The country's seven subway operators registered a combined deficit of 412.9 billion won from the free rides, accounting for 51.6% of their total net losses of 801.0 billion won in 2013[4]. The deficit incurred by the welfare program has steadily increased over the past seven years, from 263.3 billion won in 2006 to 412.9 billion won in 2013, data showed. As of 2013, about 989,041 legal non-paying passengers per day used the program, accounting for 15.6% of all subway users. The deficit the beneficiaries cause is expected to rise further as the national forecast showed the population of seniors over 65 will increase to 15.7% in 2020 from 10.7% in 2010.

GMRTC recorded a ratio of 32.0%, the highest among subway operators in 2012. The operators are advised to seek detailed and feasible measures to overcome their structural weakness. When launching a new project as a way of business diversification, they need to find where they have a competitive edge. Gwangju Metro's operator does not receive any financial subsidies from central government. Under the current system, the financial soundness of the subway operators will further deteriorate.

---

4 Nocutnews (2014.5.13.)

4. Gwangju Metro Transit Policy

4.1. Formulation of Preferential Public Transport Policy[5] (PPTP)

It is very important for GMC to set the directions of PPTP and to establish strategies for its effective implementation in accordance with the opening of Gwangju Metro Line 1. To do this, GMC is first required to devise and further the Gwangju Public Transit Master Plan. A sufficient budget in GMC should be secured in order to improve Metro transfer system and to increase municipal support for better bus transit services. A transport policy team is responsible for the establishment of sustainable public transit systems and the consideration of the implementation strategy in the city. The top priority of the GMC is to create a pleasant and sustainable transport environment for pedestrian and public transit riders. It is worth designating Gwangju as a public transport and cultural modal city based on the public transportation promotion law. In connection with this, it is necessary to improve the pedestrian environment in the old Gwangju CBD. GMC should support city promotional programs to publicize public transport opportunities. A major emphasis will be on changing citizens attitudes about public transport and then their actions. The city needs to ensure that road improvements address public transport needs. It must consider transit infrastructure needs in advance project planning and design. It can make public transport an integral part of the city's transport network and reduces the need for expensive and disruptive retrofits of the road network.

4.2. Integrated Public Transit System (IPTS)

An integrated public transit system is a public transport system that has ideally two or more forms of public transport (buses, transit rail and suburban

---

5 State of Montana(2005), pp.14-18.

rail) working together to adequately provide for the transport requirements of the metropolitan area. A metropolitan area transport association is needed to organize for the realization of an integrated public transit system. The introduction of this structural reform allows for more co-ordinated policy and investment and a common fare system on bus, subway and urban rail services.

The objectives of the IPTS for Gwangju are to: develop high quality and sustainable bus transit system in participating cities to improve mobility along strategic mass transit corridors; improve accessibility to public transportation for the transport disadvantaged; and build greater institutional capacity in the metropolitan public transportation institutions in order to formulate integrated urban transport policies, and to improve urban transport planning and traffic management. GMC first needs to implement capacity building: this component is aimed at: a) strengthening the city government's capacity to formulate urban transport strategies; b) improvement of the institutional capacity of transportation entities in participating cities to ensure adequate implementation of BRTS; c) strengthening of the operational capacity of participating cities with respect to the implementation of urban development and transport strategies.

4.3. Bigger Financial Burden of the Central Government on Metro Projects

Public transit has multiple roles: in addition to operating as a transportation system, it is typically expected to operate as a social service for people who have no other way to get around. For this reason, there may well be light rail and subway lines that turn an operational profit, but they're part of a larger system that is expected to provide basic transportation for everyone who can't use the publicly-funded road and highway system. The more parts of the city are built up in sprawling, car-oriented ways, the more expensive it is to provide that social service transit.

Funding for urban transit comes mainly from the central government, local government and other sources. Restricted funding levels place constraints upon the level of service provided and the existence of services in a metropolitan city. GMC is the owner of a public corporation, which is responsible for the metro system. One of the main factors leading to profitability of a metro is population density. If density is high enough, then the ratio of rides to mile covered is higher to begin with.

According to the Metro Act and its Enforcement Ordinance, the funding source of urban metro is made up of three elements such as government budget (60%), city budget (30%) and municipal bond (10%). But the present system of funding for metro construction is irrational and on a uniform standard. The reason is that the funding criteria applies to the building of urban metro in metropolitan cities, and has no consideration for the financial condition of a metropolitan city. For instance, the GMC is low on finances right now. That is, its financial situation is not very sound. Therefore, the central government should determine the flexible size of government financial support to construct a metro, based upon the examination results of financial status in each metropolitan city. It is suggested that GMC should ask the central government to pay 70% of the total construction cost of Gwangju Metro, with consideration for the financial vulnerability and weaker economy of GMC.

4.4. A Decline in the City's Operational Deficit

The metros of metropolitan cities in Korea are operating at a structural loss, since income from fares, limited by a social level of fares, does not cover the operating costs of the system. The funding of this deficit is mainly carried out through the Metro Act. Operating cost/revenue comes down mostly to how many people are riding public transits, and fares. If the city government is running public transits that have few people on them most of the day, that's costing a lot but bringing in little revenue. If GMC have a line with high all-day demand in both directions, it's more likely to come out on top. In general, irrational metro Line 1, the west-east bound single metro line, low modal share of the Metro, and free riding contribute to an increasing operating deficit of Gwangju Metro.[6]

In terms of capital, suburban rail routes are likely to require more infrastructure per trip served due to longer average trips. On rail or bus, if a very large proportion of transit use happens at peak hour / peak direction, then you may have much of your fleet only in use for several hours each day, and that's expensive. The Gwangju Metro doesn't operate at a profit, which means it doesn't cover its operating costs without taking construction costs into account. Expecting a transit system to cover both construction and operation costs from user fees would not be economically viable, which is why transit entities are almost always public or quasi-public. In fact, much of the loss in Gwangju Metro is tied to capital costs of expansion. GMC is now faced with an increase in the city's operational deficit for the metro in recent years. If deficits aren't reduced, it will continue to make extra demands on financial resources in Gwangju. Operating at a profit for Gwangju Metro is a moot point unless the expenses are a ridiculous drain on the tax base.

4.5. Separation of Building from Operation of Metro[7]

Urban railroad projects are to be implemented in accordance with the Urban Railroad Act (URA). This act aims at promoting the construction of subways to improve the traffic conditions in urban traffic zone, advancing urban transportation, and enhancing safety and convenience of passengers by rationalizing operation and managing equipment efficiently. The mayor of a metropolitan city should make up a transportation master plan and propose it to MLTA for authorization. Metro construction is a long-term

[6] Jeong, Bonghyun(2007), pp.8-9.

[7] Lee, In-keun(2004), pp.23-24.

project with construction period from 5 years to 12 years. It is very expensive to construct an urban metro in the city. Nobody can deny metro, as a main public transit mode in the city, is superior to other public transport, with respect to speediness, punctuality and comfortableness. Nevertheless, the mayors of metropolitan cities are somewhat reluctant to adopt Metro policy readily. It is because a metro project demands vast budgets, and it also takes a long-period of 5-12 years to complete a railroad line, while it takes a long time to have the cost-recovery effect on the project. Financial resources are the most significant of all for metro construction. Once the metro construction work is started, it is impossible to cease work on the building, and a massive budget should be invested in the construction by year. According to the law, a metropolitan government should decide to construct an urban metro in the city, and devise measures to fund the metro project in advance. In Korea, metro projects don't go well, because metropolitan government should work out both financial and construction plans of the metro project, and is fully responsible of its construction work. On the other hand, central government subsidizes a part of the total construction expense. Therefore, it is necessary to separate the building from the operation of Gwangju Metro Line 2. Central government thus takes the responsibility of the construction of urban metros, and city government should be in charge of the operation of the metro later on. It will take a change in the urban railroad act to separate the building from operation of an urban metro project.

4.6. Expansion of Park-and-Ride Facilities

Park-and-ride facilities are car parks with connections to public transport that allow commuters and other wishing to travel into city centers to leave their vehicles and transfer to a bus, rail system, or carpool for the rest of their trip. Park-and-rides are generally located in the suburbs of metropolitan areas or on the outer edges of large cities. Park-and-ride schemes are often marketed as a way to avoid the difficulties and cost of parking in the city centre, but it has also been suggested that there is 'a lack of clear-cut evidence for park-and-ride's widely assumed impact in reducing congestion.[8] In theory, park-and-ride facilities allow commuters to avoid the stress of driving a congested part of their journey and facing scarce, expensive city-centre parking. Park-and-ride facilities serve the needs of commuters who live beyond practical walking distance from the railway station or bus stop which offers service to the city center. Most facilities provide services such as passenger waiting areas and toilets. Travel information, such as leaflets and posters, may be provided.

4.7. Encouraging the Development of Station Area (SI)

A station area in a metropolitan city has high land development potential for further urban development and management, and is required for a comprehensive urban development scheme. It is also effective to spatially distribute urban functions and to induce multi-centric urban structure in a metropolitan city. Therefore, its systematic development can contribute to the improvement of urban environments and the facilitation of balanced urban development. Developing SIA can be seen as a way for helping improve earning of a metro by leading to increased land development gain. It will have a positive effect on the convenient public transit transfer systems, balanced urban development and better public transport services for the citizen. Based upon SIA development rules, GMC established the initial SIA development plan after a feasibility study and a conceptual development plan in 1996. The proposed sites included Namgwangju, Nongsung, Songjeong, and Sangmu metro stations. The SIA development projects need to promote an investment plan independent of a profitable project in terms of finance. It is desired that land use characteristics should be worth consideration and lawful and institutional devices are needed for the effective implementation

[8] Manns, Jonathan(2010).

of SIA projects in Gwangju.

4.8. Decision on the Rational Construction Types of Metro Line 2

Urban metro should be built to ease the traffic congestion and to accommodate the increasing traffic in Gwangju. The Ministry of Land, Transportation and Maritime Affairs (MLTM) announced the basic plan of Gwangju Metro Line 2 on November, 2011. According to the plan, Gwangju Metro was supposed to be built as a railroad along an elevated road above ground. The overall route was characterized by an enlarged circular line which covers most of the city's new housing sites. The original construction method of the metro caused a lot of problems for the GMC in terms of noise, urban aesthetic and environments. It first doesn't create a clean, beautiful urban landscape. Most of the residents along the tracks regularly experience levels of noise that over time can leave them hard of hearing for life. It can partially deteriorate the living environment of the city in the future.

On the other hand, the increasing building costs impose additional financial burdens on the GMC. The construction methods of the Metro are classified into two items, including single or mixed construction method. GMC planned to construct Metro Line 2 based on a mixed construction method. GMC applied for the MLTM to change the construction method of Gwangju Metro line 2 on March, 2013. The changed plan has finally approved by the MLTM on December, 2013. Most Gwangju Metro Line 2 will be built at a low depth underground or on roads in order to cut down the total construction cost of the metro, to reduce its construction period and to improve the appearance of the city. The details of the city's plan for metro construction has been made public.

Subway mirrors urban, national growth.

Seoul's rapid growth has driven the development of its public transport system, especially the subway, which has evolved into one of the world's most extensive networks in less than four decades. Owing to the network's intricate structure and rapid growth, Korean subway constructors and operators acquired engineering technologies, which went on to boost the nation's exports.

"Seoul is one of the few cities in the world which has as many as nine subway lines, together with several intercity railroads," said an official of Seoul Metro, which operates subway line Nos. 1-4. "Considering its relatively short history, this was a drastic expansion, not only in terms of scale but also in terms of the technology involved."

The first-ever underground railway in Seoul opened in 1974, connecting Seoul Station to Cheongnyangni Station. In 1981, the Seoul Metropolitan Subway Corporation, the former body of Seoul Metro, was established to operate the metro.

"Despite its relatively late start, Seoul's subway business soon took an upturn, in step with the construction boom and urban expansion in the 1980s and 1990s," the official explained. The geographical features of the city, incorporating several mountains and the Han River, also helped Korean companies build competitiveness in special features such as sub-riverbed tunnels and railway bridges

One of the most dramatic examples of technological innovation was the construction of the Subway Line No. 9 section of Express Bus Terminal Station in 2009.

Subways around the world

Year of introduction

Ranking	City	Year opened
1	London	Jan. 10, 1863
2	Chicago	June 6, 1892
3	Budapest	May 2, 1896
4	Glasgow	Dec. 14, 1896
5	Paris	July 19, 1900
14	Tokyo	Dec. 30, 1927
15	Osaka	May 20, 1933
24	Nagoya	Nov. 15, 1957
35	Beijing	Oct. 1, 1969
37	Sapporo	Dec. 16, 1971
41	Pyongyang	Sept. 6, 1973
43	*Seoul	Aug. 15, 1974

Seoul is the world's 43rd and Asia's 7th

Number of passengers (As of 2012)

Ranking	City	Number per year (million)	
1	Tokyo	3,176	
2	Beijing	2,763	
3	Seoul		2,518
		• Seoul Metro	1,509.64
		• Seoul Metropolitan Rapid Transit	835.33
		• Seoul Metro Line 9	109.5
4	Moscow	2,390	
5	New York	1,580	

Number of subway stations

Ranking	City	Number	
1	New York	468	
2	Paris	381	
3	Madrid	299	
4	Seoul		293
		• Seoul Metro	120
		• Seoul Metropolitan Rapid Transit	148
		• Seoul Metro Line 9	25
5	Tokyo	290	

Subway's share of transportation in Seoul

(Unit: %)

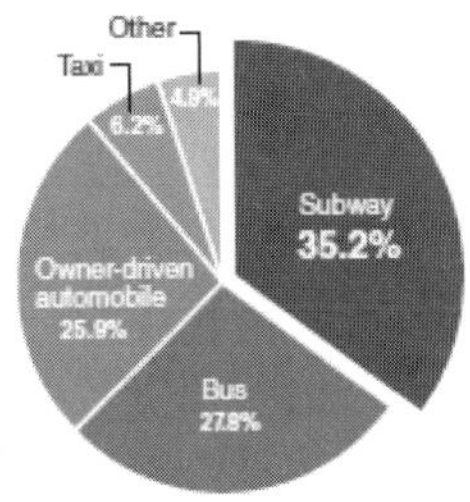

Trends of national economic development and Seoul subway expansion

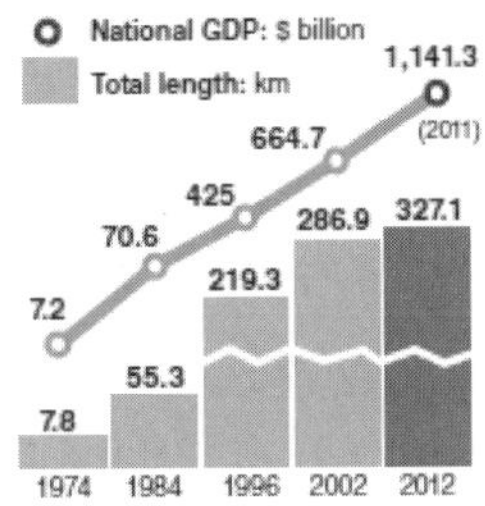

Current status (As of 2012)

Lines, length: nine lines, 329.1 km
Carriers: Seoul Metro, Seoul Metropolitan Rapid Transit, Metro 9
Daily number of passengers: 6.9 million
Annual number of passengers: 2.5 billion

Seoul Metro
Lines: four lines (1, 2, 3 and 4)
Total length: 137.9 km, 120 stations
Number of passengers per day: 4.13 million

SMRT
Lines: four lines (5, 6, 7 and 8)
Total length: 162.2 km, 157 stations
Number of passengers per day: 2.46 million

Metro 9 (private)
Lines: one line (9)
Total length: 27 km, 25 stations
Number of passengers per day: 0.3 million

Construction cost: $105 million per km (as of 2010)
Operating cost: $6.4 million per km (average among three operators)

Source: Seoul Metropolitan Infrastructure Headquarters

The station was not only the intersection point for Line No. 3 and 7, but also located under huge commercial buildings such as Shinsegae Department Store, JW Marriott Hotel and the Express Bus Terminal Station. "The construction area was a mere 15 centimeters below the conventional Line No. 3," said an official of Ssangyong Engineering &Construction, which implemented the project.

In order to guarantee the stability of the surrounding features, the builder had to simultaneously apply two separate excavation skills, an unprecedented practice which ended in success. While constructors made leaps in the subterranean civil engineering sector, Korean rolling stock manufacturers, too, gained recognition in the global market.

Hyundai Rotem recently set to expanding its leverage in the overseas market. The company, which went public last month, recorded 1.47 trillion won ($1.37 billion) in sales in the first half of this year, of which 686 billion won was in railway business. "The proportion of our sales made overseas reached 51 % last year and is expected to grow further in the coming years," said a company official.

Prompted by the growth of private companies, Seoul Metro has also entered the global market for railway operating systems. The public corporation is currently mapping out the subway network in Ho Cho Minh City, Vietnam, and offering consulting services to Bangladesh on improving its railroad signal system, officials said.

Also, its smart card system, which allows users to charge a card and use it to pay fares at discount rates, has been exported to New Zealand and Colombia, resulting in some 40 billion won ($37 million) in profits. The subway sector brought a breakthrough to the construction industry, especially in the overseas market.

The most notable success was that of Samsung C&T, which secured last month a 2.2 trillion won deal to build a subway network in Saudi Arabia, marking its fourth such order so far this year. "Middle East countries, which were struck by the 2008-2009 global financial crisis, took an upturn in recent years and set to improving their transportation infrastructure," said an official of the International Contractors Association of Korea. Dubai, for instance, is expected to invest some 7 trillion won in building new roads and railways, according to the official.

"Korean companies were able to respond with agility to such surging demands, due to their years of experience in the market and successful portfolio," he said. "While the global construction industry in general continues to struggle, special sectors such as subway construction may become the key to a breakthrough."

*** Source: The Korea Herald (2013.11.15)**

References

Edwards, John D., JR. (ed.), Transportation Planning Handbook, Institute of Transportation Engineers, New Jersey: Prentice Hall, 1999.

Gwangju Metropolitan City (GMC), Reformation Plan of City Bus Route Networks, Seminar Papers, 1996 (in Korean).

GMC, Gwangju Transportation Improvement Midterm Plan, 1996 (in Korean).

GMC, Travel Pattern Survey and Analysis for the Bus Route Planning, 1997 (in Korean).

GMC, City Administration White Paper, 2000-2011 (Each Year) (in Korean).

GMC, Statistical Yearbook, 2000-2011 (Each Year) (in Korean).

GMC, Gwangju Metropolitan Transportation Master Plan, Final Draft, August 2007 (in Korean).

GMC, Gwangju Metropolitan Public Transportation Plan, 1st Draft, December 2011 (in Korean).

Gwangju Metropolitan Rapid Transit Cooperation (GMRTC), Yearly Balance Sheet, Each year (in Korean).

Jeong, Bonghyun, Changes in the Proposed Gwangju Metropolitan Subway Line 2 and its Improved Access to Chonnam National University, Gwangju, The studies in Regional Development, Gwangju: The Center for Regional Development, Chonnam National University, Vol. 39, No.2, December 2007 (in Korean).

Jeong, Bonghyun, Conceptual Framework of the Urban Railway Networks in Gwangju City, Korea: Review of the Existing Urban Railway Route Master Plan, The Studies in Regional Development, Gwangju: The Center for Regional Development, Chonnam National University, Vol. 40, No.2, December 2008 (in Korean).

Jeong, Bonghyun, New Transportation Policy in Regional Metropolitan City: Gwangju, Korea, CNU Press, 2005 (in Korean).

Jeong, Bonghyun, SOC and Regional Development: Standing Transportation Problems and Solutions in the Jeonlla Provinces, Korea, CNU Press, 2010 (in Korean).

Lee, In-keun, Experiences in Seoul Subway Developments, ITA 2004, 2004.

Manns, Jonathan, Park-and-ride - Politics, Policy and Planning", Town and Country

Planning, Vol 79, No. 3, London: Town and Country Planning Association. March 2010.

State of Montana(SOM), Public transportation / policy paper, Tranplan 21, Department of Transportation, State of Montana, 2007.

Walmsley, David and Perrett, Ken, The Effects of Rapid Transit on Public Transport and Urban Development, State of the Art Review 6, London: Transportation Research Laboratory (TRL), Department of Transport, 1992.

White, Peter, Public Transport: Its Planning, Management and Operation, Third edition, London: UCL press, 1995.

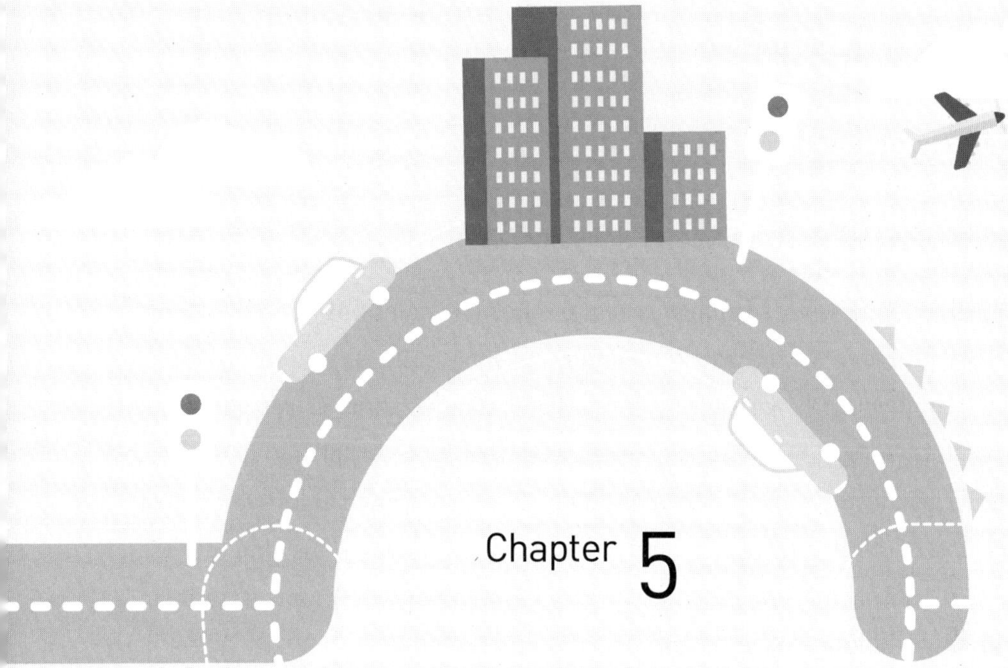

Chapter 5

Transport Demand Management Policy

1. Concept of TDM

1.1. Introduction to TDM

Definition of TDM[1]

Cities in Korea need innovative and effective solutions to solve their transport problems in the short, medium and long-term. Increased economic growth, coupled with a resulting increase in motorization in recent years, has resulted in the worst traffic congestion that the world has ever seen. Solutions to these problems are possible, not only through improvement of conditions of public transport and conditions for pedestrians and bicycle users, but also in the implementation of measures which promote a rational use of the automobile by means of TDM instruments.

TDM is a wide range of policies, programs, services and products that influence how, why, when and where people travel to make travel behaviours more sustainable. TDM refers to a variety of strategies that change travel behavior (how, when, and where people travel) in order to improve transportation system efficiency and achieve key regional objectives, such as reduced traffic congestion, increased safety and mobility, and energy conservation and emission reductions.[2] It can therefore often include the more efficient and effective use of existing transportation infrastructure. Typical TDM programs reduce Single Occupant Vehicle (SOV) trips through ride-sharing initiatives such as car-pooling and van-pooling; alternative work schedules and teleworking; and the use of transit, biking, and walking to work. However, TDM strategies should not be limited to just commute trips. TDM is a strategy which aims to maximize the efficiency of the urban transport system by discouraging unnecessary private vehicle use and promoting more effective, healthy and environmental-friendly modes of

---

1 Andrea Broaddus(2009), pp.8-9.

2 Elizabeth Young et.al. (2012), p.1.

transport, in general being public transport and non-motorized transport. TDM strategies, programs, and plans are most effective when considered for all trips and at all geographic levels — from a specific site, to a neighborhood, city, and regional or state levels — creating a comprehensive and coordinated approach.

TDM can also be described as a set of measures to influence traveller behaviour in order to reduce or redistribute travel demand. Demand for transportation follows the general economic theory of supply and demand for normal goods. For most goods, supply and demand are balanced by pricing. Many components of the transportation system are inefficiently priced, creating conflicts and inefficiencies.

Although automobiles are expensive to own, most of the costs are fixed. Consumers pay about the same for vehicle purchase, financing, insurance, registration and residential parking regardless of how much they drive their vehicle. Many cost of automobile travel are external, that is not paid directly by users, including traffic congestion, accident risk, pollution emissions and parking subsidies. Many countries subsidize motor vehicle fuel, or impose low taxes that do not even recover roadway costs. In most situations, two-thirds of motor vehicle costs are either fixed or external.

Benefits of TDM[3]

TDM strategies address key regional policy objectives related to quality of travel, livability, and sustainability. At the regional level, a TDM program coordinates a number of programs that increase the number of people who carpool, vanpool, use transit, bike, and walk to work, as well as providing information on telework and alternative work schedules. However, for TDM to be truly effective, it must be supported by land use policies and neighborhood design that reduce the need to drive for daily tasks. Including TDM in the municipal planning and development process offers a broad range

[3] Elizabeth Young et al. (2012), pp.3-4.

of economic, environmental, and public health benefits to local governments, their citizens and businesses:

First, TDM maximizes returns on infrastructure spending and reduces the need for new or widened roads. TDM is a cost-effective way to build capacity in a community's transportation system by expanding participation in alternative modes (carpools, vanpools, transit, biking, walking, and teleworking) instead of widening or building new roads, which are costly to construct and maintain. Second, TDM reduces parking demand. TDM incorporated into development reduces SOV auto trips and the need for parking, reducing the cost and burden for jurisdictions and developers to provide more parking capacity.

Third, TDM helps to meet environmental and air quality goals. TDM improves air quality by encouraging alternatives to the SOV, reducing congestion, and corresponding vehicle related emissions. TDM can help to preserve green space by reducing the amount of land needed for roads and parking facilities. TDM can reduce storm water management costs by encouraging more efficient land use patterns. Fourth, TDM is adaptable and dynamic. TDM can be customized for specific events, neighborhoods, corridors, work sites, and time frames. Unlike new infrastructure, TDM programs can easily adapt and respond to economic and population conditions.

TDM provides benefits to the public: First, reduced costs for commuters. TDM is not only cost effective for local governments but access to low-cost commuting alternatives can cut individual transportation costs by half or more. Second, reduced costs for businesses. Pre-tax programs offer savings to employers as well as employees. Transit subsidies can be deducted as a business expense. When funds are removed from paychecks before taxes are applied, employers save on payroll taxes. Third, saves time. Carpools and vanpools can get commuters to work and back faster than driving alone by using HOV lanes and HOV bypass facilities. Fourth, it improves public health. Biking or walking to work or transit increases physical activity, and reduced vehicle emissions improve air quality.

Fifth, it benefits employers and employees. Research demonstrates that adding commuter benefits to employees' compensation is a low-cost benefit that can help to attract and retain employees, and increase employee productivity. TDM can reduce employer overhead costs too. Teleworking and alternative work schedules reduce office space requirements and parking demand, and many companies are finding that it costs less to pay employees not to drive than it does to provide them with free or cheap parking spaces. Offering cash to employees who choose not to drive alone to work can amount to significant reductions in parking acquisition and maintenance costs. Sixth, it encourages sustainable development. TDM contributes to leadership in environmental and energy design (LEED) certification. Seventh, TDM increases safety. Reduced traffic congestion and complete streets can make roadways safer for all users, including bicyclists and pedestrians.

Table 5.1. Benefits of TDM

Benefits	Detailed contents
Benefits to the entire city	■ Maximizes returns on infrastructure spending and reduces the need for new roads. ■ Reduces parking demand, adaptable and dynamic ■ Helps to meet environmental & air quality goals ■ Customized for events, neighborhoods, corridors, etc.
Benefits to the public	■ Reduces costs for commuters and business ■ Benefits employers and employees, saves time ■ Improves public health, encourages sustainable development, increases safety

Source: Elizabeth Young et al. (2012)

1.2. Types and Implementation of TDM

Types of TDM

TDM is applied to regulate traffic flows and to reduce traffic growth to match the growth in road capacity. As an initial effort to identifying TDM, it is appropriate to list and define major categories of TDM measures. The literature review conducted for this paper revealed a wide range of measures which have been used or, more often, proposed for use in cities. In practice, there is considerable overlap between them and most measures would need to be reinforced by combination with others for greatest effectiveness. For ease of presentation, they tend to fall into a limited number of categories.

The volume of literature on TDM is large and the range of management measures is wide. The review of measures which have been applied or are proposed on a big city base illustrate some clear overall trends in Korea. The most common form of measure has been characterized by the legal restraints. However, the use of price and physical restraint as TDM measures is quite rare in Korea.

Table 5.2. Categories of TDM Measures

Authors	Categories of TDM Measures
May (1986)	Traffic restraints, Traffic regulations, Traffic avoidance
Wayte (1991)	Improved Access Utilization, Physical restraint, Pricing, Urban and social change
Korea Transport Institute (1990)	Physical restraints, Fiscal restraints, Legal restraints, Alternative traffic modes

Based on the literature and for this paper, we have narrowed the subject to some extent, as a result of the brief, by our own interpretation of what is most significant at this time in an Gwangju City context. TDM measures are confined to legislative restraint measures for this paper. The measures have been used or, more often proposed for use in metropolitan cities of Korea. Legislative measures include car running in shifts (CRS), alternative working hours (AWH), ride sharing programs (RSP), parking managements (PM) and road pricing (RP).

Table 5.3. Identification of TDM Measures

Measure	Technique
Car running in shifts	Car running in ten-day shifts, Car running in five-day shifts
Alternative work hours	Staggered work hours, Flexible work hours
Ride-sharing programs	Carpool, Vanpool
Parking management	Residential parking permit program, Parking lot card
Road pricing	Congestion pricing, Area entry licensed

Role of Local Government in TDM[4]

It is necessary to clearly delineate who is responsible for managing demand, since transport decisions are based upon a variety of factors, from time of day to comfort to cost. Transportation agencies are responsible for designing, building and managing road network and transport services, and for regulating vehicles. TDM measures can be implemented by transportation agencies, local, regional and national government, and private entities like employers.

In fact, Local government plays a critical role in TDM planning and implementation. Land use, urban design, and parking policies are all under the jurisdiction of local governments and are essential in influencing travel choice and demand. Efficient land use and urban design can reduce the need for auto travel for daily trips, and appropriate parking supply and pricing can encourage the use of alternative modes of transportation. The metropolitan government and its affiliated district offices are in a unique position to implement a broad range of TDM strategies at many different points in the development process. While the central government can enact legislation and set broad policies, local governments have the ability to guide the implementation of TDM strategies through the planning process using

[4] Elizabeth Young et al. (2012), p.2.

short and long-range plans, and can implement TDM strategies through development agreements, zoning, policies, and ordinances. The metropolitan city is becoming increasingly aware of the link between travel choices and land use patterns and policies. It is recognized that an individual traveler's mode choice - be it auto, carpool, vanpool, transit, walking, or biking - is significantly influenced by how communities are designed and developed.

2. Transport Conditions and TDM Measures in Gwangju

2.1. Transport Conditions of Gwangju

Socio-economic Growth

In 2012, Gwangju's population numbered 1,484,000, which accounted for 2.9% of the national total. It increased at an annual average growth rate of 0.8% during the 2000-2012 period. The total number of household in 2012 increased by 1.3 times from 430,000 households in 2000. The average growth rate over the last 12 years in car ownership has been 4.2% per annum. It was the most reliable determinant of travel demand in Gwangju. To conclude, the unsustainable situation has been heavily affected by the drastic increase in the city's socio-economic condition.

Table 5.4. Trends of Socio-economic Growth

Division	Unit	2000	2005	2012	AAGR ('00-'12)
Population	1,000 persons	1,351	1,444	1,484	0.8%
Household	1,000 hou.	430	482	556	2.2%
Car registration (Private car's ratio)	1,000 vehicle (%)	337 (67.5)	436 (73.5)	551 (79.3)	4.2% **(+11.8)**

Note: AAGR refers to average annual growth rate.
Source: GMC(each year)

Trends of Transport Indicators

The growth in road traffic volumes in Gwangju closely parallels the increase in socio-economic indicators. The total traffic population increased at the average annual growth rate of 0.92% during the 2000-2012 period. The total length of constructed road grew from 1,151 km in 2000 to 1,634 km in 2012. This was mainly due to the road construction-oriented policy of GMC. The number of cars per road-km increased from 292 cars in 2000 to 337 cars in 2012. This indicates the increasing intensity of the road network problem in Gwangju.

Table 5.5. Trends of Transport Indicators in Gwangju

Division	Unit	2000	2005	2012	AAGR ('00-'12)
Traffic population	Thousand	1,252	1,324	1,397	0.92%
Road length	Km	1,151	1,363	1,634	2.96%
Road ratio	%	18.5	20.5	23.1	+4.6
Cars per road	Cars/km	292	319	337	1.20%
Cars per person	Cars/1000	247	300	371	3.44%

Note: AAGR refers to average annual growth rate.
Source: GMC(each year)

2.2. Travel Characteristics

Share of Modal Split

The taxi share as a proportion of the total daily trips by traffic mode decreased from 23.8% in 2000 to 15.2% in 2012. This was primarily caused by travelers being diverted from taxi among other factors. As a result of the drastic increase in the number of private cars in Gwangju, the share of private cars by traffic mode grew rapidly from 13.9% in 2000 to 36.4% in 2012. This resulted in heavy traffic congestion and air pollution in the built-up area of the city.

Table 5.6. Share of Modal Split (%)

Mode	2000	2005	2012	Changes ('00-12)
Bus	49.4	37.5	36.3	−13.1
Taxi	23.8	20.2	15.2	−8.6
Private car	13.9	27.3	36.4	+22.5
Subway	-	1.7	2.7	+1.0
Walking, others	12.9	13.3	9.4	−3.5

Note: AAGR refers to average annual growth rate.
Source: GMC (each year)

Travel Speed and Congestion Cost

Congestion is a problem in Gwangju, with relatively high levels of car ownership and poor road infrastructures. The severity of congestion increased with the size of the city, and it extends as far as the suburbs. In considering congestion, it is helpful to compare average travel speeds. For instance, there was a steady decrease in average travel time in the outskirts of the city between 2005 and 2012. It is very difficult to estimate the true costs of congestion as it depends very much on the definition chosen. The total congestion costs in Gwangju grew at an average rate of 2.6% per annum during the 2000-2012 period.

Table 5.7. Changes in Travel Speed and Congestion Costs

Division		Unit	2000	2005	2012	Change('00-'12)
Travel speed	CBD	km/hour	16.9	18.8	34.6	+17.7
	Outskirts		40.2	45.8	42.4	+2.4
Congestion cost		Billion Won	711.0	788.3	965.5	AAGR: 2.6%

Note: AAGR refers to average annual growth rate.
Source: GMC (each year)

2.3. TDM Measures in Gwangju

Transportation Impact Fee (TIF)[5]

TIFs are authorized under the Urban Transportation Maintenance ACT. TIF for the building owners are probably the most commonly imposed of all types of impact fees. The purpose of impact fees is not just revenue for transportation system but traffic reduction. Impact fees for transportation facilities are calculated based on average trip, gross floor area, parking area, main land use of the facilities, and other factors. One of the variables that is used in the vast majorities of impact fee systems is trip generation. Trip generation data is used in TIF to measure the demand that different land uses create for roadway capacity. TIF systems limits the number of land use categories to a few in each of the following general categories: residential, commercial, industrial, institutional, office, recreational and services. But a number of difficulties have been encountered in using TIF trip generation data. These are because of a lack of trip generation data and the administrative difficulties involved in maintaining a system that contains a long list of land use categories.

Rapid growth and development in GMC has placed increased pressure on the transport system and it has stressed the importance of TDM. GMC has placed TDM as one of crucial elements of urban transport policies and developed various TDM strategies. However, it is judged that Gwangju is still experiencing severe traffic congestion, undermining the urban competitiveness and quality of life.

TIF ensure that new development and redevelopment pays a proportional fair share contribution for the cost of new transportation infrastructure that is deemed necessary and reasonably related to accommodating the impact of new development within the city limit. Government law allows the city to impose TIF on new development to help effectively manage the growth

---

[5] Seongil Shin(2008), pp.87-89.

of our community. TIF has been implemented in order to ensure that urban facilities pay a proportional share of the cost to internalize externalities since 1990 with a base share of 350 won per 1,000 m^2. GMC revised the TIF system so that the total amount of fees could be refunded according to participation rates of the TDM program since 2003. Despite this effort, the participation rate of the TDM program was no more than 5.2% in 2011.

The total amount of TIF in Gwangju increased at the average annual growth rate of 9.84% during the 2000-2010 period. The collection rate showed a gradual increasing trend during the same period. There are many ways to pay less TIF in Gwangju. According to the TIF ordinance in Gwangju, total amount of TIF can be reduced according to the participation rates of the TDM program per year. That is, if a project produces less transportation impact, then there is a corresponding reduction in TIF cost. TDM programs for reduction in TIF cost consist of the 10th-day-no-driving system, car running in five-day shifts, alternate-day car running, fee parking lots, operation of commuter bus, public transit usage subsidies, TDM programs of united companies, car-pooling, bicycle-riding, staggered office hours, and public transport day. With the right incentives (or disincentive) travelers may be influenced to use the transportation system in a way that contributes less to congestion. It is thus time to evolve into the more flexible TIP systems in terms of equality of charging and effectiveness of TDM.

Table 5.8. Trends of Transportation Impact Fees in Gwangju

(Unit: Million won)

Division	2000	2005	2010	AAGR('00-'10)
Imposition	2,143	4,245	5,479	9.84%
Collection	1,844	3,806	5,169	10.87%
Collection rate	86.0%	89.7	94.3%	+8.3

Note: AAGR refers to average annual growth rate.
Source: GMC(each year)

Public Bike-Sharing System (PBS)

One of the biggest trends in sustainable urban transport is called bike sharing. Bike sharing's success began in France and it took over a lot of cities worldwide. A simple definition of PBS is a bicycle rental system which allows someone to (without additional charge) take a bicycle at one point and to return it at a different one, where the bicycle can be rented by another user. It's important to distinguish between bike sharing system and bike rental service: The last type implies the kind of service, where you can rent a bike for a specific time and you usually have to bring it back to the exact same place. Such a service is common for tourist areas.

On the other hand, we have bike sharing systems with multiple stations in a certain area. The intention of a bike sharing system is that it enhances mobility without having the burden of using one's own bike and the possibility of returning it to a location other than where it was picked up. PBS is very convenient and almost always available. Instead of buying a bicycle, you can just rent one for a reasonable price. PBS enhances mobility of low-income house-holds and other groups. It has several advantages as a sustainable transportation mode such as the promotion of public transport through multi-modality, the reduction of automobile dependency, and the contribution to healthy life-styles. These advantages are why most urban planners try to apply the bike sharing concept to parts of the city or sometimes even to the whole city.

Compared to Europe and Japan, Korea began to promote cycling late. Therefore, the percentage of bike ridership is very low with 1.2% of all trips made in 2005. Since 2006, cities acknowledged that there is a need for bike infrastructure and facilities. The government invests heavily in the development of bike sharing programs. In 2007, Seoul originally planed to establish a bike sharing program similar to the Velib bike sharing system in Paris. The priority was to encourage citizens and tourists to use bikes instead of cars. As of Feb 2012, Korea has bike sharing systems in 14 cities and a total of 9,373 bikes at 493 stations.

Gwangju's PBS is in operation and managed by the district itself and Gwangju Metropolitan Transit Cooperation (GMTR). There are 875 public-sharing bikes and 74 bike stations in Gwagnju as of 2012. In 2006, GMTR introduced a PBS for the first time. At subway station with a high frequency of visitors there is a bike sharing station. Dong-gu, Seo-gu and Gwangsan-gu introduced a PBS in 2007 extensively. A PBS is not in operation in Buk-gu. Gwangju's PBS is not a very affordable service and it doesn't improve the mobility of large proportion of the population.

Gwangju is not a good example for a successful inner-city bike sharing system. Gwangju's big problem is that it is still very unfriendly to inner-city biking. The sidewalk in Gwangju is divided into a section for bikes and one for pedestrians. It doesn't provide a good-working service, and the infrastructure is insufficient. Almost every sidewalk in Gwangju doesn't have a bike lanes separated through a different surface/color. There is a rise in the usage of bicycles but the number of fatalities with vehicles and bikes grew, too. There are insufficient service personnel to manage Gwangju's PBS. It doesn't enhances the usage of public transport because it disconnects neighborhoods with bus stations. Also Gwangju's citizens lack understanding on the PBS in Gwangju, and are little interested in the PBS. The districts in GMC have difficulties managing PBS because of a state of neglect and breakdown, and bicycles being stolen. The city should work on that and then a well-functioning system for bike sharing can be introduced. This means that Gwangju has to build a bike network with a lot of safety measures to avoid accidents with pedestrians and vehicles.

Riding a bike to work is good for health. and sustainable urban development. as well as improving the quality of life of urban areas. Bike sharing systems enhance inner-city cycling and the usage of public transport.

Table 5.9. Public Bike-Sharing System in Gwangju

Division	Dong-gu	Seo-gu	Nam-gu	Gwangsan-gu	GMTR	City hall	Total
Bike stations	15	18	2	23	15	1	74
Bikes available	129	170	46	247	268	15	875

Source: Chung(2013)

Employer-Based TDM Programs

Employer-based programs can be among the most effective of transportation demand management (TDM) programs, in part because the program can be tailored to the commute needs of employees at their specific place of work. Employers can provide opportunities for employees to escape a congested commute through options such as alternative work schedules or telecommuting.

Employers are also in a position to influence employee commute choices with incentives (such as a subsidized bus pass) or even by removing/reducing subsidies that encourage drive-alone commutes (such as the provision of unlimited free parking). Research indicates that financial incentives and disincentives such as these are particularly effective commute trip reduction measures. Numerous studies conclude that parking charges, telecommuting, flexible work hour provisions including compressed work weeks, guaranteed ride home programs, and incentives for biking and walking all can be effective in reducing drive alone commuting. In addition, programs that encourage carpooling and vanpooling have proven successful in a number of localities, particularly if vans are provided.

Employers in Gwangju are encouraged to implement travel demand management (TDM) programs to reduce their employees' use of private vehicles for commuting. The observed traffic amount may not accurately reflect actual demand since TDM programs adopted are likely to suppress the demand to some degree. Gwangju has been implementing an employer-based TDM composed of 11 programs, including non-free parking, vehicle number plate rationing programs, commuter bus operations, and carpool options. These programs provide various incentives such as a reduction in the annual traffic impact fees. The incentives are designed to be proportional to the actual reduction of vehicle use as a result of the individual programs. GMC statistics indicate that popular TDM measures for office buildings are parking fees and vehicle number plate rationing programs.

Bus Exclusive Lane (BEL)

BEL in Gwangju is made legally available to buses, and covered with 47.2 km in sections on 8 major arterial roads in 2012. BEL is located in the right side of each direction in major roads, and blue color separates it from other lanes. Private cars are allowed to enter a BEL to turn to the right. One lane for each direction is reserved for BEL, and operation hours are designated as am 07:30~09:30 and pm 17:30~19:30 for both directions during the week. An impact analysis of BEL revealed that the average speed of buses improved a little for the city, while the average speed of private cars declined slightly. There are several problems associated with a successful implementation of BEL. First, BEL conflicts with right-turn cars, since BEL is placed at the right side and street design allows numerous entrances to the secondary streets. Second, a series of disruptions exist between BEL and bus-stops, commercial vehicle parking, and traffic lights.

Car Running in Ten-Day Shifts (CRTS)

As a kind of stick measure, Car Running in Ten-Day Shifts (CRTS) regulates the parking lot access of vehicles when the last digit of the number plate matches with the last digit of the date. Gwangju participants of CRTS have been government, public organizations and large firms suffering from parking difficulties. According to the effectiveness analysis, it was estimated to reduce about 5% of daily total traffic volumes. There are a few problems related with its continuation.

First, since vehicles of CRTS are prohibited from entering parking lots, individual situations of drivers are not taken into account. It is necessary to provide information of Carpool matching partners to car users who are without other traffic alternatives. Second, impacts of CRTS are not clear. Cars rejected can find free or paid parking lots near the destination. Cars left at home can be used by other members of family during the daytime.

Public Transport and Carpooling Campaigns

Public transport is frequently put forward as a principal means by which cities will be able to cope with increasing travel demand. The city government encourages people to use public transit and carpool more often for reducing traffic congestion in Gwangju. For increasing bus ridership, the city maintains cheap bus fares, private operation of buses and regular bus services. However, if public transport is to be an effective alternative, upgrading the quality and service of city buses is essential.

The city government also supports car pooling and ride-sharing for reducing traffic congestion. To support this encouragement, there are several designated carpool depots. The measure is not company based, and don't include financial and other incentives to the users. For instance, a simple fare structure, improved frequency, reliability of service, and improved security of travel encourage people to use public transport more in Gwangju.

Parking Managements

The city divides Gwangju area into 2 parts and sets different parking fares for public parking lots. In general, privately operated parking lots charge the same amount as public parking fares. The city increases parking charges almost every year for significantly altering travel behaviour in favour of high occupancy vehicles, as well as reducing traffic congestion. Main issues of using public parking lots are concerned with traffic queues near parking entrance/exit and inconvenience of paying cash for each use.

Enforcement of illegal parking is the key to TDM success. The city designated most major arterial roads as no parking area. Some of the regional transport department work exclusively for controlling illegal parking, and policeman and some city officials also reserve the same right. In general, the possibility of being fined is very low, so effective enforcement measures need to be developed.

3. TDM Policy Direction for Gwangju

3.1. Review and Considerations for TDM Measures

Review of TDM Measures

Urban transport problems of Gwagnju are similar to those in Korean metropolitan cities. The transport problems step from excessive transport demand, the shortage of transport facilities, poor public transit services, and traffic accident increases. Even though several transport policies were introduced to solve the transport problems, urban transport conditions have not improved as much as expected. In the 1900's and 2000's, the city government began to concentrate on both managing the current transport system and increasing its efficiency. During the past several decades, daily household trips have grown at a much faster rate than the population. As a result, the reduction of traffic congestion, vehicle emissions, and fuel consumption policies have become major urban policy objectives. In particular, TDM policies are designed to slow this transport trend. TDM policies are designed to shift peak-period SOV trips to other modes or times or reduce peak period travel. In general, TDM measures have diverse targets; one is to increase transit ridership, vehicle occupancy, walking and cycling, and the other is to reduce the lengths of some trips or move them to off-peak periods.

Considerations for Future TDM Measures

The overall quality of life and the national living standard has increased in Korea. Because civil awareness of environmental issues and the development of technology in transport fields have advanced, higher speed, safety, low air pollution and improved efficiency in urban transportation will be pursued. Accordingly, the traffic environment is being prepared for the 21st century so that it can cope with the socio-economic changes due to continuous economic growth and improved national living standards.

Table 5.10. Evolution of Urban Transport Policy in Gwangju

Transport supply-side policy			
Public transit policy			
Transport demand management			
Century	1980s	1990s	2000s

3.2. Choice of TDM Measures

In order to maintain and enhance mobility and access in an environment of rapid growth, it is necessary to choose a reasonable and suitable TDM measures in Gwangju. To compare the characteristics of TDM measures is important to GMC. TDM measures can be divided into two basic types: command and control measures and market-based measures. Command and control measures impose some form of performance standard which must be attained by all members of the regulated group. Therefore these measures are considered a more equitable way of achieving the desired objectives and are more politically acceptable. Market-based measures are as much a matter of regulation as command and control strategies are. They, thus, are based on economic principles to alter supply or production decision. Command and control methods impose on all the people a uniform standard of performance that must be achieved, whereas market-based methods offer incentives and dis-incentives in order to change people's behavior via the individual response to pricing.

It is said that market-oriented TDM measures have been more effective in reducing travel demand and air pollution. Therefore, it is important to choose alternative TDM measures with respect to how they are implemented and to what extent they are individually relied upon to improve overall mobility and access.

Table 5.11. Advantages and Disadvantages of TDM Approaches

Means	Advantages	Disadvantages
Command & control	▪ Perceived certainty of outcome ▪ Equity-uniform treatment	▪ No incentive to perform better than standard ▪ Incentive to exaggerate costs of compliance ▪ Little relationship between contribution to problem and cost of compliance ▪ Administrative and enforcement costs
Market	▪ Incentive to perform better than standard ▪ Costs incurred closely related to contribution to problem	▪ Uncertainty of outcome ▪ Equity-unfair to lower income groups ▪ Licence to pollute ▪ Administrative and enforcement costs
Direct	▪ Applies to all member of group ▪ Easier to enforce	▪ Less politically acceptable
Indirect	▪ More politically acceptable costs of regulation less obvious	▪ Less politically acceptable

Source: FWHA(1992)

TDM strategies should be based on achieving three objectives: Improving the efficiency of various components of current transport facilities; Managing travel demand by modifying the operating environment in which travel choices are made; Implementing significant road-capacity expansion. To achieve these three objectives, TDM measures should be combined with diverse tools related to land-use planning, economics, and sociology.

3.3. Congestion Charging

Modern traffic congestion in metropolitan city results mainly from the recurrent congestion in a specific area, causing detrimental effects to that area, as well as the adjacent areas. The characteristics of traffic congestion in city centers are particularly complicated all day long. The traditional methods (infrastructure construction, traffic facilitation) dealing with traffic congestion are no longer feasible. Transportation authorities can thus shift their focus from supply side policies to transport demand management. Urban road pricing as an instrument of traffic management has generated a great deal of interest for dealing with traffic congestion in metropolitan cities. Current awareness of the levy of congestion charges can be described to the changing public perceptions about congestion, limited budget for transportation, and growing concerns about environmental degradation.

Road pricing is specific to the charge which is relevant to road use, and congestion pricing is more specific because it focuses on reducing congestion[6]. The concept of congestion charging is based on the assumption that optimal traffic volume decide the balance between the total amount of money that road users are willing to pay for road use, and the marginal social cost that arises from road use congestion. The primary objectives of congestion charging schemes is to reduce the need for travel and to raise revenue to fund transport projects, such as road constructions. There are four types of

[6] Kim(2003), pp.92-93.

congestion charging methods: cordon tolls, distance-based charging, time-based system, and congestion-based charging.

The obstacles confronting the introduction of congestion charges are mainly public acceptability and political feasibility implementation costs or technical problems such as types of charging. However, congestion charging is the best instrument for solving the urgent traffic problems in urban areas. Public acceptability was low in general in the first introduction of congestion pricing. It was known that acceptability and political feasibility increased considerably, as time went by, in the areas where congestion charging programmes had been introduced.

3.4. Integrated Transport and Land Use Planning

Land use pattern have significant potential to influence the need for travel, trip length, and modal choice. This is why many planner require the integration of land use planning and transportation planning. This strategy aims to reduce the demand for auto travel through the management of land use planning and design. To avoid congestion in the future, careful attention should be concentrated on zoning and land use plans, in coordination with the strategic provision of transport services, to influence where development occurs. Although there are few constraints in implementing these strategies, the integration of TDM policies with land-use policies and community planning should be implemented rather than being treated as an add-on to the current process.

3.5. Weekly No Driving Day

In order to improve the flow of traffic in a city in which the majority of people seem to have a car and a large area of which was never designed for automobiles, GMC can institute a No-Driving Day Campaign. Car owners who sign up for the program commit to using other forms of transportation one day a week. As participation grows, there will also be a positive impact on air quality in the city. Cars participating in the No-Driving Campaign sport colour electronic stickers in the corner of their windshield on which is indicated a specific day of the week. These electronic stickers allow access to public parking stalls while participation in the programme results in a variety of benefits such as a reduction in automobile tax, discounts on parking fees, priority for residential parking, car maintenance discounts, free or discounted car washes/detailing as well as a number of other incentives.

GMC should collaborate with various NGOs and private enterprises to plan the 'No Driving Day' Programme. The principle is based upon a voluntary scheme, using incentives to enroll commuters to drop their cars for a day and travel to work via public transportation or other means. The system functions when the car owner registers their vehicle to stay at home one day a week, between Monday and Friday, 7am - 10pm. An electronic sticker is issued to that car which can then be monitored by radio frequency identification systems (RFID) located around the city. If throughout the year, the car is not identified as travelling on its allocated no drive day, the owner will receive a number of incentives and rewards. The programme is commercialized through sponsorship, generating a solid business model for the upfront cost of infrastructure and maintenance.

Car owners should be rewarded for their dedication to reducing car use through a number of incentives. Participants can receive: 5% reduction in car tax; 20-30% discount at selected public parking locations; priority parking in areas close to home. There are many primary advantages regarding "Weekly No Driving Day, including decrease in traffic volumes, operating speed increase, fuel cost-savings, reduction in noise, health benefits, better air quality and local living conditions, indirect promotion of public transport and alternative modes of commuter transport, and promotion of walking and cycling.

3.6. Other TDM Measures

More roads and public transit infrastructure should be provided to cope with increasing transport demands. These strategies, however, meet some financial limits. Thus it is better to rely on efficient use of existing transport facilities. Today, ITS is regarded as the most efficient traffic management tool throughout the world. An efficient linkage between TDM and ITS will effectively reduce congestion problems.

Table 5.12. Advantages and Disadvantages of TDM Approaches

Measures	Main objectives				
	Time	Route	Mode	Efficient use	Reduction travel
Parking fee controls	●	●	●	●	●
Parking information service	●	●			
Congestion pricing	●	●	●	●	
Rationing of car use			●		
Car pool campaign			●		
Park-and-ride services				●	
Transit service improvement				●	
Staggered work hours	●				
Compressed work days					●
Tele-banking, shopping					●
Job-housing balancing	●	●	●	●	●
Pedestrian, transit mall			●		

Source: Hwang (2000), pp.442-443.

Citizens find car sharing to be cheaper and more convenient

Car sharing can reduce traffic, while easing the financial burden on those who need a car occasionally. As the word spreads about car-sharing - services through which a variety of people use a single car - the concept is spreading into diverse areas of life. An increasing number of people are opting not to own a car but rather simply to rent one when necessary.

On June 12, the Hankyoreh's Jeju correspondent met graduate student Kim Yo-han, 28, on the campus of Jeju National University in the Ara neighborhood of Jeju City. Kim said that he had just returned to school after doing some volunteer teaching. Since April, Kim has been borrowing a vehicle from a car-sharing company once or twice a week and using it for about two hours.

"I like how I can use a car at a time and place that are convenient for me," Kim said. "It's really useful when I have to go a long way to do my volunteer work." This time, Kim used the car for about two and a half hours and spent 15,000 won (US$13.30), including gas. "If two or three people use the car together, it becomes so much cheaper to get around."

Car-sharing is also used by startups and other small companies for getting work done. The staff of Hello Nature, a company in the Gangnam district of Seoul that sells environmentally friendly farm products, use car sharing about 50 times a month. The company explains that they typically make use of the service when visiting food producers in other regions or meeting with marketing firms. "When you rent a car overnight, the price is similar to standard rental companies, but if you go somewhere close or just use it for three or four hours, car-sharing is much cheaper," said Park Byeong-yeol, 38, the president of the company. "I would say it has helped us save us at least half of the price of renting cars."

■ *From Seoul to the provinces*

In a bid to help reduce the parking crunch and traffic congestion in downtown Seoul, Green Point Consortium (Green Car) partnered with SoCar in January to create the "Share Car" system. Share Car operates 486 cars in 292 parking lots (including 86 public parking lots in Seoul). As of Jun. 2, Share Car had 77,970 members. 89% of the members are residents of the greater Seoul area (including Seoul and Gyeonggi Province), but the number of members who live outside of this region is increasing.

An average of 503 people use the service each day, which represents a 40% increase (140 people) from the 363 average daily users when the service began three months ago at the end of February. The average time that the cars are used each day is 4 hours and 18 minutes. 43% of users are in their 20s, 38.5% in their 30s, and 15.6% in their 40s. In order to aid the growth of Share Car, the city of Seoul has made its public parking lots available and has cut the parking fee by 50%.

Aside from Share Car, the number of people who are sharing electric cars is also on the rise. Seoul signed agreements with four companies LGCNS (City Car), Korail Network (YouCar), Korea Car Sharing (Han Car), and KT Rental Car to secure a supply of eco-friendly electric cars. Starting in May 2013, they have started sharing 184 electric automobiles.

Car sharing is rapidly expanding to more regions. Green Car has brought car sharing to 27 cities: Goyang, Gwacheon, Gwangmyeong, Gwangju, Guri, Gunpo, Gimpo, Bucheon, Seongnam, Suwon, Siheung, Ansan, Anyang, Yongin, Uijeongbu, Paju, and Hwaseong in Gyeonggi Province; Asan and Cheonan in South Chungcheong Province, Cheongwon in North Chungcheong Province; and Daegu, Daejeon, Busan, Sejong, Incheon, and Jeju.

So Car, which got involved with car sharing by setting up parking zones in 40 locations on Jeju Island, is expanding to Seoul and other regions. Clients in Jeju are mostly university students and men in their 20s and 30s. A representative with SoCar said that 60-70% of users are residents of Jeju, with the remainder being tourists and other visitors.

Choe Ji-young, 37, from Paju, Gyeonggi Province, who visits Jeju once a month with her friends to hike on an oreum (the name locals on Jeju use for the volcanic hills on the island), picks up a vehicle from the parking lot as soon as she arrives at Jeju International Airport. Choe said that car-sharing on her recent trip to Jeju Island cost her 33,000 won for renting the car, or slightly above 50,000 won including gas. Since she was joined by three friends, the cost for each of them was less than 20,000 won. "The cost of insurance is already included in car-sharing vehicles, so the only extra thing we have to pay for is gas," Choe said. "It's convenient since we don't need to meet any employees and we can unlock the car door using our membership card."

■ *'Three birds with one stone'?*

A very literal form of car sharing is taking off in Northern Europe, with drivers borrowing each other's cars. In South Korea, drivers use businesses to rent cars as needed. The law currently prohibits renting anything other than work vehicles for a profit.

The car sharing companies that Seoul City Government is supporting would seem, at first glance, to be car rental agencies. But Lee Su-jin, who heads the city's transportation demand management team, said the project serves the public in many ways. "It allows people to use [a car] as much as they need without owning one themselves, which reduces transportation costs for families," she said. "And the more car sharing people do, the fewer cars there are on the road, which reduces traffic jams in the city. In particular, it promotes the mobility of the disadvantaged, since low-income people now have inexpensive transportation for when they have to go to the hospital."

Hong Ji-young, who heads the marketing team at SoCar, explained that drivers can borrow cars for 30-minutes increments. "All you have to do to book one is visit the website or use a smart-phone app to find the location of a nearby car and the time when it's in the parking zone," Hong said.

The biggest complaint among users is that they have to return the car to the place where they borrowed it. Lee explained the reasons for this policy, saying the cars "would all end up being driven from the periphery into the city center if we allowed 'one-way cars' that people could park somewhere else. It also works against the goal of reducing traffic, and there would be additional costs because someone has to then move the cars to a garage somewhere else."

Observers have called car sharing a clever way of cutting traffic, parking needs, and pollution. Programs are in place in around 1,000 cities in 60 countries around the world. In Europe, systems have sprung up linking communities with public transportation. In the US, expansions in response to booming market demand have led to successful private models like Zipcar. Local and national governments overseas have also provided various benefits to individuals and companies sharing cars, including public parking spaces and discounts, funding, and even co-investment.

*** Source: The Hankyoreh (2013.6.17)**

References

Ann Arbor Downtown Development Authority (ADDA), Public Parking and Transportation Demand Management Strategies Plan, April 2010.

AUSTROADS, Road Demand Management, Victoria: Australian Road Research Board, 1994.

Balmer, A., L. J. French, R. Eck, and J. Legg. "Trip Generation Rates of Consolidated Schools." ITE Journal, Vol. 70, No. 8 (2000): pp. 30-34.

Broaddus, Andrea et al., Transportation Demand Management: Training Document, Germany: Deutsche Gesellschaft fur Technische Zusammenarbeit(GTZ), April 2009.

Chung, Hawook, Transport Demand Management Strategies Responding to the Change of the Transport Environment in the Downtown of Gwangju Metroplitan City, Basic Research 2013-09, Gwangju Development Institute, 2013 (in Korean).

Collins, Michael F. and Timothy M. Pharoah, Transport Organization in a Great City: The Case of London, London: George Allen and Unwin Ltd, 1974.

Ecola, L. and Grant, M., "Impacts of Transit Benefits Programs on Transit Agency Ridership, Revenues, and Costs." Journal of Public Transportation, Vol. 11, No. 2 (2008): pp.1-18.

Ewing, R., Deanna, M. and Li, S., "Land Use Impacts on Trip Generation Rates." Transportation Research Record, Journal of the Transportation Research Board, 1518 (1996): pp.1-6.

Ferguson, Eric, Transportation Demand Management: Planning, Development, and Implementation, Journal of the American Planning Association, Vol 56, No.4, P 442-456, 1990.

Georggi, N. L., P. Winters, S. Rai, and L. Zhou. "Measuring the Impacts of Employer-Based Transportation Demand Management Programs on an Interstate Corridor." Journal of Public Transportation, Vol. 10, No. 4 (2007): pp.51-77.

Gwangju Metropolitan City (GMC), Gwangju Metropolitan Administration, Gwangju, 2000-2011 (in Korean).

GMC, Traffic Volume Survey Report. 2000-2011 (in Korean).

Hwang, Keeyeon, Transportation Demand Management and IVHS: Linking IVHS with TDM, Workshop Paper of the 2nd Anniversary of Seoul Development Institute, Seoul Development Institute, pp.137-162, 1994.

Institute of Transportation Engineers (ITE), A Toolbox for Alleviating Traffic Congestion, Washington, DC: ITE, 1988.

Institute of Transportation Engineers. Trip Generation, 8th edition, Washington, DC, USA: ITE, 2008.

Ison, S. and T. Rye. The Implementation and Effectiveness of Transport Demand Management Measures. Ashgate, Hampshire, U.K., 2008.

Jeong, Bonghyun, A Preliminary Approach to the Development of an Advanced Public Transport System in Gwangju City, Korea, The Journal of Regional Development, Vol. 31, Chonnam National University, 1995 (in Korean).

Jeong, Bonghyun, New Transportation Policy in Regional Metropolitan City: Gwangju, Korea, CNU Press, 2005 (in Korean).

Jeong, Bonghyun, SOC and Regional Development: Standing Transportation Problems and Solutions in the Jeonlla Provinces, Korea, CNU Press, 2010 (in Korean).

Kim, Jin-Baek, How can We Make Urban Transportation More Sustainable in Korea, A Master's Thesis, University of Sheffield, December 2003.

Ko, J., D. Park, and S. Lee. "Transit Ridership Evaluation Using Aggregate-Level Causal Analyses of Subway Mode Shares in Seoul, South Korea." Transportation Research Record: Journal of the Transportation Research Board, 2219 (2011): pp.59-68.

Ko, J., Y. Cho, J. Choi, and T. Kim. "Evaluation of Travel Demand Management Strategies Using Importance-Performance Analysis." Transportation Research Record: Journal of the Transportation Research Board, 2118 (2009): pp.67-74.

Korea Transport Institute (KOTI), A Master Plan for the Improvement of the Transportation System and Parking System in Gwangju City, 1990.

KOTI, Transportation System Management Project II for Gwangju City, 1993.

McCormick Rankin, Ottawa Transportation Demand Management Plan: Downe Revitalization, LansFinal Report, October 2011.

Neilon J. Rowen, Donald L. Woods and Vergil G. Stover, Alternatives for Improving Urban Transportation: A Management Overview, Technology Sharing Report 77-215, The Federal Highway Administration, 1977.

O'Flaherty, C. A., Highways: Traffic Planning and Engineering, Volume 1, London: Edward Arnold, 1986.

Park, Soo-Young, Transportation Problems and Policies in Seoul, The Journal of Korean Planners Association, Vol 25, No 2, 1990.

Rowe, D., Bae, C. and Shin, Q., "Assessing Multifamily Residential Parking Demand and Transit Service." ITE Journal, Vol. 70, No. 8 (2010): pp. 20-24.

Shin, Seongil et al., Improvement Strategies of the Transportation Impact Fee for Effective Transportation Demand Management, Research Report 2008-PR-26, Seoul Development Institute, 2008 (in Korean).

Young, Elizabeth Young et al., Integrating Transportation Demand Management into the Planning and Development Process: a Reference for Cities, HNTB Consultant and Sandag Committees and Other Working Groups, May 2012.

Yun, Pan, A Study on the Operation of Bus Exclusive Lanes in Gwangju, Journal of Municipal Administration, Vol.10., Gwangju City, 1994 (in Korea).

Vivian, G. "Trip Generation Characteristics of Free-Standing Discount Superstores." ITE Journal, Vol. 76, No. 8 (2006): pp.30-37.

Zhou, L. "Modeling the Impacts of an Employer-Based Travel Demand Management Program on Commute Travel Behavior." Ph.D. Dissertation, University of South Florida, 2008.

Chapter 6

Urban Parking Problems and Policy

1. Introduction to Urban Parking

1.1. Concept and Importance of Parking

Concept of Parking

Parking is the act of stopping and disengaging a vehicle and leavings it unoccupied. Parking on one or both sides of a road is often permitted, though sometimes with restrictions. Parking may be provided in public parking facilities that serve any and all who wish to use them or in private parking facilities that are reserved for specific users. Commercial facilities are those operated for a profit, often by a professional parking operator. Commercial facilities are usually public. However, some commercial facilities may be entirely reserved for a specific group of users and therefore are 'private'.

Parking facilities are constructed together with some buildings to facilitate the coming and going of the building's users. The ancestors of modern parking were the development of the first on-street parking spaces and the first off-street parking facilities. Off-street parking facilities today range from driveways, carport, and multi-car garages at residence to parking structures. The vast majority of parking in Gwangju City is provided in surface lots and free to the user. In most cases, the parking fee is still subsidized below the actual cost of owning and operating the space, due to market forces. When most of the other parking in the community and parking at competitors is free, it is difficult to charge the full cost. The vast majority of parking facilities are operated as self-park. In the past, mechanical parking structures employed elevators and other devices to move the vehicle away to parking stalls not accessible by pedestrians. This facility type fell out of favor due to reliability problems and the high cost of maintenance as the facilities aged.

Importance of Parking[1]

The availability and cost of a parking space is an important determinant of whether or not people choose to drive to a particular destination, and also whether they choose to own a car at all. It is likely that the relatively lower levels of car ownership in inner cities of developed countries (London, Munich) are partly a result of the lack of on-street parking, as well as the above average levels of public transport accessibility and service.

Local governments have direct control over the use of kerbspace in their areas, and therefore of the supply and price of on-street parking. In some cases, this extends to public off-street car parks. The extent to which local authorities are the provider of public off-street parking varies from locality to locality. In fact, there may be little formal off-street parking available, whether owned by the municipality or not. Through the development control process for new buildings, local governments can also have some control over the level of parking that is provided in new developments.

While parking controls and prices are rarely popular with the public, they are policy options that are relatively well-known and accepted even in large Korean cities. If there is an obvious shortage of parking spaces many people may accept that there is a need for parking controls. Parking demand and pricing are transport demand measures implemented frequently by local governments, yet little of the academic literature deals with experiences of this policy, preferring instead to concentrate on the politically "more lucrative" topic of congestion charging.

1.2. Modes of Parking

For most motorized vehicles, there are three basic modes of parking, based on the arrangement of vehicles — parallel parking, perpendicular parking, and angle parking.[2] These are self-park configurations where the vehicle

[1] Tom Rye(2011), pp.1-2.

driver is able to access the parking independently.

Parallel parking is the most common mode of streetside parking for cars. It may also be used in parking lots and parking structures, but usually only to supplement parking spaces that use the other modes. With parallel parking of cars, these are arranged in a line, with the front bumper of one car facing the back bumper of an adjacent one. This is done parallel to a curb, when one is provided.

With perpendicular parking of cars, these are parked side to side, perpendicular to an aisle, curb, or wall. This type of car parking is more scalable than parallel parking and is therefore commonly used in car parking lots and car parking structures. Often, in car parking lots using perpendicular parking, two rows of parking spaces may be arranged front to front, with aisles in between. If no other cars are blocking, a driver may perform a "pull-through" by driving through one parking space into the connecting space to avoid having to reverse out of a parking space upon their return. Sometimes, a single row of perpendicular car parking spaces is marked in the center of a street. This arrangement eliminates reversing from the manoeuvre; cars are required to drive in forwards and drive out forwards.

Angle parking is similar to perpendicular parking for these vehicles, except that cars are arranged at an angle to the aisle (an acute angle with the direction of approach). The gentler turn allows easier and quicker parking, narrower aisles, and thus higher density than perpendicular parking. While in theory the aisles are one-way, in practice they are typically wide enough to allow two cars to pass slowly when drivers go down the aisles the wrong way.

Angle parking is very common in car parking lots. It may also be used in streetside car parking in the U. S. when there is more width available for car parking than would be needed for parallel parking of cars, as it creates a larger number of parking spaces. Some cities have utilized angled parking

---

[2] Edwards (1999), pp.499-505.

on-street. This has been done mostly in residential, retail and mixed use areas where additional parking compared to parallel parking is desired and traffic volumes are lower. Most angled parking is designed in a head-in configuration while a few cities have some back-in angled parking (typically on hills or low traffic volume streets). Angle parking is considered dangerous by cycling organizations, especially in the head-in configuration, but unwelcome in either form.

Table 6.1. Type of Parking

Modes of Parking	Detailed Contents
Parallel parking	■ Arranged in a line, with the front bumper of one car facing the back bumper of an adjacent one. ■ Done parallel to a curb, when one is provided.
Perpendicular parking	■ Parked side to side, perpendicular to an aisle, curb, or wall. ■ Commonly used in car parking lots and structures.
Angle parking	■ Used in streetside car parking ■ Done mostly in residential, retail and mixed use areas

Source: http://en.wikipedia.org/wiki/Parking#Modes_of_parking

1.3. The Automobile and Parking: Facts of life

It is acknowledged in transportation and urban planning that our resources are not limitless and that greater efficiency in the use of transportation resources must be achieved. Parking availability and price are key determinants in mode choice, which in turn, is the most fundamental element in transportation planning. Reliance on the private car and the need to park it at both ends of each trip, has increased in the last decade even as transportation demand management (TDM) and the reduction of single occupant vehicle (SOV) trips has been a focus of transportation and urban planners.

The largest single factor in these trends is suburbanization. The population in the city center where transit is more widely available and price incentives to use alternative modes exist has declined. Other factors contributing to the increased reliance on the private car are the maturation of baby boomers, more woman in the workplace, more trip changing, higher levels of automobile ownership, the democratization of mobility, the shift from an industrial to a service-based economy, and corporate downsizing and re-engineering. All have combined with suburbanization to increase the modal split of SOV trips. And all contribute to the ever-increasing need for parking. As a result, the traditional and still widely held view in Gwangju is that adequate and convenient parking must be provided for commerce and a community to survive, let alone thrive.

2. Parking Problems and Characteristics

2.1. Identification of Parking Problems[3]

Progress in parking has been made in spite of discord and difficult circumstances. The parking problem is very important in a metropolitan city such as Gwangju, because it affects everyone- not only the individual driver, but also his immediate community. In stating the problem, it is necessary to locate several causative factors, which can be used to help uncover possible solutions. The problem should not be stated so narrowly at the beginning that its full scope and impacts remain hidden. The parking problem has been aggravated by several factors which affected the actual parking situation. Previous works in the identification of parking problems can generally be classified as three types.[4]

First, the parking problem is ascribed to the fact that the amount of usage of vehicle has increased in the city. Frequently, the number of parking spaces were not developed to keep pace with this growth. The increase in car

[3] Jeong (1991), pp.16-24.

[4] Jeong (1991), pp.16-24.

ownership requires the development and implementation of a sound parking policy. Second, the parking problem stems from the fact that there is not sufficient parking space to accommodate all parkers in the urban area. Historically, insufficient expenditure for parking facilities in the U. S. A. has compounded the traffic congestion and parking problem in many areas. The lack of appropriate parking facilities can result in congestion and frustration in an urban area. Third, parking problem in an urban area often results from the dynamic interaction of physical and human elements in the modern city. Parking problem are either human or physical in character. It is suggested that an appreciation of downtown dynamics can be gained through a comprehensive and continuos assessment of the character of parking. Here physical elements of parking problems are mainly linked to environmental circumstances. Two human factors include shifts in parking distribution and the influences of land use controls and planning.

Approaches to the parking problem are directed to transport technology or facilities rather than the issue of urban planning and transport policy. It is necessary to analyse parking problems from the stand-point of urban planning and the transport system.

Figure 6.1. Identification Framework of Parking Problems

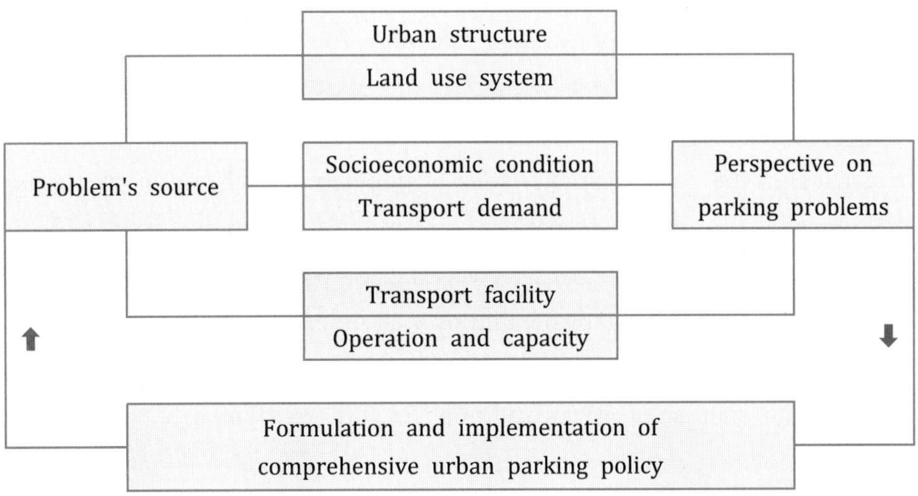

2.2. Sources of Parking Problems

The parking situation in a metropolitan city is affected by three factors, namely urban structural, socio-economic and transport facility factors.[5] First, urban structural factors emerge from the matrix of elements within the land use system in the city. Urban structure is determined by the land use system that refers to the spatial distribution of urban functions. Since urban parking is a major determinant of the traffic generation characteristics of land use as well as a major urban land use, parking constraints are key factors in the modal-choice.

Parking needs are most important in the CBD (Central Business District) which is the area of complex urban function and high-density land use. The CBD becomes an area where extensive parking problems are found. The influence of land use controls and planning leads to parking problems. Parking facilities also affect the dynamics of land use and transport performance in a manner not dissimilar to a highway bottle-neck. The types and densities of land uses and their relationship account for most automotive traffic in the CBD.

Second, socio-economic factors are fundamental to the consideration of transport demand. Transport demand becomes an original factor that creates a practical change in parking demand. It is very much related to increased car ownership and decreased transit ridership. The parking problem becomes more pronounced as the size of the city increases. The total size of parking supply increases as the size of the city increases, but at a decreasing rate. In particular, the basic characteristics of population such as car ownership and personal income, affect parking demand. For instance, an increase in urban population accompanies an increasing transport and parking demand, and leads to increased car ownership as well as increased demand for office accommodation. These attributes, in turn, bring increased traffic and parking facilities. The number of private automobiles has contributed to the increase,

[5] Jeong (1991), pp.16-24.

in parallel with a rapid increase in personal income and increased car ownership. Other natural factors that have a direct effect on the need for transport and parking are the quantity of travel and its pattern. The parking problem thus is affected by the increasing transport demand.

Third, transport facility factor refers to the operation and capacity of urban transport facilities. The urban transport system consist of the terminals, the roadways and the vehicles. As an integral part of urban transportation, parking is not an isolated function, but it is directly related to traffic on the road and thereby capacity and provision of roads and to the viable use of public transport. The parking problem is intimately related to the form of road network of a community. For instance, a gridiron road system with more or fewer random local variations, is obviously a basic cause of traffic and parking problems in the city. In addition, the problem of terminal design, its regulation and control must be tied to problems of traffic flow requirements, and vehicle and parking characteristics. The parking problem is also aggravated by the following three elements: rapid expansion, peaks in vehicular traffic and poor transport systems. The parking problem is thus affected by operation and capacity.

Table 6.2. Source Factors of Parking Problems

Factors	Detailed factor by group
Urban structural factors	▪ Increase in employees, central management organizations ▪ Mono-nucleated CBD urban structure, high-density land use ▪ Central management functions, building floor space,
Socio economic factors	▪ Urban population increase, increase in local travellers ▪ Increasing trips per person, increase in personal income ▪ Rising car ownership
Transport facility factors	▪ Amount and timing of travel, public transport services ▪ Traffic volumes of private cars, radial road outside CBD ▪ Subway network and transfer systems, ▪ Construction difficulties of parking facilities, road facilities,

Source: Jeong(1991)

2.3. Parking Characteristics[6]

Parking characteristics can be explained in terms of parking supply and parking demand. They mean not only the physical marks of parking facilities on the ground which delineate parking spaces, but also the habits of parkers in an urban area. In past parking studies, primary emphasis was mainly given to the issue of parking demand. Demand is very much related to the behaviour and habits of parkers. Parking characteristics can be also found through the analysis of parking inventory and usage data.

Information on the characteristics is necessary and a prerequisite to the development and implementation of an urban parking policy. Moreover, the information can be used to help plan and design the type of parking facilities that are required, and that will operate in the most economical and efficient manner.

The term "parking characteristics" has been widely used in parking studies. A consensus of what is included in parking characteristics has not developed and not been accepted. The common threads in past parking studies are these elements related to parking supply and parking activity in an urban area. Several parking studies have been made of downtown parking characteristics related to city size. Such parking studies generally show similar patterns of parking characteristics as a function of urban area population levels and parking facility type. Parking characteristics can be analyzed by the use of secondary data and research reports.

Table 6.3. Types of Parking Characteristics

Division	Parking characteristics	Remarks
Supply of parking space	■ Facility type, facility usage ■ Facility location, facility distribution	Physical character
Demand for parking space	■ Travel purpose, parking duration ■ Walking distance, turn-over rate	Usage character

[6] Jeong (1991), pp.16-24.

Comprehensive parking inventory data can give the actual number, type, distribution and location of parking facilities. On the demand side of parking, parking characteristics consist of trip purpose, parking duration, walking distance and turnover rate.

3. Parking Characteristics and Systems in Gwangju

3.1. Trends of Transport Condition

Gwangju's population grew at 0.8% annually during the 2000-2012 period. The total number of households increased at an annual growth rate of 2.2 during the same period. Gwangju's 2,335 km of total road length in 2012 increased by 1.4 times from 1,845 km in 2000. The total number of vehicles in Gwangju increased rapidly at an annual average rate of 4.2% during the 2000-2012 period. The total number of private cars accounted for 79.3% of Gwangju's total number of vehicles in 2012, showing an annual average growth rate of 11.8% during the 2000-2012 period. The total number of driver's license holders experienced a rapid increase between 2000 and 2012. To conclude, the parking problem in Gwangju has been heavily affected by the growing number of driver's license holders and increased private car ownership.

Table 6.4. Trends of Socio-economic Growth in Gwangju

Division	Unit	2000	2005	2012	AAGR ('00-'12)
Population	1,000 persons	1,351	1,444	1,484	0.8%
Household	1,000 hou.	430	482	556	2.2%
Road length	Km	1,845	1,946	2,335	2.0%
Car registration (Private car's ratio)	1,000 vehicle (%)	337 (67.5)	436 (73.5)	551 (79.3)	4.2% **(11.8)**
Driver's license holder	1,000 persons	538	669	827	3.6%

Note: AAGR refers to average annual growth rate.
Source: GMC(each year)

3.2. Supply of Parking Spaces

Trends of Parking Facilities

There was an overall drastic increase in parking spaces, showing an annual growth rate of 8.4% on average from 2000 to 2012. This reflected the growth of Gwangju. By type of facility, the total space of garages increased at an average annual rate of 9.2% during the same period. Even if the space available for lot parking was insufficient to accommodate all vehicles demanding it, lot spaces increased steadily as Gwangju grew.

The parkers were separately identified in their use of curb, lot or garage spaces. The utilization of parking garages increased with the population increase of Gwangju, whereas curb parking lots decreased. In 2012, curb parking facilities accounted for only 6.0% of the total parking supply in the city and accommodated 2.7% of all the parkers. Off-street facilities(garages and lots) provided 94.0% of the total supply in 2012.

Table 6.5. Trends in Parking Spaces

Facility Type	2000		2005		2012		AAGR
	Place	Space	Place	Space	Place	Space	('00-'12)
Garages	10,792	158,933	19,676	294,831	28,815	458,329	9.2%
Lots	442	16,190	602	26,717	684	30,301	5.4%
Curb parking	588	15,828	530	13,842	519	13,133	−1.5%
Total	11,822	190,951	20,808	335,390	30,018	501,763	8.4%

Note: AAGR refers to average annual growth rate based on space.
Source: Gwangju Statistical Yearbook (each year)

Security of Parking Spaces

The parking problem of Gwangju has become an important and urgent social issue in the 2000s. The rapid increase in private car ownership and usage have resulted in a heavy parking problem in the built-up area. Parking is still in a chaotic state due to the shortage of parking facilities and lack of comprehensive parking policy. As a result of the additional construction of housing development projects, the parking space deficiency in the city showed a declining trend between 2000 and 2012.

General parking conditions across the city have improved during the 2000-2012 period. The reason for this was that there was a rapid increase in parking garages of the massive housing development sites and buildings during the same period. For instance, the security of parking space increased from 56.7% in 2000 to 91.1% in 2012.

Table 6.6. Trends in Security of Parking Spaces

Items	Unit	2000	2005	2012
Parking spaces(A)	Thousand	191	335	503
Vehicle ownership(B)	Thousand	337	436	551
Securing rate of parking space (A/B)	%	56.7	76.9	91.1

Source: Gwangju Statistical Yearbook (each year)

3.3. Forecast of Parking Facilities in Gwangju

The total parking demand at night is estimated to increase from 490,100 spaces in 2010 to 649,900 spaces in 2025. In addition, the total parking supply is expected to grow from 362,300 spaces in 2010 to 482,300 spaces in 2025. During the same period, the securing rate of night parking spaces is forecasted to show a slight decreasing trend. This shows that parking difficulties will last further, because of the imbalance between supply and demand of parking in Gwangju City. That is, parking facilities are not equally distributed on a block by block basis in the built-in area. It is suggested that GMC should not only continue to expand parking facilities, but also to manage overall parking demand in the city.

Table 6.7. Forecast of Parking Spaces by year

(Unit: 1,000 spaces)

Year/Item	Parking demand		Parking supply	Securing rate(%)	
	Day	Night		Day	Night
2005	391.8	435.7	335.4	85.61	76.97
2010	435.6	490.1	362.3	83.19	73.85
2015	485.0	557.2	413.7	85.29	74.24
2020	521.1	613.6	441.4	84.70	71.94
2025	551.1	649.9	482.3	87.52	74.21

Source: GMC(2008)

3.4. Parking Controls and Management System

Parking Violations and Illegal Parking

The traffic routes and the movement of public transport in Gwangju are hampered by illegally parked cars on streets. The total number of illegally parked cars in Gwangju increased from 162,700 vehicles in 2000 to 273,631 vehicles in 2012. This suggests that the current level of parking enforcement does not appear to be effective in discouraging illegal parking, especially given the low fine structure for parking violations. Lax controls over illegal parking have caused parking violations to increase in the city. An excessive amount of illegal parking indicates inadequate enforcement and the cultural standard of parkers. Disorganization at ticket offices can contribute to more delay and overcrowding of public transport.

Table 6.8. Trends of Parking Violation

Item	Unit	2000	2005	2012	AAGR %
Vehicle ownership	1,000	337	436	551	4.2
Parking spaces	1,000	191	333	502	8.4
Parking violation	1,000	163	157	274	4.4

Note: AAGR refers to average annual growth rate.

Source: Gwangju Statistical Yearbook(each year)

Parking Management System

Gwangju Metropolitan Government(GMC) holds the responsibility of developing and implementing parking policy without recourse to special legislation. Examining its administrative organizations can help identify problems in coordination and responsibilities, and leads to a better understanding of the GMC's capabilities.

Table 6.9. Parking Administrative Organization

Facility type	Parking management		Parking controls
	City government	District(Gu) office	
Garages	TSD	TAD	TAD
Lots	TSD	TAD	TAD
Curb parking	TSD	TAD	TAD

Note: TSD means Traffic Safety Division, and TAD means Transportation Administration Division.
Source: http://www.gwangju.go.kr

The Traffic Safety Division of GMC takes charge of the provision and operation of parking facilities in Gwangju. The Traffic Section of each police Station is responsible for enforcing curb parking regulations. The parking sector in Gwangju is characterized by the multiplicity of organizations associated with it. The structural weakness in the machinery of GMC has prevented the implementation of a comprehensive parking policy for Gwangju. A lack of coordinated action among the various divisions has affected the successful implementation of a comprehensive parking policy in Gwangju.

4. Parking Problems and Policy in Gwangju

4.1. Parking Difficulties in the City

The GMC has implemented parking policies to improve parking problems in a isolated way. The level of connectivity between parking management strategies has not increased yearly in terms of time and region. It has not helped GMC reduce parking difficulties in the city, and there is still much room for improvement of parking problems. This has resulted in a serious parking situation. Parking problems are mainly caused by a rapid increase in vehicle ownership and insufficient parking facilities. This has led to a regional imbalance between demand and supply of parking in the city, and has also exacerbated the parking problem. In fact, the total public and private parking facilities have not been provided sufficiently so far. Parking facilities annexed to buildings have expanded gradually.

Other causes of parking difficulties in GMC are illegal parking and traffic disorders. There are lots of illegally parked cars on roads, and drivers do not obey the traffic laws. These problems have negative effects on traffic safety and advanced traffic order. In addition, traffic in secondary streets is very congested and delayed as well. As the private automobile oriented transport environment will continue to persist, the parking situation in Gwangju is not expected to improve very much.

Table 6.10. Types of the Parking Problem

Items	Parking demand	Parking supply	Parking management
Types	Increase & concentration, Excess and disparity, Illegal parking	Shortage & distribution, Utilization & controls, Zoning	Administration, Parking policy & plan, Law, Parking rates

4.2. Parking Problems and Solutions

Parking Problems in Gwangju

The people who get to use parking spaces are those that arrive there first, but this might not be the most beneficial use where parking spaces are scarce. On-street parking causes safety and traffic congestion problems by blocking one or two traffic lanes, narrowing streets to one lane, reducing visibility and forcing pedestrians to walk in the road, if no proper footpath are provided. In addition, it obstructs access for emergency services.

Poor management of on-street parking and/ or lack of information about parking availability in areas of high demand lead to a large amount of traffic circulating looking for a parking space, contributing to congestion and pollution. Parking regulations are not enforced, or poorly enforced, and enforcement and management are sometimes informal and or corrupt. Parking on pedestrian areas, such as footpaths, or across street corners makes streets inaccessible to parents with push-chairs and physically challenged people, and discourages people from walking. This renders the urban environment less attractive and hence reduces economic activity. In return, it makes people more car-dependent.

Where on-street parking is priced, it is often cheaper than off-street parking. As a result, people look for a scarce space on the street whilst off-street car parks lie half empty. The fact that there are parking spaces available in city centers encourages people to drive there, while congestion and pollution could be reduced by having less parking in town to encourage people to use other modes of transport instead. City centers are concerned about losing custom to urban-edge developments with lots of parking, so they respond by trying to make it easier to park. It is necessary and possible to better manage parking and solve parking problems there.

Parking is a vital urban and transport resource that needs to be efficiently managed. Proper parking management would reduce the need to travel longer distances, reduce the amount of short trips and also initiate a modal shift to other climate friendly modes of travel.

Parking Problems and the Solutions

The following table contains a list of typical parking problems on the left.

On the right are some actions that can be taken to deal with these issues and references to further information.[7]

Table 6.11. Guide of Parking Tactics as to the Problems

Parking problems	Parking management tactics
Lacking parking spaces	■ Restrict maximum length of stay ■ Cheaper short-term parking rates ■ Provide off-street parking lots
On-street parking	■ Restrict parking for rush hour ■ Restrict parking owing to safety ■ Price/advertise off-street parking
Poor management of on-street parking Lack of information on parking availablilty	■ Provide more parking information ■ Price/advertise off-street parking ■ Park and ride facilities
Parking regulations Informal regulations	■ Improve enforcement ■ Change organizational practices ■ Change institutional structure
Parking on pedestrian areas	■ Better parking enforcement ■ Self enforcing measures
Cheaper on-street parking	■ Change pricing structure ■ Better advertising of off-street parking ■ Improve quality of off-street parking
Free parking spaces in city centers	■ Gradually reduce supply, park and ride facilities ■ Limit maximum lengths of stay ■ Increase price of parking
Losing custom in city center's shops	■ Provide more, cheaper parking ■ Use space-efficient modes (BRT, etc.) ■ Use pedestrian and parking management

Source: Tom Rye(2011)

[7] Tom Rye(2011), pp.8-10.

4.3. Evolution and Changes of Parking Policy

Parking Policy Evolution

Evolution of urban transport and parking policy in Gwangju has been marked by periods of continuity and change. The share held by city buses among all the transport modes decreased during the second part of the 1980s, owing to increased private car ownership. The share of taxis maintained a stable growth. Most transport policy in Gwangju mainly concentrated on the construction of urban transport facilities. In that period, the parking problem started to become an integral part of the transport problem in Gwangju.

Table 6.12. Transport System and Parking Policy

Items	The 1990s	The 2000s
Major traffic mode	City bus	Multi-traffic modes
Features	* Decreasing share of city buses	* Increasing share of autos and taxies
Transport policy	* Expansion of road facilities * Transportation system management * Urban railway plan	* Expansion of road facilities * Operation of urban railway
Parking policy	* Establishment of parking plan	* Implementation of parking policy

In the 1990s, the share held by city buses decreased, while the share of private cars increased steadily owing to the rapidly increasing private car ownership. Transport policy in Gwangju was generally typified by the construction of roads and the transportation system management. In urban parking policy, more efforts were made to construct additional parking spaces in the CBD. Despite the parking policy being concentrated primarily on the expansion of parking facilities in the 1990s, little contribution has been made to the solutions of parking problems.

Changes in Parking Policy

GMG's statement of parking policy reflects an awareness that there are serious problems with both parking and transport policy, and the process that has formed and implemented that policy.

Parking policy in Gwangju has been traditionally associated with urban transport policy toward the car and its concomitant impacts. In the late 1980s, most objectives of urban transport policy were concerned with the accommodation of travel needs through road construction, and with public transport provision by construction. More emphasis on parking policy in the late 1980s is found in the construction of parking facilities. Therefore, the parking policy of Gwangju remains unchanged and has not properly coped with the change in the past transport system.

Table 6.13. Changes in Gwangju's Parking Policy

Strategy type	1990	1995	2000	2005	2012
Management of parking demand				IT	IT
Restrictions on car traffic					
Improvement of parking facilities					DT
Construction of parking facilities	DT	DT	DT	DT	DT
Efficient use of parking facilities			IT	IT	
Improvement of parking management system			DT	DT	DT
Establishment of parking culture					DT
Cultivation of consciousness					DT
Parking problems			PR	PR	PR

Note: DT refers to a direct tactic of parking policy; IT, an indirect tactic of transport policy; PR means that parking problem became an integral point of urban transport problems.

Source: GMC(each year)

4.4. New Parking Management Policy (PMP) for GMC

Definition of PMP[8]

Parking management strategies is a term adopted to describe the parking policies and actions that can be employed by cities to alleviate parking and other related transport problems. Most of these strategies are equally applicable to major activity centers, both institutional and commercial. The goals of PMS are to minimize auto usage and traffic congestion, maximize transit patronage, provide adequate parking, and foster economic growth. There is no one parking strategy that can simultaneously achieve all hypothetically desired goals. This is partly due to some fundamental conflicts among various goals. For example, strategies that increase parking supply are likely to reduce the incentive to use mass public transit, Some of these strategies may be quickly discarded for failure to meet the goals and objectives of a community or institution. Others require more detailed consideration.

Types of PMS

The types of PMS or its categories include pricing, on-street supply, enforcement and adjudication, off-street supply, and marketing. Pricing is a major force in determining parking conditions, especially in the dynamic circumstances found in activity centers where fees are charged for parking. Generally speaking, there may be one or more purposes in pricing of parking: generating revenue, controlling who parks where, and encouraging alternative modes of transportation. On-street parking is often a critical parking resource to activity centers despite the limited capacity it can provide. The goals for management of on-street parking relate to controlling who parks where and preventing spillover parking into adjacent neighborhoods. Illegal parking not

---

8 ite(1999), pp.536-559.

only allows parkers to avoid paying their fair share and subverts the entire parking management system, but it may also negatively affect traffic flow on critical streets. The level of enforcement and the rate schedule are more important determinants of parking behaviour than the fine schedule. Strict enforcement and higher fees are more beneficial to a system as a whole. Local officials can restrict supply by setting maximum rather than minimum parking requirements in the zoning process. While marketing in itself will not increase parking supply or reduce demand, it will be very valuable to publicize any and all steps to improve parking in a activity center. There are strategies available to meet almost any parking management goal for an activity center or a community. Obviously, the first step is to articulate the goals.

Table 6.14. Guide of Parking Tactics as to the Problems

PMP	Detailed contents of PMP
Pricing	■ Change parking rates: Increase rates, Decrease rates, Free parking in CBD, Differential pricing programs ■ Merchant shopper discounts: Stamp programs, Token programs ■ Employer parking subsidies: Reduce subsidies, Transit/HOV subsidies
On-street parking supply	■ Add or remove spaces, Change mix of short-and long-term parking ■ Parking restrictions, Residential parking permit programs ■ Carpool/vanpool preferential parking, Loading zone regulations
Off-street parking supply	■ Expand or restrict off-street supply in CBD & activity centers ■ Zoning requirements, Constrain normal growth in supply ■ Construct new lots and garages, Change mix of short-and long-term parking, Preferential parking ■ Restrict parking before or during selected hours of the day
Enforcement	■ Enforcement: Non-police enforcement, Ticketing, Towing, Booting ■ Adjudication: Administrative, Judical
Marketing	■ Advertising: Brochures, Maps, Media ■ Convenience programms

Source: ITE(1999)

Appropriate Technology Use for Payment and Data Collection[9]

Technology can help make parking management more efficient based on easier data collection and analysis. Multi-space parking meters and pay-by-phone services, for example, can make it easier for drivers to comply with parking fees. Such technologies can help cities track on-street parking use in real time and adjust prices across a whole area through a central computer, giving managers better control over the whole parking system. Cities across Europe have implemented these technologies. When cities do not have the internal capacity to implement and manage a modern parking system, it is appropriate to outsource the system or component tasks to a competent private sector partner. Cities like Barcelona and the City of Westminster in London have found success with such an arrangement.

In Gwangju Metropolitan City, parking enforcement is mostly carried out by parking wardens patrolling the streets on foot or by car. This is often quite inefficient, requiring a large number of employees, each of whom has limited range. GMC needs to implement an enforcement scheme that requires fewer people to execute. Scan cars accompanied by wardens on scooters can take over enforcement responsibilities. The scan cars use cameras and automatic license plate number recognition technology to identify illegal parkers. The scan car will travel at 40 kmh up and down the streets taking 160 scans per second. Wardens follow the scan cars on scooter and issue tickets for any violation they find.

Centralized Management of Parking Inventory

Traffic congestion has become a major problem in old and new CBDs of GMC in the last several years. GMC should put together an integrated set of solutions that make it more expensive to park in the old city center and dense commercial districts and give residents and visitors more ways to get

9 ITDP(2013), p.36.

around the dense area. GMC needs to launch an integrated parking program called "Green Zone".

Its purpose is to regulate visitor parking supply by limiting parking time with a pricing mechanism and by giving priority to residents. Pay and display parking is available in several districts with varying pricing. Residential and preferential parking permits can allow residents in the green zone to park at a lower rate while preferential permits can allow non-residents to park in exchange for paying the city's highest hourly rates. The project will contribute to converting parking spaces into motor cycle parking and biking stations. The revenue generated by on-street parking fees should be used to fund the city's bike share system. GMC must have a parking management corporation that oversees both on-and publicly owned off-street parking and try to harmonize prices.

Increased Parking Fees

The parking spaces are insufficient in Gwangju's old CBD and new commercial districts. In particular, the shortage of parking spaces is most severe in the areas within the 1st ring road where hospitals, business and commercial centers are located. This is one of the factors causing the notorious traffic congestion in GMC.

GMC has attached great importance to the parking issue and adopted various parking policies to address it. One innovative measure is the adjustment of parking fees. The measure is to charge based on the area the car is parked in-the nearer to the city center, the higher the charge. Parking fees are raised for the cars parked in the designated key areas. It is designed to provide disincentives for parking in the city center and thus encourage people even more to the use public transport.

A Centralized Management of all Parking Activities

For a parking management system to be efficient and effective, both on-and off-street parking must be managed together as a whole city. This is best achieved by putting one entity in charge of the overall supply and demand it to alter prices based on parking demand. When on-street parking spaces are underpriced or managed independently of off-street parking supply, the city sees excess demand for the former and low use of the latter. Such imbalances lead policy makers to believe that there is a parking shortage when, in fact, there is hidden capacity. Limited but convenient on-street parking spaces should be the most expensive, nearby off-street spaces less expensive, and remote off-street spaces the cheapest. San Francisco, Barcelona, and several other European cities have used this approach to varying degrees.

Rigid Parking Enforcement with High Technology and Physical Design

Most systems are only as good as their enforcement. A good enforcement system starts with reliable car registration records that allow the authorities to find violators and collect fines. Drivers should expect to face penalties if they park illegally or fail to pay meter fees. New technologies like van-mounted license plate readers, in-street sensors and smart meters can efficiently target tens or hundreds of enforcement officers that cities normally hire for this task. Amsterdam is one city that has made extensive use of vehicle-mounted license plate readers.

Physical design approaches can reduce the need for human enforcement as they ensure that drivers do not park illegally or unsafely. Treatments like bollards that block cars from driving onto sidewalks and clearly delineated no-parking zones can ensure that drivers use only legal spaces and stay out of cyclist and pedestrian zones, increasing overall street safety. Zurich and Paris have both used bollards and other physical elements to make clear where drivers can and can't park and to show vehicle speeds in certain residential neighborhoods.

Implementation of Performance Standards for Parking Management

Drivers gravitate toward parking spaces right in front of their destination. Studies show that if those spaces are free or cheap, people will complete to use them, which results in over-consumption and perceived shortages while parking in other area lies under-utilized. This often means that all on-street spaces will be occupied during peak hours, forcing drivers to circle in search of an open space, slowing traffic flow around them, and parking illegally, creating safety risks. Seatle and San Francisco, most notably, have started to adjust parking prices to ensure on-street parking availability at all time by setting an occupancy performance target.

This can ensure that drivers unwilling to pay higher fees either use less convenient spaces or take public transport. Those willing to pay for a space can find one quickly, which reduces traffic congestion. This strategy should include introducing on-street parking fees where demand exists and using pricing to ensure that there is an available space approximately every 50 or 60 meters (or 1 space per block face).

Provision of Clear Information on Parking Supply to Ensure its Effective Use

Electronic displays that show where available off-street parking spaces are can help drivers find those spaces efficiently. More broadly, such displays can also help ensure that an area's whole parking supply is better utilized. GMC needs to implement such systems. Gwangju is a dynamic metropolitan city that is used as a case study for application of these parking strategies. Parking issues are rising to the forefront of Gwangju's urban concerns. Drivers complain about parking shortages. Illegal parking is on the rise as citizens choose to pay fines or expect authorities to look the other way.

With Gwangju's motorization rate rising, parking issues are only expected to get worse. The many entities involved in seeking to solve this problem have led to policies that mostly increase parking supply. In addition to increasing minimum parking requirements for developers, the city should introduce formalized on-street parking in some areas, encouraging shared parking while also working to build new off-street parking spaces. The solutions sometimes conflict with other strategies for the GMC. The strategies will alow the city to continue developing thriving commercial centers around public transit.

A self-portrait in the newspaper

Parking difficulties in Seoul's CBD

Seoul drivers hunting for a parking place represent one of the best growth industries in the world, says Australian parking operator Wilson Parking, which began operating in the capital last month. Introducing an all-day rate of 5,000 won, the company has reaped quick attention by Seoul drivers.

"Car parking has been a serious problem to motorists in Seoul, the capital with 2.78 million registered vehicles on the limited land. But for us, the city is one of the most lucrative markets in the world," said Albert Auckett, managing director of Wilson Parking Korea.

Since March, Wilson Parking, the largest parking operator in the Asia-Pacific region, has reached deals to handle parking at Gateway Tower, Ace Tower and Seoul City Tower. The car parking business, although quite unfamiliar to many Koreans, has long been a profitable venture in the West and especially crowded Asian cities like Hong Kong and Singapore.

"People should understand the car parking business as a special form of property investment, a daily business, a service industry which requires a strong customer focus," said Auckett. Wilson Parking, according to Auckett, has been recognized as the largest and most experienced parking operator in Asia-Pacific controlling more than 900 car parks throughout Australia, Hong Kong, New Zealand, and Singapore. Korea is its fifth business destination.

The Korean operation involves adopting Wilson's experience to local needs. Auckett said, "Car parking business is not as simple as it looks. It needs to understand changing variables in limited space. So, only experience can make the business successful." However, Wilson has found difficulties in educating building owners about car parking as a revenue source. "Building owners don't think of a car parking area as a business unit. It is important to equalize property value of offices and parking places," added the director.

Wilson plans to manage parking at 10 high-rise buildings in Seoul within this year, including Seoul Financial Center. It plans to extend its business to the full range of parking facilities including airports, universities, hotels, shopping centers, hospitals, conference venues and landmark properties.

The director said that shopping centers will be the biggest target for its business. "We have already conducted a survey about complaints that occurred at a car parking area in a shopping center in Seoul. We will continually monitor and review our operations for ways in which improvements can be made in the shopping center where the car parking site is the first and last stop to satisfy customers' need," said Auckett.

Wilson Parking Korea is a wholly owned subsidiary of Wilson Group Asia Pte Ltd, a private company incorporated in Singapore to hold the shares of Wilson Parking companies in Asia-Pacific. The holding company is owned by the Kwok family, who is the major shareholder of Sun Hung Kai Properties Limited, listed on the Hong Kong Stock Exchange.

*** Source: The Korea Herald (2005.5.16)**

References

Brierly, J. Parking of Motor Vehicles 2nd ed, London: Applied Science Publishers Ltd, 1962.

Burrage, R.H. and E.G. Mogren, Parking, Connecticut: The ENO Foundation for Highway Traffic Control, 1957.

Chung, Hawok and Kim, Hanghee, The Establishment Strategies and Considerations of Parking Governance for the Happy Communities in Gwangju City, The Journal Focus Gwangju 2012-20, Gwagnju Development Institute, December 2012 (in Korean).

Collins, Michael F. and Timothy M. Pharoah, Transport Organization in a Great City: The Case of London, London: George Allen and Unwin Ltd, 1974.

DiRenzo, John F., Bart Ciam, and Edward Barber, Parking Management Tactics: A Reference Guide, Report No.FHWA-PL-80-010, Washington, DC: Federal Highway Administration, 1981.

Edwards, John D., edit., Transportation Planning Handbook, Second Edition, Institute of Transportation Engineers (ITE), 1999.

Ellis, Raymond H., Direnzo, F. and Barber, Edward J., New directions in Central Business Districts Parking Policies, Transportation Research Record 845: 40-51, 1982.

Gwangju Metropolitan City (GMC), Municipal Parking Ordinance, Gwangju (in korean), 2009.

Highway Research Board (HRB), Parking Principles, Special Report 125, Washington, DC., 1971.

Jeong, Bonghyun, Evolution of Urban Parking System in Seoul's CBD during the 1977-87 Period and its Implications, Journal of The Korean Regional Development Association 4, 2: 89 - 101, 1992.

Jeong, Bonghyun, Public Acceptability in the Implementation of Parking Policy, The Journal of Korea Planners Association 28, 1: 171 - 185, 1993.

Jeong, Bonghyun, New Transportation Policy in Regional Metropolitan City: Gwangju, Korea, CNU Press, 2005 (in Korean).

Jeong, Bonghyun, SOC and Regional Development: Standing Transportation Problems and Solutions in the Jeonlla Provinces, Korea, CNU Press, 2010 (in Korean).

Korea Research Institute for Human Settlements (KRIHS), Strategies for the Development of Parking Related Policies, Seoul(in korean), 1987.

Korea Transport Institute (KOTI), A Master Plan for the Improvement of the Transportation System and Parking System in Gwangju City, 1990.

KOTI, Transportation System Management Project II for Gwangju City, 1993.

KOTI, A Feasibility Study of the Urban Railway Construction in Gwangju city, 1992.

Levinson, Herbert S., Parking in a Changing Time, in Herbert S. Levinson and Robert A. Weant, eds, Urban Transportation: Perspectives and Prospects, Connecticut: ENO Foundation, 1982.

Ligocki, Clemenc and Zonn, Leo E., Parking Problems in Central Business Districts, Cities 1, 4: 350-355, 1984.

Ministry of Transport (MOT), Parking-The Next Stage, London: Her Majesty's Stationery Office, 1963.

Murphy, R.E., The Central Business District, Second Edition, Chicago: Aldine Atherton, Inc., 1972.

O'Flaherty, C. A., Highways: Traffic Planning and Engineering, Volume 1, London: Edward Arnold, 1986.

OECD, Evaluation of Urban Parking System, Paris, 1980.

Rye, Tom, Parking Management: A Contribution towards Liveable Cities, Germany: Deutsche Gesellschaft fur Technische Zusammenarbeit(GTZ), November 2011.

Scully, William J., Parking Management in a Small Community: Back to Basics, ITE Journal 58, 11: 32-35, 1988.

Sharpe, D.E., Parking Practice, including Restraint, City of Leicester, A Report of the British Parking Association Seminar on Parking Policy and Practice, Brighton, November, 1975.

Smith, W. and Associates, Parking in the City Center, Washington, DC: The Automobile Manufacturers Association, 1965.

Topp, Hartmut, Parking Policies in large Cities in Germany, Transportation 18: 3-21, 1991.

Weant, R. A., Parking Garage Planning and Operation, Connecticut: The ENO Foundation for Transportation, Inc., 1978.

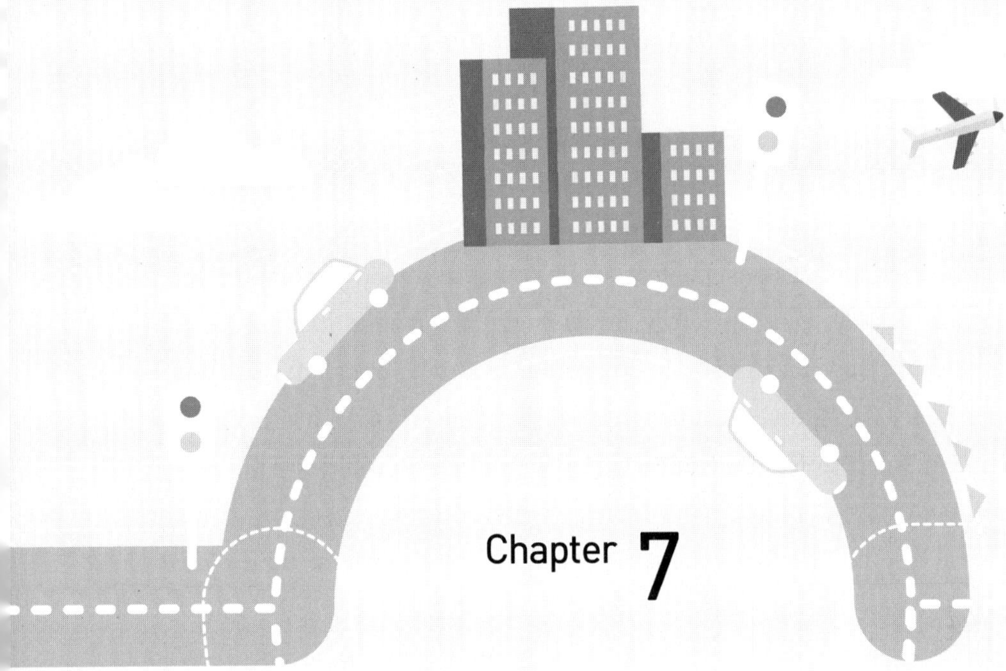

Chapter 7

Road Traffic Accidents and Safety Policy

1. Concept of Traffic Accident

1.1. Definition of Traffic Accident[1]

Traffic refers to all the vehicles that are moving along the roads in a particular area. An accident happens when a vehicle hits a person, an object, or another vehicle, causing injury or damage. If someone has an accident, something unpleasant happens to them that was not intended - sometimes causing injury or death. A traffic accident, also known as a traffic collision, car crash or road traffic accident occurs when a vehicle collides with another vehicle, pedestrian, animal, road debris or any other stationary obstruction, such as a tree or utility pole. Traffic accidents may result in injury, death, vehicle damage, and property damage.

Traffic accidents can be classified by general type. Types of accident include head-on, road departure, rear-end, side collisions, and rollovers. A number of factors contribute to the accident risk, including vehicle design, speed of operation, road environment, driver skill and/or impairment, and driver behaviour. Car collisions lead to death and disability as well as financial costs to both society and the individuals involved.

1.2. Causes of Traffic Accident[2]

Although the law requires each driver to practice reasonable care while on the road, many fail to do so and their negligence often leads to a tragic car accident involving property damages and serious injuries, including fractures, spinal cord injury, brain injury, and death. Over 90% of motor vehicle accidents involve some degree of driver behavior combined with one of the other below listed three factors. Drivers often try to blame road conditions, equipment failure, or other drivers for those accidents. When the

---

1 http://en.wikipedia.org/wiki/Traffic_accident

2 http://www.smartmotorist.com/traffic-and-safety-guideline/; Hung(2003), pp.7-11.

facts are truthfully presented, however, the behavior of the implicated driver is usually the primary cause. Most are caused by excessive speed or aggressive driver behavior.

Driver Behavior

The most common driver errors that lead to car accidents include: traffic violations, driver error and/or distraction, equipment failure, and flawed road design and layout. Driver errors caused by distractions and/or impairment are among the most common factors that contribute to car accidents. A distraction is anything that diverts the driver's attention from the road. Talking on a cell phone is the leading cause of driver distraction and causes thousands of car accidents each year.

Traffic laws are rules that govern traffic, regulate vehicles and facilitate the orderly and timely flow of traffic. Drivers are expected to obey traffic laws in order to avoid a collision with another vehicle, object, cyclist and/or pedestrian. Breaking traffic laws leads to traffic violations that could cause a car accident. The most common traffic violations include speeding, running a red light or a stop sign, tailgating, losing control of the vehicle, failing to use a turn signal, driving on the wrong side of the road, crossing the median, failing to stop for pedestrians, reckless driving, drunk driving and a number of others. Impaired driving resulted in some of the most disturbing statistics and a number of traffic movements. Drunk driving cases often results in much higher verdicts than any other type of car accident injury cases.

Equipment Failure

Mechanical failures can lead to car accidents and are, in some cases, a direct result of negligence on the part of the owner of the car, a mechanic and/or the manufacturer. Manufacturers are required by law to design and engineer cars that meet a minimum safety standard. The most cited types of equipment failure are loss of brakes, tire blowouts or tread separation, and steering/suspension failure. Combined totals for all reported equipment failure accounts for less than 5% of all motor vehicle accidents.

If you suspect that equipment failure or a manufacturing defect contributed to your car, bicycle or truck accident, you should contact an experienced auto accidents attorney who can help further investigate your claim and obtain compensation for your property damages and injuries. The amount of personal injury settlement depends on many factors, including the extent of property loss and medical bills.

Roadway Design

Motorists may blame roadway design for accidents, but it's rarely the cause. Consultants spent years getting road barriers, utility poles, railroad crossings and guard-rails to their current high level of safety. Civil engineers, local governments and law enforcement agencies all contribute to the design of safe road layouts and traffic management systems. The government provides guidelines for their construction, with design flexibility to suit local conditions. Roadways are designed by engineers with special consideration given to the following elements, such as hazard visibility, roadway surfaces, traffic control devices, behavioral control devices, traffic flow, roadway identification signs, and weather conditions.

Poor Maintenance

Although road conditions can be affected by many factors, including bad weather, road conditions, and flawed design, some poor road conditions may also be caused by negligence. Roadway maintenance contributes to some motor vehicle accidents, but not to the extent that drivers use it as an excuse. The most common road conditions that lead to car accidents include: lack of traffic control and/or devices, failure to display warning signs during construction, debris on the roadway, faded or obscured road signs, potholes, salting, and sanding.

Table 7.1. Factors Contributing to Traffic Accidents

Factors	Detailed contents
Driver behavior	Traffic violations; excessive speed, aggressive driver behavior, cellular phone, watching DMB
Equipment failure	Loss of brakes, tire blowouts or tread separation, steering/suspension failure
Roadway design	Hazard visibility, roadway surfaces, traffic control devices, behavioral control devices, traffic flow, roadway identification signs, weather
Roadway maintenance	Debris, faded road signs, potholes, roadway construction, salting and sanding.

1.3. A Model for Traffic Accident[3]

Traffic accidents bear strong elements of human-environment adjustments and maladjustment. A model for a traffic accident is characterized by three main components. The vehicle which describes vehicles in its composition, age, technical conditions, and safety equipments, such as seat belts in a car. The environment, comprising the road system and the wider physical and built up environment. And the physical environment, which splits further into different aspects such as; daylight and climate (weather conditions and road conditions), spatial conditions (arrangements and macro structures), settlement pattern, situation of areas of residence and working areas, principle of traffic separation, topography, and road constructions qualities.

The behavior of the population includes characteristics such as age and sex ratio as well as attitudes and general traffic behavior. It goes further into driving behavior, driving experience, driving style, risk compensation,

[3] Deus D. Komba(2006), pp.10-19.

and risk driving (influence of alcohol and drugs) Superimposed on this model is a system of traffic laws, regulations and modes of enforcement designed to ensure that the population adheres to the controls and regulations so as to maintain some level of road safety i.e. traffic rules, speed controls and convictions for various road traffic offences. The model is used as a framework for understanding the multiple causes and prevention of traffic accidents that occur in developing cities. Available literature identifies traffic accidents in a place as having been caused either by physical factors in the road system (environment), the vehicle or behavior factors, or how they interact with enforcement regulations in unique settings.

Figure 7.1. A Model for Traffic Accidents

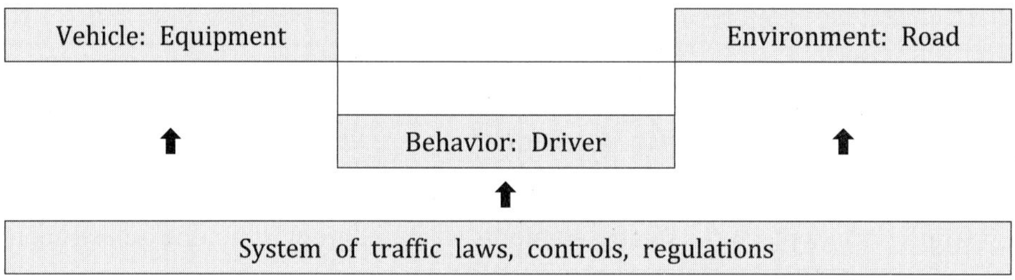

2. Condition of Road Traffic Accidents

2.1. Changes in Transport Condition

Gwangju Metropolitan City (GMC) is situated in the southwestern part of the Korean Peninsula. Gwangju's land area is estimated at 501.25 km^2, and Gwangju had a population of 1.48 million people as of 2012. The city of Gwangju is currently divided into five district offices with an elected political representative for each district. The major part of Gwangju's road system is accounted for metropolitan roads which had a combined total length of 1,697 km in 2012. Vehicle ownership has increased gradually by year.

In 2012, the total number of registered vehicles stood at 606,100 cars.

Private vehicles comprised 79.3% of the total, and other vehicles 20.7%. The number of driver's license holders grew greatly during the 2000-2012 period. In comparison with the statistics of 2000, the number of registered vehicles and driver's license holders increased by about 5.02% and 3.52% respectively in 2012.

Table 7.2. Trends of Road Transport Conditions in Gwangju

Year	Population (thousand)	License Holders (thousand)	Road Length (km)	Vehicle Registration (thousand)
2000	1350.9	538.0	1,169	336.6
2005	1,443.9	668.5	1,354	487.2
2008	1,447.1	715.5	1,495	525.6
2010	1,450.2	751.4	1,621	569.6
2012	1,484.0	814.4	1,697	606.1
AAGR	0.8%	3.52%	3.15%	5.02%

Source: GMC(2001-2013)

Note: AAGR refers to average annual growth rate.

2.2. Trends of Traffic Accidents

Despite the rapid increases both in the number of vehicles and of licensed drivers, the number of accidents and injuries slowly decreased. On the other hand, the number of fatalities decreased only slightly. For example, the number of traffic accidents in 2012 was 8,600 incidents, and the number of fatalities involved in these accidents was 114 persons, and the number of the injured was 13,886 persons. The total number of deaths decreased at the AAGR of 2.48 % during the 2000-2012 period. In comparison with the statistics of 2000, the number of injuries due to traffic accidents increased by 1.32 times in 2012. The year 2012 had death rates of 7.5 deaths per 100,000 population, 1.9 deaths per 10,000 vehicles, and 1.4 deaths per 10,000 licenses.

Table 7.3. Trends of Road Traffic Accidents in Gwangju

Year	Accidents(cases)	Deaths(person)	Injuries(person)
2000	7,853	154	10,528
2005	7,797	103	12,361
2008	8,260	140	13,598
2010	8,894	126	14,618
2012	8,600	114	13,886
AAGR	0.76%	−2.48%	2.33%

Source: RTA(2013)

Note: AAGR refers to average annual growth rate.

In short, the traffic conditions in Gwangju since 2000 can be characterized as a slow population increase as well as a rapid increase in the number of vehicles and licensed drivers. As a consequence, various traffic problems such as traffic congestion, high accident rates, traffic pollution, and parking difficulties came about in the built-in area.

2.3. Characteristics of Traffic Accidents

Traffic Accidents by Collision Type

By accident type, about 77.4% of road traffic accidents were caused solely by a collision between vehicles, and 20.6% by a crash between vehicle and pedestrian in 2012, respectively. This means that accidents caused by human factors amount to as much as 95%.[4] Efforts thus should be made to minimize driver's error to reduce road traffic accidents.

Pedestrians are also vulnerable to road accidents and accidents involving pedestrians. Pedestrian accidents have been identified as a major cause of deaths and injuries in Gwangju. Pedestrians account for approximately 20.6%

[4] Sul edit.(2013), pp.69-70.

of all road accidents in Gwangju. In the past, there has been a tendency to address the needs of motorized traffic only, while largely neglecting pedestrian needs. There has also been a marked increase in traffic in disadvantaged communities with a corresponding increase in conflict between drivers and pedestrians.

Table 7.4. Road Traffic Accidents by Type (2012)

Collision type	Accidents		Casualties (person)	
	Cases	%Share	Deaths	Injuries
Car vs. people	1,768	20.6	56	1,859
Car vs. car	6,743	77.4	41	11,567
Car alone	359	4.2	17	460
Total	8,600	100.0	114	13,886

Source: RTA(2013)

Traffic Accidents by Violation

Many drivers fail to practice reasonable care while on the road. Their negligence often leads to a tragic car accident involving property damages, serious injuries, and death. Over 90% of motor vehicle accidents involve some degree of driver behavior combined with one of the other three factors.

By driver's violation, approximately 48.5% of the total traffic accidents in 2012 were caused, first of all, by unsafe driving (driver's carelessness). About 16.0% of 2012's total accidents in Gwangju were due to the unsafe following distance on the road, and 13.3% traffic signal violations, respectively. It is suggested that if people drove more carefully, there would be fewer accidents.

Table 7.5. Road Traffic Accidents by Violation(2012)

Violation types		Accidents		Casualties (person)	
		Case	%Share	Deaths	Injuries
Driver	Violation of centerline	460	5.3	8	837
	Traffic signal violation	1,146	13.3	12	2,071
	Unsafe following distance	1,375	16.0	2	2,584
	Unsafe driving	4,172	48.5	67	6,033
	Traffic offence at crossing	737	8.6	3	1,282
	Others	710	8.2	22	1,079
	Sub-total	8,600	100.0	114	13,886
Poor vehicle maintenance		0	0	0	0
Pedestrian's negligence		0	0	0	0
Total		8,600	100.0	114	13,886

Source: RTA(2013)

Traffic Accidents by Location

In 2012, about 51.6% of the total traffic accidents occurred on road crossings. The total number of traffic accidents which happened on roads (single route) accounted for approximately 44.9% of the total in Gwangju. Unusually, the total deaths of traffic accidents on roads showed 2.2 times that of traffic accidents at crossings in 2012. It is mainly attributable to the speeding caused by unsafe driving on roads.

Table 7.6. Road Traffic Accidents by Location (2012)

Collision spot	Accidents		Casualties (person)	
	Case	%Share	Deaths	Injuries
Crossing	3,861	44.9	33	6,643
Single route (on road)	4,438	51.6	74	6,811
Others	301	3.5	7	432
Total	8,600	100.0	114	13,886

Source: RTA(2013)

Traffic Accidents by Vehicle Type

By vehicle type, passenger cars are thought to have caused 5,507 traffic accidents for the year 2012. This accounted for about 64.0% of the total traffic accidents in Gwangju. The rates are shown as follows: 11.9% for taxi, 8.3% for truck, and 3.5% for bus, as of 2012.

Table 7.7. Road Traffic Accidents by Vehicle Type (2010)

Vehicle type	Accidents		Casualties (person)	
	Case	%Share	Deaths	Injuries
Passenger car	5,507	64.0	66	8,639
Bus	299	3.5	3	463
Taxi	1,025	11.9	14	1,637
Truck	721	8.3	10	1,211
Motorcycle	303	3.5	1	417
Bicycle	130	1.5	3	137
Others	615	7.3	17	1,382
Total	8,600	100.0	114	13,886

Source: RTA(2011)

3. Issues of Road Traffic Safety

3.1. Implications

Traffic crashes have increased steadily during the years 2000-2012. Currently most crashes involve vehicle vs. vehicle. The major cause of traffic accidents is unsafe and reckless driving. Unsafe following distance, traffic signal violation, and traffic offence at crossing are other important causes of traffic accidents in Gwangju. The high rate of road traffic accidents in conjunction with the absence of traffic order on the road have long been considered a critical social problem in Gwangju. There are still substantial publicity and discussion about how to correct the problem.

Today, more attention is paid to the issue of road traffic accidents for three main reasons.[5] Firstly, Gwangju's accident rate is much higher than those of metropolitan cities in both Korea and advanced industrialized countries. GMC considers the high traffic accident rate to be a barrier to the city expressing the city spirit of democracy, peace and human rights. Secondly, Gwangju needs to improve its city image, particularly in the field of road traffic safety. Thirdly, recognizing the enormous social costs involved with traffic-related injuries and fatalities, several nongovernmental organizations (NGOs) aggressively took part in the policy formulation process. The NGOs pushed both city council and the government to implement new legislations and to enforce pre-existing regulations. Owing to their efforts, combined with a mass media campaign focusing on traffic-related social costs, the various efforts to reduce road traffic crashes have been accepted as a national movement by the public.

3.2. Outline of Traffic Accident Issues[6]

It can be seen that the traffic safety problem of Gwangju has been aggravated by the various elements of the problem which affects road traffic safety. Those elements identified most frequently are lack of public education and enforcement, poor and unreasonable design, and reduced respect for law enforcement. Most apparent here is the rapid growth of travel demand, and traffic disorder. The residents of the city are closely and constantly affected by the traffic accident risk in diverse ways. They are dissatisfied with local driving behaviour and road facilities. Road traffic safety policy could be related to the task of reducing traffic accidents and promoting traffic safety in the city. The traffic safety problem is the summation of the things which people dislike about traffic accidents.

Because the scope of traffic accident problems is broad, it is often necessary to identify main problem types which are influenced by the road

---

[5] Yang et.al(2003), pp.89-90.

[6] Erik Cempel(2007), pp.5-22.

traffic system. The main problems identified are seen as common problems facing both GMC and the residents of Gwangju. As shown in Figure 2, poor driving behaviors are mainly caused by the affiliative interaction of lack of public education and enforcement, and negligent law enforcement. It results in traffic accidents and reduced road traffic safety.

Figure 7.2. Overview of Gwangju city's Traffic Safety Issues

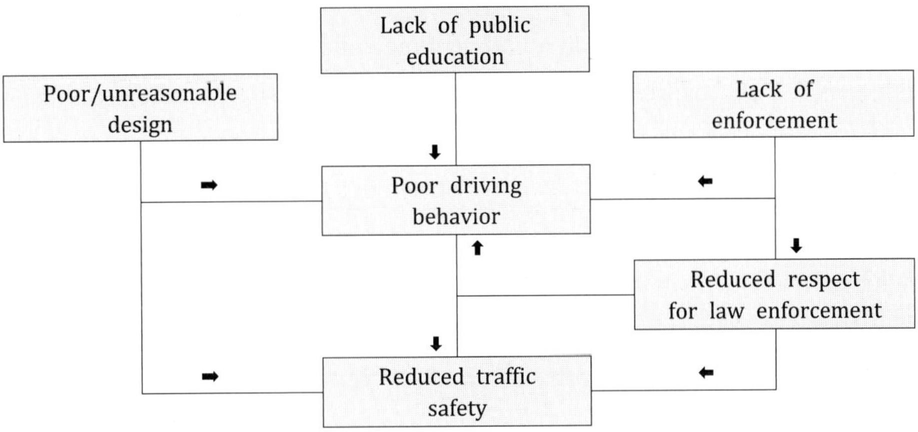

3.3. Problems of Traffic Accidents

Facilities and Geo-metrics

Because of the topographical conditions and mono-nucleated urban structure, the road network of Gwangju is a grid pattern in the built-up area, and radial and circular type toward outlying areas. In particular, there are enormous intersections at the gridiron-network of the built-up area streets. The heavy city traffic with its endless delays at lights, crosswalks, and intersections increases the dangers of traffic accidents. A lack of sight distance at the intersection of minor roadways is a cause of traffic accidents. It is important on minor roadways for safety considerations such as driver sight distance to be considered. There are too many access points on busy streets. At-grade intersections and private driveways greatly increase the number of conflicts involving vehicles, cyclists, and pedestrians.

Road Traffic Signals

Any cyclist or driver who fails to comply with traffic signals is a danger to themselves and other drivers. Partially signalized intersections do not contribute to reducing traffic congestion and traffic accidents. They foster unclear procedures and priorities of drivers. Besides, dangerous and unpredictable geometric design and striping causes fatal traffic accidents on major roads and expressways. It is very hard for drivers to follow confusing and non-standard pavement markings and road signs at major roads in the city. Drivers can be confused and distracted at the wheel. Confusing and non-standard signs lead to dangerous and last-minute lane changes on roads. Different pavement markings of major roads are apt to provide drivers with inconsistent meaning and traffic information while driving. There are a lack of 'yield' or 'stop' signs at streets, and different number lanes are striped on opposite intersection legs.

Table 7.8. Problems of Road Traffic Accidents in Gwangju

Division	Detailed problems
Facilities: geometrics	• Enormous intersections • No sight distance at intersection • Too many access points on busy streets • Dangerous/unpredictable geometric design
Facilities: striping/signs	• Confusing/non-standard pavement markings • Confusing/non-standard signs • Lack of 'yield' of 'stop' signs • Different # lanes striped on opposite intersection legs
Behavior/ enforcement	• Lack of enforcement • Behavior/not respecting rules • No 'nexus' of road capacity and parking capacity • Businesses not exactly following rules; making interpretations

Sources: Jeong(2005); Cempel(2007)

Behavior and Enforcement

Cars parked illegally on streets generally obstructs traffic flow on minor roads, and are a reason for some on-street traffic accidents. Illegal use of shoulder as well as vehicles entering and exiting traffic aggravate traffic delays and congestion, and bring about traffic accident on major roads. They are infractions of the traffic laws. The GMC and the metropolitan police agency need to adopt stringent regulations for traffic control, and should exercise strict control over illegal parking and speeding up on roads. This is probably the best safeguard against traffic accidents in Gwangju City.

Moreover, traffic accidents are most likely to occur when drivers are less well-disciplined. Reduction in accident rates can come as a result of more effective disciplining of the driver, elimination of drunk drivers, safer vehicles and roads. An excessive amount of illegal parking indicates inadequate enforcement and the cultural standard of parkers.

4. Road Traffic Safety Promotion Policy

4.1. Objectives of Traffic Safety Policy[7]

The identification of objectives and direction is a first essential step in the development of road safety plans and policy. The objectives provide direction for road safety projects and plans. Road safety plans and projects focus on development opportunities within the city and the development challenges facing Gwangju City. The main goal is to improve road safety and reduce accidents in the city. The detailed goal for road safety policy is to improve the safety and security of the transport system, and to ensure a high level of safety and security for all users of the transportation system in the city. The main objectives of road safety plan and policy are to integrate

[7] COT(2009), pp.10-12.

engineering measures, education, awareness, and law enforcement to ensure reduction in fatal accidents and fatalities, and to create an environment where all road users, including vulnerable groups, can travel freely and safely.

Figure 7.3. Goals and Objectives of Traffic Safety Plan

【Goal】

- To improve road safety
- To reduce accidents in the city

⬆ ⬇

【Objectives】

- To integrate engineering measures, education, awareness and law enforcement
- To ensure reduction in fatal accidents and fatalities, and to create an environment where all road users can travel safely

4.2. Road Safety Treatment

Road Safety Treatments

It is important to select those measures that will be most cost-effective in addressing the particular safety issue at a site. This can require more than one measure or a combination of measures. A list of road safety measures provide an overview of measures that are likely to be effective when addressing particular safety issues in the city. These are the measures that seem likely to be more cost-effective.

For example, the introduction of chevron signs on a sharp curve could significantly reduce run-off accidents in return for a relatively small investment. At locations where there are problems with unsafe overtaking, the use of centerline rumble strips could be an effective alternative to the provision of passing lanes. In locations where large volumes of pedestrians are using a roadway, the provision of walkways and traffic calming measures can be effective in addressing road safety issues.

In the selection of road safety measures, it is important to realize there is no single solution that can address all issues. One measure will seldom provide a complete solution to a safety issue and it will often be necessary to apply a combination of measures. On higher order mobility routes, traffic calming can significantly affect the flow of traffic and increase travelling costs.

Table 7.9. Road Safety Improvement Treatments in Urban Area 1

Issue	Safety measures	Implementation cost		
		Low	Medium	High
Pedestrians	Separate pedestrian and traffic		×	×
	Public transit facilities, eg-bus bays	×	×	
	Pedestrian barries on high-speed road		×	
	Pedestrian median refuge	×	×	×
	Pedestrian bridges/subways			×
	Walkway and cycle tracks	×	×	
	Street lighting		×	×
	Remove parking lots near crossings	×	×	
	Traffic calming	×	×	
Speed-related	Traffic calming measures	×	×	
	Speed enforcement cameras	×		
Intersections and accesses	Access management	×	×	
	Intersection closure or relocation	×	×	
	Roundabouts		×	×
	Right-and-left turn lanes		×	×
	Road signs, markings and studs	×		
	Sight distance	×	×	×

Source: COT(2009)

Table 7.10. Road Safety Improvement Treatments in Urban Area 2

Issue	Safety measures	Implementation cost		
		Low	Medium	High
Traffic signals	Remove unwarranted traffic signals	×	×	
	Provide right-and-left turn lanes		×	×
	Ensure TSM compliance	×	×	
	Ensure correct signal timing	×		
	Provide overhead traffic signals		×	
Parking	Parking restriction	×		
Run-off road	Remove fixed objects	×	×	×
	Breakaway devices	×	×	
	Safety devices		×	
	Guard-rails	×	×	
	Trees near to roadway	×	×	
	Poles (electrical, telephone, etc)		×	×
	Road signs, markings, delineators	×		
Accidents on curves	Sharp curve chevrons	×		
	Flatten sharp curves			×

Source: COT(2009)

Human Factors and Road Safety Treatments

Particular attention should be given to human factors in the engineering design of road safety measures. The engineering design of a road safety measure should not only accommodate human limitations but could also be used to influence human behaviour. Road improvements can lead to unexpected changes in driver behaviour which could have a significant impact on road safety, sometimes in unexpected ways.

For example, widening of a roadway will tend to increase speeds, and can result in an increase in accidents. It is particularly important to take the information needs of road users into account. Safe decisions can only be made when road users have sufficient information to inform them of hazardous conditions. Formal information is provided by means of road signs and markings while informal information is obtained from the road itself and the environment. Both types of information should be utilized to inform the driver regarding possible hazardous conditions.

Pedestrian Safety

Pedestrians are one of the road user groups that are most vulnerable and most at risk in accidents. The safety problem is not only the result of pedestrians in greater danger of being seriously injured or killed, but also because of basic incompatibilities between pedestrians and motorized traffic. Even if walking is the most basic form of transportation, the needs of pedestrians are frequently neglected in road provision. The fundamental principle in the accommodation of pedestrians is to provide separation between pedestrians and vehicular traffic. Separation can be achieved by providing a separate pedestrian walkway system. The need for road crossings should be provided for by means of pedestrian bridges or subways in urban expressways. The security of pedestrians and cyclists should be taken into account.

Comfort and convenience are also important considerations in the provision of pedestrian and cyclist facilities. The natural action for the pedestrian or cyclist is to cross the road at the desired point.

Traffic Calming

Traffic calming is fundamentally aimed at reducing the adverse safety and other impacts of traffic on residential areas. Traffic calming emphasizes the needs of pedestrians, cyclists and residents by placing restrictions on vehicles. Road safety for pedestrians and cyclists, can be significantly improved by the introduction of traffic calming measures. Lower vehicle speeds resulting from such measures reduce the likelihood of accidents as well as their severity. Traffic calming can be implemented in business nodes with highly concentrated pedestrians to protect pedestrians from the adverse impacts of motorized traffic.

The more important objectives of traffic calming are to improve traffic safety of communities, and bring about calmer, quieter and more tranquil neighborhoods, reduced noise and air pollution. Traffic calming should mostly be considered on access roads which are given to the needs of the local community and residents. Traffic calming can be subdivided into two classes, such as speed calming measures and traffic intrusion methods. The typical measures of speed calming include speed humps, raised pedestrian crossings, traffic circles, and chicanes. The speed calming measures, such as chokers, semi-closures, and semi-closures are effective for traffic intrusion.

Law Enforcement Cameras

Law enforcement cameras can be used on high-speed roads where a sudden reduction in speeds is required and where it is not possible to install traffic calming measures. A typical application is where a major road or freeway enters an urban area and where drivers find it difficult to immediately adjust to the changing conditions. The camera installation itself must be visible and road signs warning drivers of the camera must be installed.

Traffic Signals

An inappropriate signal could in fact lead to severe disruption of traffic and result in lengthy delays, particularly on main roads. Excessive delays result in significant fuel wastage, higher vehicle costs, and air pollution. Another potential disadvantage of a traffic signal is that it can lead to diversion of arterial traffic into residential streets, which could significantly affect road safety on and the liveability of the streets.

The inappropriate installation of signals can in fact increase the number of accidents. Road safety at traffic signals can be improved by introducing improvements such as those described below: ensure that traffic signals are warranted; provide right-and left-turning lanes on higher speed roads; ensure that the traffic signals comply fully with the requirements of the Korea Road Traffic Signs Manual; ensure optimum traffic signal phasing and timing; check that yellow and all-red intervals are appropriate, etc.

4.3. Education and Awareness

Visible Political Support

The main objective of education and awareness is to ensure that communities understand the dangers of road traffic and the purpose of the proposed road safety measures. Road safety projects in the city are normally undertaken on the basis of a partnership of technical practitioners, traffic law enforcement agencies, educational institutions and nongovernmental organizations (NGOs). Through this action, the role of these other institutions and organizations is acknowledged and a platform is created for the inclusion of innovative inputs into the awareness campaign.

Large-scale regional projects are normally launched by a political incumbent of the city, such as city mayor and metropolitan council. At the launch, the project is officially handed over to the community by mayor and council. The launches can involve a series of dramatic plays, street events and recitals on the theme of the promotion of road safety. This has been found to be a highly effective and popular method of making the public aware of the project and of the potential dangers posed by traffic. Follow-up awareness campaigns focus mainly on schools and community centers, and should coincide with the implementation of the proposed engineering measures.

Educational and Awareness Programs

The following are examples of educational and awareness programmes that can be introduced and incorporated into road safety master plans: road safety promotion and education at schools; distribution of educational and awareness pamphlets to the public; road safety education of residents in frequent accident areas; community meeting and workshops; involvement of local print media; erection of information billboards along streets; driving along streets.

Youth and Road Safety Campaign

The campaign can consist of the following: visits to schools by a team consisting of the councillors and officials from the Traffic Safety Section and the metropolitan police department; presentation on traffic hazards and tips on road safety improvements; distribution of posters, flyers and reflective strips. The police department needs to be involved with education programs at schools. These programs are presented with the assistance of provincial road safety officers, NGOs, and road safety forums.

Teacher Patrol

Teacher patrol standards and requirements are managed through strict national guidelines in regard to the approval and registration of teacher crossings, administrative and operational procedures, training, and regular inspection of teacher patrols. A teacher patrol manual should be formulated through the Road Traffic Authority or the Transport Safety Division, etc. In particular, traffic enforcement officers are very closely involved with the inspection of the specific sites and the training of teacher patrol team and their supervisors. Training of scholar patrols provides an opportunity to convey various road safety issues to children and at the same time create a relationship of trust between the children and the traffic law enforcement function.

4.4. Law Enforcement Plans

Law Enforcement and its Strategy

Law enforcement is an essential element of road safety and specific provision should be made for law enforcement plans in the road safety master plan. It is not possible to address all road safety issues by means of engineering measures or education and awareness campaigns alone; proposals should therefore be included for specific law enforcement actions.

The Metropolitan Police Agency and affiliated police station are responsible for the implementation of the law enforcement plans. The agency should be closely involved in the development of the law enforcement plans to ensure that it will be possible to implement and integrate these plans within the agency's overall strategy. The agency should be involved in most stages of the development of the road safety master plan. The department can also assist in the planning of road safety measures and provide support for the successful implementation of engineering measures.

Law Enforcement Plan

Provision should normally be made in the road safety master plan and policy for law enforcement as one of the measures required to improve road safety. The law enforcement aspects would typically focus on matters such as speed, drunken driving, moving offences, and driver and vehicle fitness. Although provision is made in the National Road Traffic Act for pedestrian offences, there is some difficulty in enforcing the legislation.

The reasons are that pedestrians are not required by law to carry identification on their person, and pedestrian offenders are mostly community members going about their day-to-day business therefore arresting them is not really a socially acceptable course. Pedestrian-related issues need to be addressed by engineering measures or through education and awareness campaigns. It is particularly important that the law enforcement plan should not focus on law enforcement alone but also engender community support for law enforcement. The plan should make provision for informing the community of the need for and importance of law enforcement in road safety.

The law enforcement plan can provide for the following elements, inclusive awareness and education, road safety committees, and integrated involvement of role players. Traffic enforcement officers involved in community safety programmes should receive focused training, over and above their normal operational training. This should involve a basic understanding of community development issues, communication, and the education of children. When required, provision should be made in the law enforcement plans for such training.

A self-portrait in the newspaper

Safety consciousness. Regulation alone cannot prevent accidents

The government last week announced a set of measures aimed at reducing casualties from traffic accidents, including obliging all passengers to wear seat belts on any type of road starting in 2015. It was a proper but overdue move.

In terms of traffic safety, Korea has long remained near the bottom among major industrialized nations. According to figures from the Ministry of Land, Infrastructure and Transport, the number of traffic accident fatalities in Korea stood at 2.4 per 10,000 vehicles and 10.7 per 100,000 people in 2011, compared to the OECD averages of 1.2 and 6.2, respectively. In the two categories, the country ranked 30th and 29th among the 32 member states of the Organization for Economic Cooperation and Development.

Separate data recently released by the National Police Agency showed 5,392 Koreans were killed in traffic accidents last year, up 3.1 % from 5,229 in 2011. The increase reversed the downward trend that had continued for a decade.

Against this backdrop, it has been too easy a stance to stick to the current rule that obligates only drivers and front-seat passengers to fasten seat belts with backseat passengers required to do so only on expressways. All the measures announced last week, which also includes compelling all new cars to be equipped with daylight running lamps, should be implemented thoroughly to achieve the goal of reducing traffic accident fatalities from 2.34 per 10,000 vehicles last year to 1.6 in 2017. It is hoped that the figure will be drawn down further below the target.

What may be more important than regulatory efforts by the government is that all drivers and passengers should thoroughly make a habit of fastening seat belts and also abide by other traffic rules. Local experts on road safety estimate that only 73 % of all drivers wear seat belts and a mere 10 % of backseat passengers do so in Korea, compared to about 90 % and 75 %, respectively, in other major advanced countries.

The high rate of traffic accident deaths in Korea should be understood as just partly reflecting the lack of safety consciousness among its people, which was proven again last week in two tragic cases. Five high school students drowned to death Thursday when they were swept away by a strong current after they entered the sea as ordered by unqualified instructors during a summer camp on a west coast beach. The accident came days after seven workers were killed when water from the swollen Hangang River swamped an underground waterworks construction site in Seoul. The deaths were blamed on the lack of safety warnings from their supervisors, who had paid no heed to possible dangers from the heavy downpour.

President Park Geun-hye came forward Monday to order officials to ensure that similar accidents would not happen again and warn that anyone to be found negligent on supervisory work would face stern punishment. Immediately after her instruction, state auditors launched emergency safety checks on major construction sites in Seoul, and Education Ministry officials vowed to discipline teachers who fail to accompany their students to outdoor classes.

These moves are all too familiar to the public, who have seen previous pledges do little to prevent the repetition of accidents. This time, all relevant officials should prove that it will no longer be the case. On their part, citizens must enhance their own safety consciousness and adhere to obligations required of them. It was embarrassing that some passenger cars stood in the way of rescue vehicles rushing to the flooded construction site in Seoul.

*** Source: The Korea Herald (2013.7.24)**

References

Cempel, Erik, Global Road Safety Rules and Standards to Reduce Traffic Accidents in Korea, 1st UN Global Road Safety Week, KINTEX, Research Associate, The Korea Transport Institute, April 23, 2007.

City of Tshwane (COT), Guidelines for the Development of Road Safety Master Plans, Metropolitan Municipality, Road and Stormwater Division, May 2009.

Gwangju Metropolitan City (GMC), Gwangju Transportation Improvement Midterm Plan, 1996 (in Korean).

GMC, City Administration White Paper, 2000-2011 (Each Year) (in Korean).

GMC, Gwangju Metropolitan Transportation Master Plan, Final Draft, August 2007 (in Korean).

GMC, Gwangju Metropolitan Public Transportation Plan, 1st Draft, December 2011 (in Korean).

GMC, The 2nd Transportation Safety Master Plan, November 2012 (in Korean).

GMC, Gwangju Statistical Yearbook, Each Year (2000-2011).

Hung, Wing-kei, A Review of Road Safety Strategies, the HKU Scholars Hub, The University of Hong Kong, 2003.

Jeong, Bonghyun, Changes in the Proposed Gwangju Metropolitan Subway Line 2 and its Improved Access to Chonnam National University, Gwangju, The studies in Regional Development, Gwangju: The Center for Regional Development, Chonnam National University, Vol. 39, No.2, December 2007 (in Korean).

Jeong, Bonghyun, New Transportation Policy in Regional Metropolitan City: Gwangju, Korea, CNU Press, 2005 (in Korean).

Jeong, Bonghyun, SOC and Regional Development: Standing Transportation Problems and Solutions in the Jeonlla Provinces, Korea, CNU Press, 2010 (in Korean).

Komba, Deus Damian, Risk Factors and Road Traffic Accidents in Tanzania: A Case Study of Kibaha District, Master Thesis in Development Studies, Department of Geography, Norwegian University of Science and Technology (NTNU), May 2006.

Road Traffic Authority (KoRoad; RTA), 2010 Traffic Accidents Statistics by Region, 2011 (in Korean).

Sul, Jae Hoon edit, Transport Safety Policy in Korea, KOTI Knowledge Sharing Report Issue 04, Korea Transport Institute (KOTI), 2013.

World Health Organization (WHO), Pedestrian Safety: A Road Safety Manual for Decision-makers and Practitioners, 2013.

Yang, Bong-Min and Kim, Jinhyun, Road Traffic Accidents and Policy Interventions in Korea, Injury Control and Safety Prevention, Vol.10 No.1-2, 2003, pp.89-94.

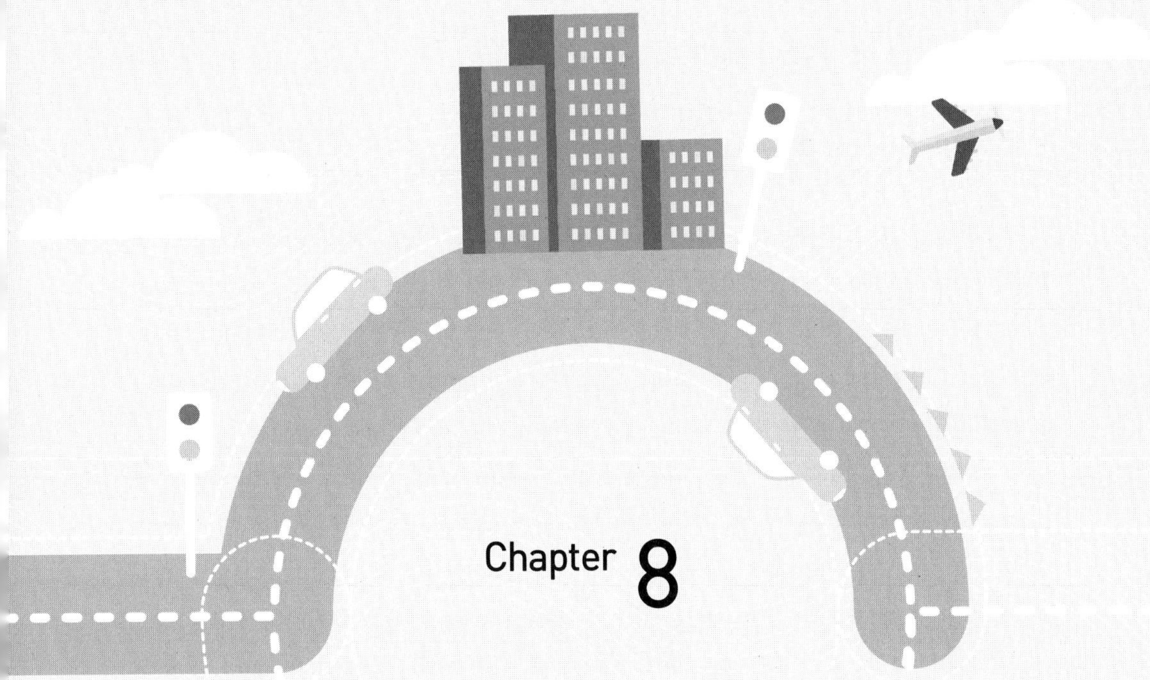

Chapter 8

Bicycle Transport Problems and Policy

1. Theory of Bicycle Transportation

1.1. Concept of Bicycle Transportation[1]

A bicycle (bike) is a human-powered, pedal-driven, single-track vehicle, having two wheels attached to a frame, one behind the other. A person who rides a bicycle is called a cyclist or bicyclist. Bicycles are the principal means of transportation in many regions. They are employed for many uses such as utility, work, recreation, racing, military and entertainment.

Around the turn of the 20th century, bicycles reduced crowding in inner-city tenements by allowing workers to commute from more spacious dwellings in the suburbs. Bicycles allowed people to travel for leisure into the country, since bicycles were three times as energy efficient as walking and three to four times as fast. Recently, several European and North American cities have implemented successful schemes known as community bicycle programs or bike-sharing. These initiatives complement a city's public transport system and offer an alternative to motorized traffic to help reduce congestion and pollution.

In Europe, especially in the Netherlands, parts of Germany, and Denmark, commuting by bicycle is very common. In the Danish capital of Copenhagen, a cyclists' organization runs a Cycling Embassy, that promotes biking for commuting and sightseeing. The United Kingdom has a tax break scheme (IR 176) that allows employees to buy a new bicycle tax free to use for commuting.

1.2. Reasons and Effects of Bicycle Riding

Reasons

Economic instability and ever-increasing climate change are just two of

---

1 http://en.wikipedia.org/wiki/Bicycle#Uses

the many reasons riding a bike is an excellent alternative to driving. It is also important to look at smart ways to start saddling up and using bicycles for real transportation. It is easier to finance a new bicycle than a new car. A bicycle has a tiny manufacturing footprint when compared to a car. Bicycles produce no meaningful pollution when in operation. Bikes save taxpayers money by reducing road wear. They are an effective alternative to a second car. Using a bike for transportation can also help you lose weight and improve your overall health. We can store a dozen bicycles in a single automobile-sized parking place. Bicycles don't burn gasoline and therefore lead to less air pollution. Bicycling may be faster and more efficient than taking a car in urban areas. Bikes cost much less to maintain and operate than automobiles. Bicycles provide mobility for those who may not qualify or afford to drive. Studies also show that bicycle commuters are healthier, more productive, and require less time off at work.

Effects and Benefits of Cycling[2]

Bicycle transportation is a growing activity in Korea, due in part to the many benefits cycling offers. Transportation by bicycle is the most energy efficient mode of transportation, and generates no pollution, except in its manufacture. Cycling is often the fastest mode of transportation from door to door for distances up to 10 km in urban cores. Ten bicycles can be parked in the space required for a single automobile. The cost of a typical car parking space in a parking structure can be up to $10,000 compared to $125 to manufacture and install a post-and-ring bike stand accommodating two bicycles, or $1,000 for a high security bicycle locker. The addition of a through traffic lane on an existing road can cost from $350,000 to $500,000 per km to design and construct in Toronto. This widening would provide an additional roadway capacity of 800 vehicles per hour. By comparison, the costs associated with the addition of a single 1.5 m bike lane, which can

2 COT(2005), pp.1-3.

accommodate approximately 2,000 trips per hour, can range from $5,000 to $10,000 for a simple restriping, or from $35,000 to $150,000 per km where a road widening is required.

Short distance motor-vehicle trips are the least fuel-efficient and generate the most pollution per km. These trips have the greatest potential for being replaced by cycling and walking. Reducing auto trips will mitigate ozone depletion, the greenhouse effect, ground level air pollution, photochemical smog, acid rain and noise pollution.

Cycling contributes to personal health by enhancing fitness and providing an enjoyable, convenient and affordable means of exercise and recreation. The most effective fitness routines are moderate in intensity, individualized and incorporated into our daily activities. Cycling and walking can both accomplish this, and at the same time provide mobility. About two-thirds of Canadians are physically inactive, resulting in about $2.1 billion of direct health care costs in Canada. Increased physical activity, such as walking and cycling, can reduce the risk of coronary heart disease and the cost of medical care, decrease workplace absenteeism, and maintain the independence of older adults. Cycling benefits one's health regardless of the age at which one takes it up.

Cycling provides access and transportation to segments of the population who would not otherwise be able to travel independently. These segments include: those who cannot or choose not to own a motor vehicle; those who do not have access to a motor vehicle for the required period; and/or those who cannot or choose not to use public transportation. Riding a bike instead of driving a car on short trips can save up to 18 to 24 cents per km, which could in turn result in thousands of dollars saved per person per year.

Table 8.1. The Benefits of Cycling

Division	Detailed Items
Environmental	■ No space consumption, No primary energy consumption ■ No CO2, no nitrogen oxides, no hydrocarbons, No CO ■ Less risk of accident
Socio-political	■ Increase individual freedom of mobility, and self-confidence ■ Greater autonomy and access to young and elderly people
Economic	■ Low purchasing and maintenance cost ■ Less cost to build infrastructure than car, less space requirement

Source: COT(2005); KOTI(2010)

1.3. Functions of Bicycle Transportation

Urban transport policy in many cities has concentrated on the expansion of transport facilities intended to smooth traffic flows on roads. It is suggested that urban transport problems are very difficult to solve, if sustainable transport policy, such walking and bicycle transport, isn't devised upon. Urban transport system is mainly divided into two elements, including city-wide transport and district transport. Bicycling is the most efficient and flexible green transport mode in urban districts. Before the era of motorization arrived, bike functioned as the major and connecting transport mode in many cities.

Traffic is very congested and parking is difficult in the current era of motorization. Cycling is regarded as the environmentally- friendly and major short-range transport mode today. Cycling is convenient to go to work and do district shopping in large city, and is widely used as the connecting transport mode in outlying areas. Bikes are thus the major and ancillary means of transportation in urban areas. Travelling by the bike is the major transport mode in local areas, such as small cities, residential or industrial districts, and university towns. In those areas, bicycle is the major transport mode for the travel purposes of commuting, shopping and leisure. Cycling is also the ancillary means of transportation for transferring to other public transit modes.

2. Bicycle Facilities and the Use Characteristics[3]

2.1. Types of Bikeway and Bicycle Facilities

Types of Bikeway[4]

The names and definitions of the various cycle facility types vary from country to country, but besides local naming conventions, one of the main subdivisions is whether the facility is physically separated by barriers, parking or bollards from other vehicle traffic, or whether the segregation is due to painted markings. The facilities have been modified over time and increased in variety as usage changes, and as cities receive feedback and experiment with improvements. Segregated cycle facilities are a form of cycling infrastructure consisting of marked lanes, tracks, shoulders and paths designated for use by cyclists and from which motorised traffic is generally excluded. The term includes bike lanes, cycle tracks, separated bike lanes, road shoulders, and side paths located within a road right-of-way.

A bikeway is a road, route, or path which in some manner is specifically designed and/or designated for bicycle travel, regardless of whether such facilities are designated for the exclusive use of bicycles or are to be shared with other transportation modes.[5] Bikeways in Korea are generally classified into bike lane, bike path, and shared-use footway (side-path), according to Article 3 of the Promoting Bicycle Usage Act in Korea.

---

[3] Korea Herald(2013.5.20)

[4] http://en.wikipedia.org/

[5] Lagerwey(2007), p.3.

Table 8.2. Types of Bikeway

Bikeway	Example figure	Concept
Bike lane	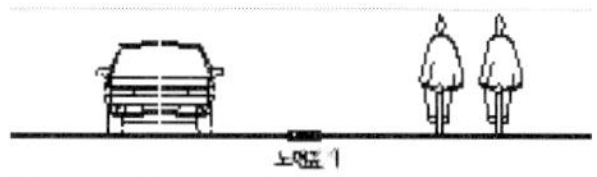	Lanes for cyclists only, marked on an existing portion of a roadway
Bike path	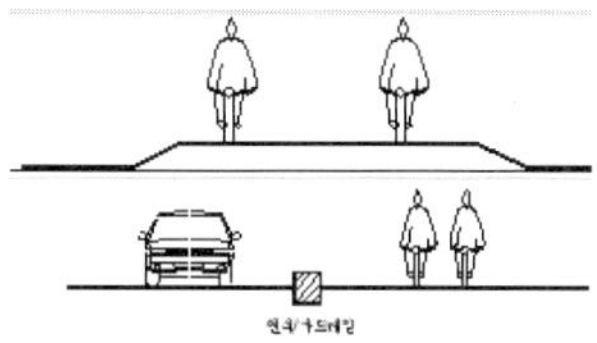	Physically separated from motor traffic and distinct from the sidewalk within the roadway
Side-path	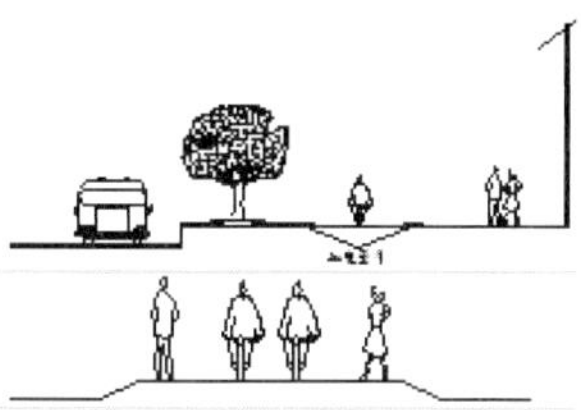	For use by both cyclists and pedestrians, lower standard that a cycle track, a shared use path

Source: Chung(2011); Choi(2012)

Existing Bikeway Facilities

As the number of bikes increases in Gwangju, the need for adequate bikeway facilities also will grow. The total length of bikeway on over 196 bikeway routes was 588.4 km as of 2012. Gwangju had approximately 455.8 km of side-path, 112.6 km of bike path and 11.6 km of bike lanes in 2012.

By type of bikeway, the share of side-path accounted for 77.5% of the total bikeway network based on its length in 2012. Those which are not wide enough don't carry sufficient volumes of bicycle traffic, because of traffic accident risk and traffic inconvenience. Two main problems here are the lack of linkage among some bikeway networks, and non-uniform spacing.

Table 8.3. Existing Bikeway Facilities (2012)

District	Route	Types of Bikeway (Length: km)			
		Bike path	Bike lane	Side-path	Sub total
Donggu	21	7.0	1.1	43.6	51.7
Seogu	45	28.3	-	98.3	126.6
Namgu	25	9.6	7.5	45.8	62.9
Bukgu	38	24.7	-	111.2	135.9
Gwangsangu	67	42.9	7.4	157.0	207.3
Total	196	112.6	16.0	455.8	588.4

Source: GMC(2013)

Figure 8.1. Bikeway Facility Network in Gwangju

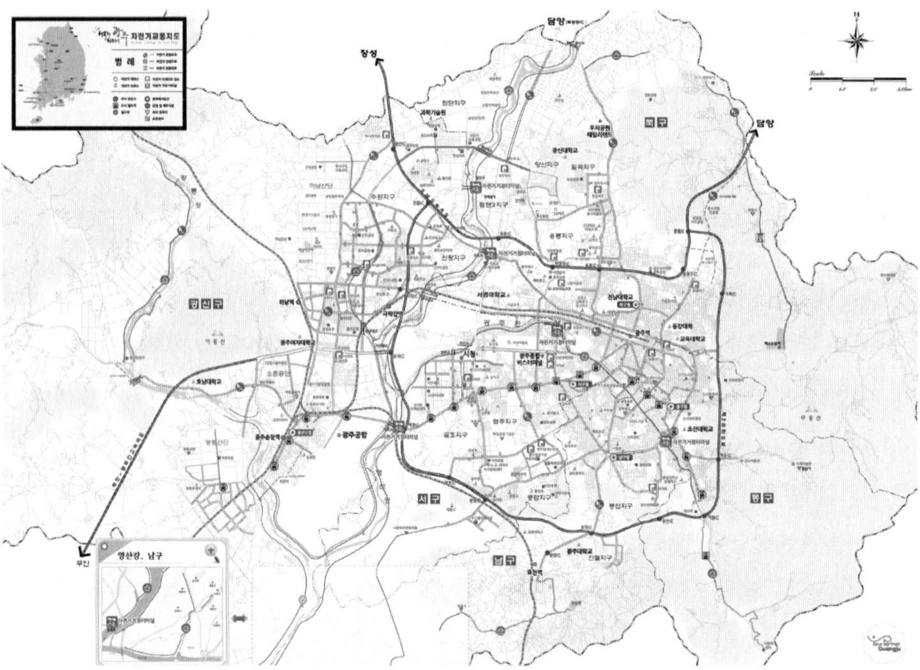

2.2. Bicycle Parking Lots and Storages

Bicycle parking relies on infrastructure and equipment (bike racks, bicycle locks etc.) to enable a secure and convenient parking of bicycles. Arrangements for this include lockers, racks, manned or unmanned bicycle parking stations including automated facilities, roofs for weatherproofing, as well as specific legal arrangements for ad hoc parking alongside railings and other street furniture.

The total bicycle parking capacity was calculated at 10,859 lots, which operate at different 733 places in 2012. By district, around 68.4% of the total parking capacity was concentrated in Bukgu of Gwangju. Bukgu shared for 23.1% of the total bikeway network based on its length. This not only induces inefficient parking lot operation, but also aggravates the bicycle parking situation across the city. In Gwangju, bicycle parking facilities are scarce, or are so inadequate that nearby trees are used.

The hitching post type of bicycle rack is an improvement over the old type that had a slot for the front wheel, not the frame, but only allow for two bicycles per post. Secure bicycle parking is argued to be a key factor influencing the decision to cycle. To be considered secure, the parking must be of a suitable design: allowing the bicycle to be locked via the frame (see bicycle parking rack). Where cycling is seen as an unwelcome or inappropriate activity, or due to lack of knowledge about best practices, bicycle parking may simply not be provided or else placed at awkward, distant, and out-of-sight locations. Cyclists may be expressly forbidden from parking their bicycles at the most convenient locations.

Table 8.4. Public Bicycle Parking Lots (2012)

District	Donggu	Seogu	Namgu	Bukgu	Gwangsangu	Total
Places	103	119	72	162	277	733
Lots	1,195	1,438	1,067	2,909	4,250	10,859

Source: GMC(2013)

2.3. Bicycle Use Characteristics

Bicycle Ownership[6]

Bicycling is an affordable mode of transportation that provides physical activity, produces no pollution, and support social interaction. As a vehicle, the bicycle is very efficient in its use of public space. Many residents in Gwangju use a bicycle as their primary mode of transportation to go to work. Thousands more cycle to school, to access transits, to visit friends, or to improve their health. Bicycling is already a popular mode of transportation in Gwangju.

As for the 7 metropolitan cities of Korea, bicycle ownership in Seoul stands at 0.46 bikes per household, the highest among the cities, and Busan has the lowest. Bicycle ownership in Gwangju stands at 0.35 bikes per household, which stands the same as 0.35 bikes, the average level for 7 metropolitan cities. The share of bike mode for the 7 cities increased from 0.8% in 2000 to 2.5% in 2010. Bike mode share of Daegu is among the highest in the 7 cities. Gwangju's bike mode share grew slightly from 1.1% in 2000 to 1.9% in 2010.

Table 8.5. Bicycle Ownership and its Mode Share in 7 Metropolis

City / Item	Bicycle ownership / household	Bike mode share(%)	
		2000	2010
Ulsan	0.38	0.9	2.7
Daejeon	0.45	1.1	2.7
Incheon	0.32	0.8	2.2
Daegu	0.44	1.4	3.8
Busan	0.17	0.4	1.3
Seoul	0.45	0.7	2.8
Gwangju	0.24	1.1	1.9

Source: KOTI(2010)

6 Choi(2012), pp.6-8.

Bike-riding Characteristics in Gwangju[7]

A cyclist travel survey was undertaken to understand the bike-riding characteristics in Gwangju in March 2009. The survey respondents were 500 cyclists and 500 non-cyclists living in Gwangju City. The Chi-square statistics were used to analyze the data of the cyclist travel survey. About 69% of cyclists were men, and 31% women. A high portion of the cyclist rode bike between 1 and 3 days a week. Regarding weekly bike-riding day by age, young cyclists even in their teens and 30's used bicycles for 1 or 3 days within a week. As for bike usage frequency by occupation, students comprised the largest number of cyclists, followed by office workers, self-employed, and housewives. By travel purpose, the cyclists with a monthly income of one to two million won (70.8%) mainly used their bikes for leisure and exercise (59%).

By occupation, cycle-riders for leisure (59%) and home-to-school transport (18%) were associated with students (50%) and employees (23.2%). The average travel time of cyclist was 21.2 minutes based on a one-way journey. Cyclists rode on bikes on average of 14.9 minutes for shopping, and 23.7 minutes while doing sports or leisure activities, respectively. Cyclists rode bicycles on between roughly 3 to 5 km roadways. Around 41.2% of the cyclists used bike 1 to 4 times, and 30.4% for 4 or 6 times in the week. Daily bike-rider made up 24% of the total cyclists. About 40.8% of the non-cyclists intended to ride bicycles 1 or 3 times a week, if bicycle transport situations are improved in the city, and 7.0% of them 4 to 6 times in the week.

---

7 Chung(2010), pp.24-29.

3. Bicycle Transport Problems[8]

3.1. A Matter of Policy

Urban transport policy in Gwangju was mainly concentrated on the construction of road networks. The increased traffic has caused traffic jams cross the city, which has necessitated the widening of roads. This shows that GMC has neglected to create a bicycle-friendly infrastructure. Bicycle networks were merely constructed in the new built-up area or the outskirts of the city. Under the car-friendly transport system, the level of connectivity among transport modes (bicycle, walking and public transits) was decreased by the improvement of road facilities. This may result in a decline in bicycle function as a transport mode.

The city government has not formulated a coherent policy for the bicycle transport system, through the institutional cooperation among district office, metropolitan government, and related organizations. A bicycle administration system for successful implementation of comprehensive bicycle transport policy is lacking in the city. For instance, the city government created an exclusive section for bicycle transport on July 2009. However, increased bicycle administration was not handled quickly and efficiently by the small-scale and nonprofessional public servants. It is thus necessary to strengthen a bicycle sector policy and institutional framework in the city government, and to formulate the bicycle transport policy monitoring system. In fact, GMC continues to implement software-driven bicycle policy, which is characteristic of small budget, small-scale investment, and facilities improvement.

3.2. A Matter of Facility Maintenance

GMC has scarcely any bicycle facilities and many bad bikeways, and largely

[8] Jeong(2005), pp.345-348; Chung(2011), pp.29-31.

lacks bicycle lanes or bicycle paths. In 2012, the share of side-path accounted for 77.5% of the total bikeway network based on its length. Most of the bike paths were mainly built in the city's outskirts. The functional and structural system of bicycle facilities network is not well formulated. Existing bikeway are so narrow and winding that bicycles are unable to pass in the built-in area. There are many missing links in the cycle facilities network, and it slows down the road function of cycle facilities. This directly contributes to travel inconvenience, accident risk and inefficient traffic flow.

The city government removed parts of existing roads or reduced their width to make the new bike lanes. Bike lanes were extensively damaged, and do not have sufficient bicycle crossings. There are illegally parked cars and stacked goods on bicycle road facilities. The connectivity between bicycle roads are not good in general. There are many missing links between bicycle roads. These can obstruct passing of bicycle and impede the smooth flow of bicycle traffic on bike lanes.

Bike-and-Ride is as an easy, environmentally friendly and healthy way to combine a bike ride with a bus/railway ride to travel around the city. Bicycle parking stations or bike-and-ride facilities near public transport terminals and in the suburbs of the city are insufficient in Gwangju. Many bicycle parking lots are nowhere near the large mixed-use complex. Bicycle parking lots on the sidewalk are significantly under-used owing to scanty bike parkers.

3.3. A Matter of System Management

In Gwangju, the greatest attention in bicycle transport policy has been paid to bicycle system management, such as improvement of bicycle parking and bicycle signs. However, most of the bicycle paths in Gwangju are mainly constructed in the city's outskirts, which don't provide good accessibility to the cyclists. In fact, the city government needs to implement a comprehensive bicycle transport policy that reflects the actual condition of bicycle transport in Gwangju. Many cyclists are unwilling to use bicycles, as they are worried about accidents on roads and the severance of bike traffic flow in bike lanes.

A prime reason for bicycle usage decrease is lack of investment. GMC didn't spend a lot of money to expand and improve the bicycle infrastructure, because of its weak funding base. It has caused the deactivation of bicycle riding in the city. In the meantime, GMC and 5 city-affiliated district offices are in bad financial condition. GMC has not been abundantly funded by the central government to expand bicycle infrastructure.

An another important thing for promoting bicycle usage is public relations. GMC and related organizations should begin active marketing and promotional campaigns to promote bicycle riding in Gwangju, and more citizens will cycle because of all the big media hype. They also need to use celebrities and cartoon characters to promote bike riding. It is important for private sector to participate more in the publicity activities as well as campaigns about cycling. The government tries to lead citizens to voluntarily participate in the bicycle riding movement, and seeks to enhance mutual cooperation with the citizens in the promotional campaigns.

3.4. A Matter of Traffic Accidents

Careful consideration should be given to issues of traffic safety. While the overall number of traffic deaths has seen a big decline since the turn of the century, the number of cyclist fatalities actually rose between 2003 and 2009, from 253 to 333. In Gwangju, the number of deaths and injuries caused by bicycle traffic accidents has increased at the average annual growth rate of 8.3% in recent years. There are risks of traffic accidents every time a passenger is on a bike in the bike lanes of Gwangju City. Cyclists numbers in the city are expected to gradually increase, because of leisure activities and owing to the revitalization of bike-riding.

It is said that Koreans are not fully prepared when cycling. The city should try to keep traffic order and to improve bike traffic safety on bike lanes and paths. Cyclists should put on safety helmets and wear safety harnesses during cycle-riding. Students should be required to undergo traffic safety training, and car drivers must obey traffic regulations. In particular, it should be compulsory for all cyclists to wear safety helmets during cycling, based on the traffic safety law.

3.5. A Matter of Culture

The critical problem is culture. Seven in 10 Koreans own a bicycle and more half of the population cycled at least once a month in 2012. But despite the obvious popularity of the bicycle for leisure, the public has yet to take up cycling as a means of transport with similar gusto. A lot of people still think bicycles are a transportation tool for poor people. In contrast to the cyclists' paradise of the Netherlands, where up to 43% of trips are by bike, or nearby Japan, where the proportion is 25%, cycling accounts for just 2.5% of transportation in Korea, as of 2010. Close to 50% of Koreans give leisure as the primary purpose of their cycling.

In fact, GMC did not invest heavily in the promotion of cycling, viewing it as a way of reducing traffic congestion and environmental pollution. The city focused primarily on leisure riding rather than daily commuting. This prioritization of pleasure riding over transportation is the major failing of city's government efforts to increasing cycling's popularity. Although, it is necessary to improve the small back roads that offer the most enjoyment to the avid rider. Soft policy such as education is more urgent. The ultimate goal is to change culture.

4. Bicycle Transportation Policy in Gwangju

4.1. Korea Bike Transport Policy

The level of bicycle use in Korea is generally low. Korean Census 2005 indicates that about 1.2% of all trips were made by bicycle. The country's overall bicycle share data was extracted from Census 2005 and the others were estimated based on the person trip survey performed by Ministry of Land, Transport and Maritime affairs in each shown year. The data illustrated higher bicycle share rates in mid-size or small cities than in metropolitan cities.

It is necessary to review the history of bicycle policies for a better understanding of the bike-sharing programs in Korea. The Korean national government has actively promoted bicycling since mid 1990's, while European countries and Japan started in the mid 1970's. Since 1995 the Bicycle Promotion Act promoted a compulsory national bicycle master plan, the installation of bicycle facilities, and statements about financial support for bicycle promotion policies. Many bicycle policies were instituted during the last two decades. Since 2008 the investment on bicycle has increased at a large scale. A variety of bicycle policies such as the bicycle model city project have been enacted. However, bicycle ridership has not significantly increased. In order to increase bicycle ridership, the Korean national government supported a bike-sharing program. The national government also selected 10 bicycle model cities as growth pole regions, and is currently investing about 8.3 million dollars per city for the initiation of new bicycle programs, including the 2012 bike-sharing program. For this reason, bikes-sharing programs have become a new trend in the history of transportation policy in Korea.

Gwangju is looking for way to guide development in a manner that is more environmentally, socially and economically sustainable. Gwangju Metropolitan Government (GMC) needs to develop a official plan which includes a vision for bike transportation in Gwangju. The transport vision focuses largely on reducing automobile dependance and encouraging green transport, such as bike and walking.

4.2. Provide Cyclists with Subsidies

Citizens cycling to subway stations or for commuting will receive subsidies as part of Gwangju City's effort to encourage bicycle use. Free bike rentals will also be made available by making use of abandoned bicycles. The city government should expand bicycle-only lanes in the built area. To boost bike use, the city can plan to give about 200-300 won subsidies to people who ride between their homes and subway stations, or work place. Kiosks are installed at bicycle parking lots near subway stations for the pilot program. Citizens can cycle from home to the station, park there, have the kiosk scan their traffic card, and take the subway to work or school. On their return, they can retrieve the bikes from the kiosk and the subsidy will be credited to their cards. They can use the money later for buying goods or taking public transportation.

The service will be expanded to more bike parking lots in Gwangju next year. City officials are also talking with nearby metropolitan governments and Gwangju subway or Korail, to link the service to buses and subway lines going beyond the city border. Free rental bikes will be available gradually. Citizens will be able to use free bikes in their residential areas as well as to and from nearby subway stations, and are required to return them at community centers or stations. The city is able to use abandoned bicycles for the service.

The city will also mend bike lane management systems, as some lanes are currently often blocked by illegally parked cars and riders sometimes risk accidents with cars driving too close beside them. At intersections or on roads near large malls where bike riders frequently face vehicles blocking the cycle paths, the lanes will be moved from the current car lanes to sidewalks. Car parking will be allowed on some bike lanes in residential districts short of parking lots during designated times. The city is pushing for lower speed limits on roads with cycle lanes, in consultation with the regional metropolitan police.

4.3. Making Gwangju more Bicycle-friendly

From an urban perspective, an increase in bicycle commuters will have many positive effects on our cities. It's obvious that other forms of transportation will be less crowded, but also it will be a ground breaking countermeasure for many issues like air pollution, climate change, gas consumption, and physical fitness.

It is suggested that making Gwangju a bike-friendly city is the only way to save all commuters. First, more showers and lockers should be accessible. This should be the highest priority because pedaling is exercise that makes riders sweat. After reaching the office, people have to change from bike wear and safety gear into business attire. Without those showers and lockers bike commuting is nearly impossible.

Hopefully, every office building will have these facilities, but opening public baths to commuters at reasonable prices will also be effective. Not many cities around the world have a public bath culture so using this facility could be unique. Second, anti-theft parking lots should be available. Considering current consumer trends, high-end brand bicycles are becoming popular, leaving most bicycle parking lots vulnerable to theft. Stealing just one component can make good money so these kinds of bicycles need complete security. GMC have to build locker-style bicycle parking lots for trial at major stations, the bus terminal and massive office buildings. You can put your whole bike in a big locker so others can't touch any parts of it. The safest way is giving secured parking spaces inside of a building, not outside.

Lastly, more bike roads are needed, especially in central districts. All well-known bike-friendly cities such as Copenhagen in Denmark, and Amsterdam, the Netherlands, have wide bicycle lanes. Unlike them, most roads in Gwangju are planned for cars. There are a lot of obstacles threatening bike commuters. Perhaps every street should be designed for pedestrians and bicycle riders first. It's the most time-consuming work, but without new roads, commuting disasters will happen again and again.

4.4. Ensuring the Safety of Cyclists

Improving the safety of cyclists is crucial to getting more people on their bikes. The treacherous nature of many of the country's roads is one likely explanation for why commuting by bike has yet to take off. Even on designated paths, cyclists must often compete with other traffic. In 2009, just 12.5% of the country's cycle routes were separated from vehicles and pedestrians. To promote cycling to work, the first thing that has to be done is to ensure the safety of bikers. Bike paths have to be on street-level but separated from the lanes for cars and a physical barrier should protect both transport methods from each other. Even if safety would seem to be improving in at least some areas, access to a bicycle itself, especially for casual riders, may be another barrier. An extensive public bicycle scheme for Gwangju should be implemented, including a city-wide bike sharing network. This would allow a commuter to get off his bus or subway and use a public bike for the last mile to his company. In the best case, the commuter would get a discount for the bike or even rides it for free.

To make bicycling popular and safe, GMC should introduce special bicycle lanes, right next to footpaths, and reserved for (non-motorized) bikes only. In addition, cyclists must respect all traffic regulations, including traffic lights. Bicycles should be used not only for recreational purposes but even more as a proper and very popular means of transport. Cycling paths should be paved and made for all types of bicycles.

With regard to commuting via bicycle, shared walking/bike paths are not well thought out in Gwangju. Many paths should be next to a road but are next to buildings where people exiting doorways are likely to be hit. Likewise, there are no protected paths for cyclists when riding on the streets, and buses and taxis pose a great danger. There needs to be a separate bike path extending throughout Gwangju to give those who can and wish to ride a safe and secure path to do so. There also needs to be bike parking areas that are secure where anyone who rides or commutes via bike can feel secure that their bike will not be stolen or damaged while they are at work or tending to business. Stricter traffic law enforcement so that cyclists don't have to be concerned about accidents caused by driver's negligence.

A self-portrait in the newspaper

A city for bicycle commuters

What stresses out city dwellers in Korea every day? It's a man-made disaster that causes severe exhaustion: commuting.

In the morning, tons of people rush into the streets like tsunamis. Downtown areas look like huge parking lots because cars can only move inch by inch. Subways and buses are overcrowded too. To stop this vicious cycle, we should revive another means of transportation we've ridden for over 100 years — the bicycle.

I started commuting by bike in 2010. Before that, getting to my workplace was so frustrating. I was sick and tired of squeezing through other passengers on the bus. Car driving was also not a good option. Leaving traffic jams aside, I'm not allowed to park my car at the building where I work due to limited space. Other parking lots nearby cost over 150,000 won a month. So I started riding two wheels instead of four and I realized it was possible to go to work with a great feeling. I was free from heavy traffic and the best part was I could commute and do exercise at the same time.

From an urban perspective, an increase in bicycle commuters will have many positive effects on our cities. It's obvious that other forms of transportation will be less crowded, but also it will be a groundbreaking countermeasure for many issues like air pollution, climate change, gas consumption, and physical fitness.

Despite all those numerous benefits, our cities don't seem to welcome bicycles with regard to infrastructure. Here are the most critical suggestions based on my three-year riding experience. It may take serious and long-term commitments, but a bike-friendly city is the only way to save all commuters.

First, more showers and lockers should be accessible. This should be the highest priority because basically pedaling is exercise that makes riders sweat. After reaching the office, people have to change from bike wear and safety gear into business attire. But where do we store these belongings after that? Without those showers and lockers bike commuting is nearly impossible. Hopefully every office building has these facilities, but opening public baths to commuters at reasonable prices will also be effective. Not many cities around the world have a public bath culture so using this facility could be unique.

Second, anti-theft parking lots should be available. Considering current consumer trends, high-end brand bicycles are becoming popular, leaving most bicycle parking lots vulnerable to theft. Stealing just one component can make good money so these kinds of bicycles need complete security. Gangnam-gu is making a good move. They have built locker-style bicycle parking lots for trial at Samseong, Hakyeoul and Suseo stations. You can put your whole bike in a big locker so others can't touch any parts of it. The safest way is giving secured parking spaces inside of a building, not outside.

Lastly, more bike roads are needed, especially in central districts. All well-known bike-friendly cities such as Copenhagen in Denmark, and Amsterdam, the Netherlands, have wide bicycle lanes. Unlike them, our roads are planned for cars. There are a lot of obstacles threatening bike commuters. Perhaps every street should be designed for pedestrians and bicycle riders first. It's the most time-consuming work, but without new roads commuting disasters will happen again and again.

Are all methods possible to be implemented? Changes already have begun and my daily commuting is a great example. With a 13-km distance to the office, over 90 % of the way is bike-only lanes; I could ease my wife's mind from fear of a car-bicycle crash. And my company has differentiated facilities for bicycle commuters: an indoor bike parking lot with ID card security gate, showers, lockers, towels and even cosmetics. I can come and go without any difficulty.

Hope I'm not the only lucky rider. Gradual changes will snowball for a sustainable bicycle-friendly city.

*** Source: The Korea Times (2014.1.13)**

References

Choi, Dong-Ho, The Strategies to Promote Bicycle Usage in Gwangju's Neighborhood, The Gwangju Journal, Vol.16 No.1, Gwangju Development Institute (GDI), 2012 (in Korean).

Chung, Ha-Wook, The Strategies for the Activation of the Bicycle Utilization in Gwangju Metropolitan City, Policy Research Report 2009-09, 2009, Gwangju Development Institute, 2010 (in Korean).

COT (The City of Toronto), Toronto Bike Plan, 2005.

Gwangju Metropolitan City (GMC), City Administration White Paper, 2000-2013 (in Korean).

GMC, Gwangju Transportation Improvement Midterm Plan, 1996 (in Korean).

GMC, City Administration White Paper, 2000-2011 (Each Year) (in Korean).

GMC, Gwangju Metropolitan Transportation Master Plan, Final Draft, August 2007 (in Korean).

GMC, Gwangju Metropolitan Public Transportation Plan, 1st Draft, December 2011 (in Korean).

GMC, The 2nd Transportation Safety Master Plan, November 2012 (in Korean).

GMC, Gwangju Statistical Yearbook, Each Year (2000-2011).

Jeong, Bonghyun, Evolution of Urban Parking System in Seoul's CBD during the 1977-87 Period and its Implications, Journal of The Korean Regional Development Association 4, 2: 89-101, 1992

Jeong, Bonghyun, Public Acceptability in the Implementation of Parking Policy, The Journal of Korea Planners Association 28, 1: 171-185, 1993.

Jeong, Bonghyun, New Transportation Policy in Regional Metropolitan City: Gwangju, Korea, CNU Press, 2005 (in Korean).

Jeong, Bonghyun, SOC and Regional Development: Standing Transportation Problems and Solutions in the Jeonlla Provinces, Korea, CNU Press, 2010 (in Korean).

Lagerwey, Peter, Seattle Bicycle Master Plan, USA: City of Seattle, 2007.

Lee, Gun-Young & Park, Kyung-Hwan edit., Korea on the Move: Korea's Current Transportation Policy and Prospects for the Future, KOTI, 1997.

KOTI, Korean Situations and Policies to Stimulate Bicycle Use for Urban Transport, OECD Working Group on Transport, January 2010.

Shin, Hee-Cheol et al., Bicycle Transport Policy in Korea, KOTI Knowledge Sharing Report Issue 06, Korea Transport Institute (KOTI), 2013.

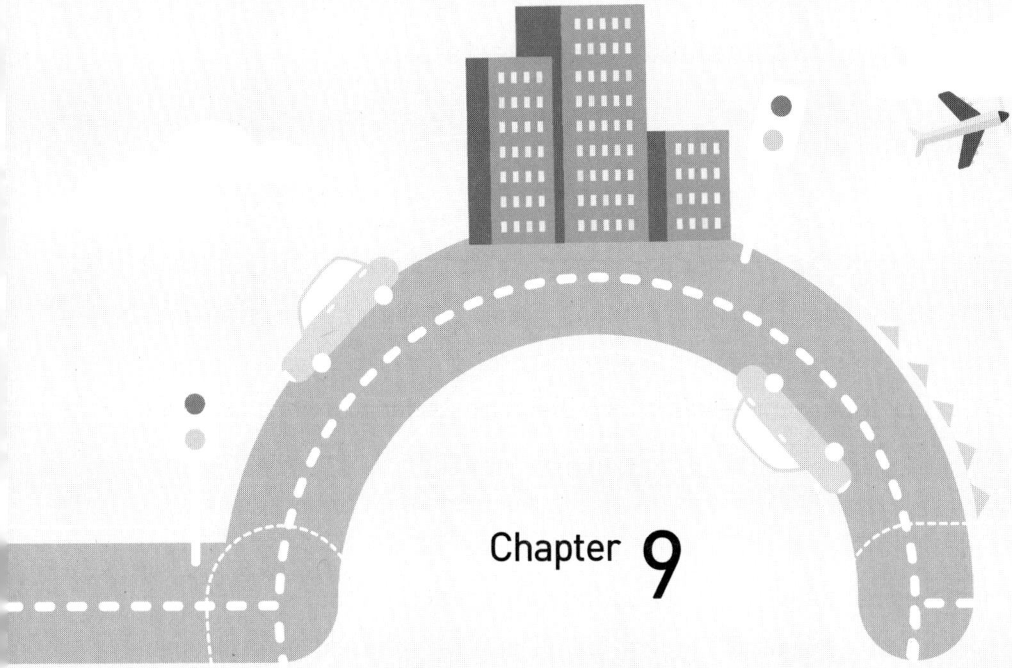

Chapter 9

Sustainable Transport Problems and Policy

1. The Idea of Sustainable Transportation

1.1 Definition of Sustainable Transportation[1]

Sustainable transportation can be loosely defined as a set of transport activities together with relevant infrastructure that collectively does not leave problems or costs for future generations to solve or bear- present builders and users of the system should pay such costs today. These costs are not limited to environmental externalities, but also include social and other economic impacts caused by transportation. Conceptually, sustainable urban transport (SUT) is transport that serves the common vision of an urban area's economic and social development. In practical terms, SUT focuses on easing access and mobility for people to reach work, services, resources, and each other. SUT needs to provide access for all groups in society in a manner that is within the environmental carrying capacity of a region and is affordable to both the providers and users of transport systems. SUT also provides for smooth movement of goods within cities.

SUT is an essential precondition to maintain and improve the quality of life in metropolitan cities and to increase the well-being of its citizens. To accomplish this, SUT will require a different way of thinking about the structure of Korean metropolitan cities and new approaches to land use planning. SUT has a direct relationship with poverty and reduction. Access to affordable transport for all groups in the population is a prerequisite to improved health and education. Effective SUT systems support economic growth without compromising economic and social dimensions to a point beyond repair. SUT has the potential to act as a catalyst in the development process.

The sustainability of transport systems is defined by its impacts on the environment and safety, as well as social and economic sustainability. Three quick checks that decision makers can apply in making decisions on urban

---

1 PSUTA(2005), pp.12-13.

transport systems are: ① How will decisions affect pollution and safety? ② Do decisions increase or decrease congestion, and promote access to transport for all age groups in society? ③ Do policies increase or decrease the economic robustness of the transport sector itself while decreasing the cost burden of transportation on ordinary citizens? These criteria or pillars of sustainable transportation have quantitative and qualitative dimensions. The former are measured or estimated scientifically and should be objective. The latter provide the weightings by which stakeholders value the former, so contain an important element of political and even personal subjectivity. Governance must provide a transparent stakeholder engagement process that both promulgates development of the objective characteristics of sustainable transport — through indicators — as well as providing a process for making decisions based on indicators and political values.

Figure 9.1. Pillars of Sustainable Transport

Government sustainability Nature of laws; enforcement mechanisms Flows of public and private resources into sustainable transport		
Safety & environmental sustainability Health of future citizens	Social sustainability Equity	Economic sustainability Innovation & efficiency
• Ambient air quality • Emissions factors • Public health records on air pollution-related disease • Accident and safety data	• Travel times & other measures of access, by gender, social class, location of housing • Crime and incidents in transit • Costs of travel; budget shares, etc	• Transport costs in national accounts • Fares and fuel costs • Financial balance of private and public transport firms • Institutional structure of transport industry
Transport system : geographical area, participants modal split, VKT, trip distribution, origin-destination		

Source: PSUTA(2005)

1.2. Key Challengs of SUT

Rapid Urbanization and Congestion[2]

Rapid economic growth in urban areas drives considerable growth in the demand for transport of both people and goods in metropolitan cities of Korea. Apart from the growth in private vehicles, the population growth and increased affluence have also resulted in strong growth, in absolute terms, in the demand for public transport. The cities have had difficulties in meeting this increased demand, leading to a decrease in the quality of services provided.

The growth in private motorization has overwhelmed the streets in almost every large Korean city, creating unbridled congestion and long commute times. Non-motorized transport and collective transport have suffered as authorities emphasize paved streets for individual vehicles. Building more roads and flyovers cannot hope to catch up with the trends. This challenge can only be met with a new approach to sustainable transport.

The expansion of Korean cities is based on an urban sprawl type of land use. Urban sprawl is partly the outcome of higher affluence, as family size shrinks while families seek larger homes. Sprawl also arises because of the absence of effective land-use planning. This, together with flawed land pricing mechanisms which transfer the environmental costs of the urban sprawl to the community at large, has favored the development of "motorized hungry transport" systems.

Air Quality and GHG Emissions

Air quality has worsened because of the rise in transportation, even as authorities have forced reductions in emissions from fixed sources. The main pollutants of concern are particulate matter (PM), NOx (Nitrogen Oxides), and

---

2 PSUTA(2005), pp.13-15.

hydrocarbons. Increasing NOx levels contribute to an increase in ozone levels. The rapid growth in the number of vehicles explains why ambient air quality levels do not meet guideline values set by the World Health Organization (WHO), despite the recent technical improvements. While technological improvements will continue to reduce emission levels on a per vehicle basis, the implementation of technological measures will fall short of reaching air quality goals.

CO_2 emissions from the transport sector form a major part of the greenhouse gases responsible for climate change. There is a growing acknowledgment that fine particulate matter emissions have climate impacts in Asia, which could be responsible for increased or decreased rainfall in specific parts of the continent.

Road Safety

The rapid increase in motorization, especially cars and trucks, has resulted in an associated growth in the number of traffic accidents. Up to 50 percent of the victims are not occupants of motor vehicles, but pedestrians or non-motorized vehicle users. The annual economic losses for Korea from road accidents are estimated at 1.9% of the annual gross domestic product (GDP), and 10.6% of the annual total budget. Additionally, an indirect consequence of rapid motorization is that pedestrians and cyclists increasingly must detour around motorized traffic to get where they are going, or risk fatal accidents while crossing traffic.

Economic Sustainability

Urban transport systems, whether run by urban authorities or the private sector, face many economic challenges. Above all, the publicly owned and operated parts of the sector often require huge subsidies, while private operators make a profit. The many concession-based systems make some money for their operators, but only because cities pay these concessionaires more than they can take in from fare boxes. Indeed, a pandemic of cheap transport provided as a public good, while understandable as a policy of providing access for low-income people, undermines the long-term viability of collective systems and encourages sprawl. This is only worsened by public investment in expensive metro and rail-based systems, whose real costs no one can afford to meet.

The greatest challenges to the collective systems' economic sustainability are two-fold. In addition to rising low direct cost mobility provided by two wheelers, a myriad of private, often "pirate" small operators are filling in gaps left by shaky public systems. Another challenge is the squeeze on transit operators between the need to hold down fares to stay competitive with private two-wheelers vs. the need for revenue to update and clean up bus fleets and fuels. A third challenge is the appearance of expensive metro and rail systems, whose fares must be held well below costs to attract riders. In short, the rapidly growing client base for motorized low-cost collective transport may be siphoned away by private transport, just as mass transport feels the pressure of the higher costs of rail-based systems. The falling customer base puts even more pressure on operators to cover costs.

Social Stainability

Social sustainability measures whether the present transport system creates inequities of access and opportunity, or disadvantages some groups over others. In much of Asia, the most obvious aspect of social sustainability reflects the social systems that have sprung up around both mass transit and small-scale transport (mini-buses) in almost every Asian country. Tens of thousands of families depend on income from small transport operators, both honest and shady. In Latin America, no meaningful transport reforms can occur without a role for these groups as stakeholders. In Asia, three-wheeler and conventional taxi drivers can be a strong force against transport reform toward larger, more efficient vehicles and lower emissions. Transport solutions that leave these groups in strong opposition are not socially sustainable.

Equally as important for social sustainability is equity of access, i.e., the way in which impacts of congestion and poor access to transport fall most heavily on the poor or other groups. This is measured by differences in modal shares, travel times, travel ease, and travel costs that arise between rich and poor, men and women, handicapped and able, or private car users vs. those using other modes. Private vehicles monopolize streets; pedestrians, cyclists, and the handicapped have fewer and fewer safe choices for moving about. Giving equal access to cars and other vehicles, as well as NMT (non-motorized transport), penalizes those who walk, cycle, or ride the bus – generally the economically weak. That is because individual private vehicles take up significantly more road-space than collective or non-motorized transport.

Since private vehicles are generally the privilege of the middle or upper classes, and public motorized transport is used mainly by the middle classes, this means that in rapidly urbanizing cities, the poor are left with fewer choices than others. Hence, they are also at a disadvantage seeking employment, since they cannot move as fast or far as others. Most subtly, there may be discrimination against women, either because they face harassment on public modes, or because they simply have less access to whatever mode is fastest or safest. In short, a transport system where affordable access is not assured for all is not sustainable, because such a system freezes some people out of the economic and personal development that transport access can bring.

Governance of Sustainable Urban Transport

Governance is required for sustainable urban transport. A regulatory framework is required for the transport sector, which includes pricing policies. Environmental regulations and monitoring are required to set emissions limits and clean air goals, as well as to monitor the results. Safety measures (including driver education, traffic laws, vehicle safety standards, protection of NMT) must be promulgated and enforced. Enforcing traffic and parking laws and other regulations and policies that increase access is also a part of good governance. A great challenge in every Asian city is to overcome the obvious gaps in governance that leave so much of transport in decay and disarray. Needless to say, without good governance, there would be no consultative processes by which stakeholders could weigh in on the social aspects of transport projects discussed above.

On a broader front, sustainable urban transport requires consistent political support and well-coordinated and transparent administrative structures and processes. Genuine efforts to strengthen the sustainability of transport systems require the involvement of all stakeholders in a structured manner and full access to information on all topics by all groups. Proactive approaches are required to set up channels and processes to ensure genuine lasting participation by stakeholders in the formulation and implementation of SUT policies and programs. For stakeholder participation in SUT planning and implementation to function well, it is important that information on the status of urban transport systems and efforts to improve it are collected on a regular basis and made available to all local stakeholders.

Future transport services will continue to be delivered by a mix of actors in the formal and informal sector. Regulators need to assess whether and how actors in the informal sector interact with the formal sector. Financing will be required for actors providing motorized transport services. Access to financing is easier for transport providers in the formal sector. A well-organized public transport sector functions better with a limited number of providers that operate in the formal economy.

1.3. Causes of Unsustainable Transportation

The various factors causing unsustainable transportation systems are noted in this section. Factors related to socio-economic growth are noted first, and then factors related to the growth in traffic. Several factors contributing to the growth of unsustainable transportation are population, employment, building floor space, personal income, and vehicle registration. Factors contributing to the increase in traffic also include vehicle ownership, traffic population, travel mode, trip purpose, and trip frequency as well as road facilities.

Figure 9.2. Causes and Situation of Unsustainable Transportation

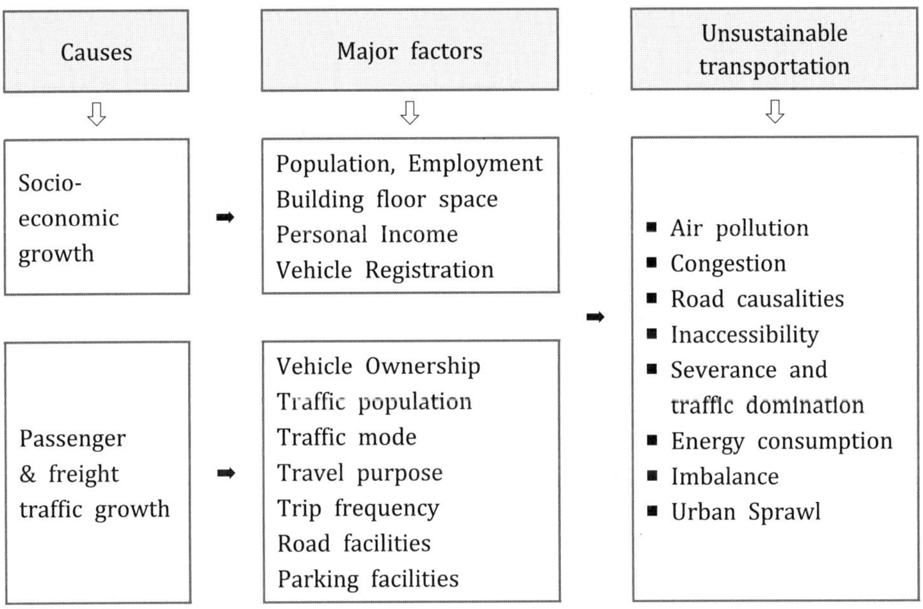

Source: OECD (1995); Jeong (2000)

2. Causes of Unsustainable Transportation

2.1. Socio-economic Growth

In 2012, Gwangju's population numbered 1,484,000, which accounted for 2.9% of the national total. It increased at an annual average growth rate of 0.8% during the 2000-2012 period. The total number of households in 2012 increased by 1.3 times from 430,000 households in 2000. The average growth rate over the last 12 years in car ownership has been 4.2% per annum. It was the most reliable determinant of travel demand in Gwangju. To conclude, the unsustainable situation has been heavily affected by the drastic increase in the city's socio-economic conditions.

Table 9.1. Trends of Socio-economic Growth

Division	Unit	2000	2005	2012	AAGR ('00-'12)
Population	1,000 persons	1,351	1,444	1,484	0.8%
Household	1,000 hou.	430	482	556	2.2%
Car registration (Private car's ratio)	1,000 Vehicle (%)	337 (67.5)	436 (73.5)	551 (79.3)	4.2% (+11.8)

Note: AAGR refers to average annual growth rate.
Source: GMC(each year)

2.2. Trends of Transport Indicators

The growth in road traffic volumes in Gwangju closely parallels the increase in socio-economic indicators. The total traffic population has increased at the average annual growth rate of 0.92% during the 2000-2012 period. The total length of constructed road grew from 1,151 km in 2000 to 1,634 km in 2012. This was mainly due to the road construction-oriented policy of GMC. The number of cars per road-km has increased from 292 cars in 2000 to 337 cars in 2012. This indicates the increasing intensity of the road network problem in Gwangju.

Table 9.2. Trends of Transport Indicators in Gwangju

Division	Unit	2000	2005	2012	AAGR ('00-'12)
Traffic population	Thousand	1,252	1,324	1,397	0.92%
Road length	Km	1,151	1,363	1,634	2.96%
Road ratio	%	18.5	20.5	23.1	+4.6
Cars per road	Cars/km	292	319	337	1.20%
Cars per person	Cars/1000	247	300	371	3.44%

Note: AAGR refers to average annual growth rate.
Source: GMC(each year)

2.3. Share of Modal Split

The taxi share as a proportion of the total daily trips by traffic mode decreased from 23.8% in 2000 to 15.2% in 2012. This was primarily caused by travelers being diverted from taxi among other factors. As a result of the drastic increase in the number of private cars in Gwangju, the share of private cars by traffic mode grew rapidly from 13.9% in 2000 to 36.4% in 2012. This resulted in heavy traffic congestion and air pollution in the built-up area of the city.

Table 9.3. Share of Modal Split (%)

Mode	2000	2005	2012	Changes ('00-12)
Bus	49.4	37.5	36.3	−13.1
Taxi	23.8	20.2	15.2	−8.6
Private car	13.9	27.3	36.4	+22.5
Subway	-	1.7	2.7	+1.0
Walking, others	12.9	13.3	9.4	−3.5

Source: GMC(each year)

3. Unsustainable Transportation Problems

3.1. Traffic Congestion

Congestion is a problem in Gwangju with relatively high levels of car ownership and poor road infrastructures. The degree of congestion's severity rose with the size of the city, and it extends as far as the suburbs. In considering congestion, it is helpful to compare average travel speeds. For instance, there was a rapid increase in average travel time in the outskirts of the city between 2005 and 2012. It is very difficult to estimate the true costs of congestion as it depends very much on the definition chosen. The total congestion costs in Gwangju grew at an average rate of 2.6% per annum during the 2000-2012 period.

Table 9.4. Changes in Congestion Costs

Division	Unit	2000	2005	2012	Change ('00-'12)
Travel speed (Outskirts)	km/hour	40.2	45.8	42.4	+2.2
Congestion cost	Billion Won	711.0	788.3	965.5	AAGR: 2.6%

Note: AAGR refers to average annual growth rate.
Source: GMC(each year)

3.2. Air Pollution

The transport emissions which cause the greatest concern include carbon dioxide (CO_2), carbon monoxide (CO), nitrogen oxides (NOx), sulphur dioxide (SO_2), volatile organic compounds (Voids), lead, particulate and smoke. Most vehicles also emit very fine particles of carbon (from diesel engines), inorganic lead compounds (from gasoline engines using leaded gasoline) and other metals used in oils to enhance engine performance. These particles cause dust, damage to health, and soil buildings.

Total emissions in Gwangju have decreased slightly during the 2000-2010 period, while total emissions from Gwangju's road traffic have also decreased slightly during the same period. Road transport is still the largest source of air pollution, accounting for 51.0% of Gwangju's total emissions in 2010.

Table 9.5. Emissions of Transport-related Pollutants

Items / Year	Unit	2000	2010	AAGR ('00-10)
Emissions	1,000kg/ year	52,371	45,186	−1.46%
Emissions from road traffic		28,243	23,045	−2.01%
Transport's share	%	53.9	51.0	−2.9

Note: AAGR refers to average annual growth rate.
Source: GMC(each year)

3.3. Traffic Accidents

Traffic accidents are, on the whole, the most dramatic and terrifying of Gwangju's transport problems. The total number of traffic accidents increased at an annual average rate of 0.76% during the 2000-2012 period. There were 114 people killed, and 13,886 people injured on the roads in 2012. In addition, the increasing number of cars still leads to a great many traffic accidents in Gwangju. Apart from the suffering caused by road causalities, the economic and social costs are high, both in Gwangju and throughout Korea.

Table 9.6. Trends of Road Traffic Accidents in Gwangju

Year	Accidents(cases)	Deaths(person)	Injuries(person)
2000	7,853	154	10,528
2005	7,797	103	12,361
2012	8,600	114	13,886
AAGR(%)	0.76	−2.48	2.33

Source: GMC(2001-2013)
Note: AAGR refers to average annual growth rate.

3.4. Imbalance of Economic Activity

There has been a tendency for Gwangju to take the lion's share of Jeonnam's economic growth. Too much growth has resulted in too much traffic; undue congestion; overcrowding of the public transport system; longer trip lengths; an expansion of the urban sprawl, giving limited access to open countryside; and to high land and property prices. In addition, Gwangju's area takes the bulk of the new employment growth at the expense of Jeonnam's other centers: And the area which attracts the higher growth frequently suffers from traffic congestion, and many other problems as a result. In Gwangju, the use of public transport is of course more concentrated in the morning and evening rush hours. The majority of buses in Gwangju are subject to considerable traffic congestion, as well as to chronic overcrowding at these times.

To conclude, transportation is a part of the daily lives of most of Gwangju's citizens, providing the mobility demanded by our society and its economy. Although there is a sign that traffic conditions in Gwangju are improving slightly, they are not improving fast enough. Motorized transportation is still causing major problems of lost time in traffic, declining life quality, and unnecessarily high levels of public investment. It also affects the environment by consuming energy in the form of fossil fuels, a non-renewable natural resource, and by generating wastes, emissions, and spills, thus contributing to ground, air and water pollution, and to the potential for climatic change. It is also imposing greatly increased costs on local businesses, and the community as a whole. This already bad situation is made worse by the fact that the partial methods of dealing with the problems are no longer able to cope.

4. Sustainable Transport Policy

4.1 Definition

The concept of ST strategies is generally gaining acceptance in Gwangju's transportation research fields. The term "strategy" means the art of planning tactics. The term "policy" is used to refer to sets of strategies-namely, statement of aims. The notion of "a sustainable transport policy" is reserved for an integrated and coordinated set of ST strategies and tactics designed to further the attainment of local objectives. An important element here is the relationship between ST policy and local objectives. Some examples of ST policy objectives are as follows: the need to reduce the necessity to travel; to reduce the use of cars and trucks; to favour more energy-efficient modes; to reduce noise and emissions; to encourage more efficient road use; to reduce traffic accidents, thus improving the overall attractiveness of the city. These objectives provide quantitative and qualitative guidelines for use in focusing and directing transportation policy.

4.2 Types of Sustainable Transport Policy

Types of ST Policies

As an initial effort to identify an effective ST policy for Gwangju, it is necessary to list and define major types of ST policies. The notion of types here is reserved for classified strategies of ST policies. Specific types of ST policies in past transportation studies were identified differently according to the character of each study. It should be pointed out that this list of major types is far from exhaustive. It is simply illustrative of the most commonly applied strategies that play major roles in the writing of ST policies. Based on the existing literature, it is therefore necessary to review some major types of ST policies.

Table 9.7. Types of ST Policy Review

Authors	Year	Major Types of ST Policies
Kim & Lee	1996	■ Improvements in technology, Improvements in vehicles & fuels, Transport demand management ■ Transport system management, Restrictions on use or ownership
Lee Jeong	1997 2000	■ Enforcing targets, Reductions on personal mobility ■ Encouraging cycling and walking, Reductions on commuting traffic
KEI	1998	■ Improvements in vehicles, Improvements in fuels ■ Improvements in technology, Transportation demand management, low and zero emission vehicles
OECD/ ECMT	1995	■ Public transport, Cycling/walking, Traffic restraint ■ Investment road/parking, Freight distribution, Road safety ■ Environmental standards & targets ■ Reductions on consumption
Goldman Gorham	2006	■ New mobility, City Logistics ■ Intelligent System Management, Livability
KOTI	2012b	■ TDM and traffic operation efficiency ■ Enhancement of walk and bicycle mode ■ Public transport improvement, Green transport technology ■ Low carbon green logistics

Source: Reference to the above mentioned theses

Strategies of Sustainable Transport Policy

From the general stand-point of land use and transportation planning, it is perhaps useful to discuss briefly some principal tactics. A wide variety of strategies and tactics are available to governments at all levels to tackle unsustainable transportation problems. Some tactics are concerned solely with land-use planning, others with land use and transport. If congestion, rising fuel consumption, casualties and environmental damage are to be dealt with effectively, it will not be enough to design and implement transport and planning policies independently. A combination of carefully selected policies that reinforce each other and avoid adverse side-effects, will be required. Based on the existing literature, and evaluated in terms of popularity and adaptability of ST policy, various tactics of ST policies are identified and grouped into two overall categories: planning strategies, and transportation strategies.

Table 9.8. Strategies of ST Policy

Division	Detailed tactics
Planning strategies	■ Land-use/transport planning, Regional policy, Restraint on central city growth ■ Designated growth area/new towns, Regeneration of city center/inner areas ■ Relocation of employment groups, Fiscal inducements to locate, Zoning regulations, Green belts
Transportation strategies	■ Road construction, Rail construction, Improved services/lower fares ■ Traffic management, Bus priority, Toll charges/road pricing, Parking controls ■ Park and ride, Car restraint, Cycle priority, Pedestrian priority, Traffic calming ■ Car pooling, Standards for noise/air pollution

Sources: OECD(1995); KEI(1998); Kim(1996); Jeong(2000, 2005)

4.3 Evolution and Direction of SUTP

Policies and Strategies Implemented

The main planning strategies used by the GMC in the 2000s included designated growth area, regeneration of city center, and land use-transport planning. On the transport side, rail/subway construction has been the most popular policy over recent decades. Road construction was thought to be the way forward two decades ago. The emphasis changed towards public transport provision later, when it was realized that road construction was not achieving the desired results. Traffic management, park-and-ride and bus priority strategies have been applied across Gwangju, and parking restraints have been the main means of controlling car traffic.

Table 9.9. Evolution of policies in the 2000s

Strategies	2000-2005	2006-2010
■ Land-use/transport planning	++	++
■ Regional policy	+	++
■ Restraints on central city growth	+	+
■ Designated growth areas/new towns	+++	++
■ Regeneration of city center/inner areas	++	+++
■ Relocation of employment groups	+	++
■ Fiscal inducements to locate	+	+
■ Zoning regulations	+	++
■ Green belts	+	+
■ Road construction	+++	+
■ Subway construction	+++	++
■ Improved services/lower fares	+	+
■ Demand management	+	++
■ Transport system management	++	+
■ Bus priority	++	+++
■ Toll charges/road pricing	-	-
■ Parking controls	++	++
■ Park and ride	++	+
■ Car restraint	+	+
■ Cycle priority	+	+++
■ Pedestrian priority	+	++
■ Traffic calming		+
■ Car pooling	+	+
■ Standards for noise/air pollution	+	++

Note: + to +++: denotes importance of measures implemented.
Sources: OECD(1995); GMC(1999-2013)

Direction of SUTP

A questionnaire was disseminated by the OECD to the Member countries. In all, 132 cities from 19 different countries responded in 1991. The cities were asked to list a range of transport and land-use policies that they had adapted and to assess their effectiveness in tacking congestion. The cities were also asked to outline any further policies planned to reduce congestion and pollution.

It was found from the survey that the most widely applied policies were: parking controls; priority for public transport vehicles and high occupancy cars; pedestrianisation; traffic management; access restrictions. Of the most widely applied policies, pedestrianisation and transit fares and service levels were the most effective strategies to solve traffic problems. The other more effective strategies were: provision of new roads; improved traffic information, and traffic calming. In contrast, access restrictions, cycle lanes, and priorities were considered to be relatively less effective. Also, future policies had a different emphasis when compared with past policies: more cities had cited new roads, cycle lanes, and LRT capacity. In addition, the more popular transport strategies were also mentioned. Few cities had mentioned land use measures and road user charges planned. Though many of the cities felt that their transport policies had been effective, perhaps in solving local congestion, the general consensus was that the overall level of congestion is getting worse.

Transport policies have been used to a greater or lesser extent in all the cities. Over the years, there has been a gradual shift emphasis in most cities from strategies geared to increasing road capacity toward improving public transport. More recently, attention has been focused on environmental issues. Past policies have not been successful in tacking these problems, and new approaches are needed. This book, therefore, sets out three strands of a concerted transport policy for Gwangju and which combines measures that reinforce each other.

The first relies on the adoption of best practice in land-use and transport planning, traffic management and the improvement of public transport found anywhere in the world. The second builds on the first by using innovative land-use and transport strategies to reduce the need to travel and converts best practice into a coherent structured policy package. The land use planning

Table 9.10. Analysis of Transport Policies Adapted

Policy descriptions	Perceived effectiveness	Importance of plan
Road infrastructure	+++	****
Traffic management	++	**
Road traffic information	+++	**
Traffic calming	+++	**
Access restrictions	+	***
Parking control	++	****
Road user charges		
Pedestrianisation	++++	**
Cycle lanes	++	****
Priorities: buses and HOV	++	***
New light rapid transit	++	****
New rail capacity	+	**
Coordination & information	+	***
Transit fares and service levels	++++	****
Land use zoning systems	+	
Development control/planning guidance	+	**
Green belts/green spaces	+	*
Development corporation	+	
Staggered work/school hours		
Other environmentally friendly policies		***

Notes: + to ++++ indicates the strength of the perceived effectiveness positively.
* to **** denotes importance of future policies planned.

Source: OECD(1995)

strategies would be concerned with the types of settlements which should expand and the provision of local facilities. Land uses would be integrated with public transport routes, roads, cycle and walkways. Speed limits would be applied more extensively on through roads, and traffic calming would be extended to most residential areas and school areas. The integrated package of traffic management tactics would include congestion pricing, reductions in city-center parking, bus priorities, park-and-ride services, and investment in traffic infrastructure. The third applies progressive increases in fuel taxes to reduce vehicle kilometers and CO_2 emissions, and to augment the other policy measures. Only strands 2 and 3 would bring about significant improvements in travel and the urban environment.

The Need for Sustainable Transport Policy[3]

A sustainable urban transport policy is needed to protect and enhance our natural and built environment. GMG must implement a range of measures to reduce pollution and traffic, develop a sustainable internal transport infrastructure, and persuade people out of cars by providing practical alternatives such as improved bus services, cycle tracks, and footpaths. Higher car use leads to increase in congestion, local air and noise pollution, and road injuries. The need to provide for the motor car puts pressure on our environment and its use also results in less physical activity and, consequently, a less fit and healthy society. The issues are congestion, local air and noise pollution, global greenhouse gas emissions, reduced physical activity, the built environment, road injuries, access for everyone, and oil dependency. These are recognised issues throughout Korea and the developed world. Unless metropolitan cities embrace more sustainable ways of travelling in Korea, such issues can only get worse.

3 SOJ(2010), pp.19-20.

4.4. SUTP for Gwangju Metropolitan City

Promotion of Walking and Cycling[4]

Walking environment improvements include pedestrian preference zone (PFZ) and walking trail establishment. The purpose of implementing the pedestrian preference zone is to arrange roads in residential/commercial area with poor walking conditions or high risk of traffic accidents, and to create convenient walking environment, by applying traffic calming measures. GMC needs to designate the zone in the city and to offer for a detailed design plan. The PFZ project should be promoted for the promotion of the transport convenience of the mobility disadvantaged. Sustainable walking trails, which connect public transport roads (station, bus stops) and residential/commercial areas, can contribute to the increase of public transport use. It also can improve people's leisure and cultural possibilities by making spaces for a range of leisure activities through the route development in connection with riverside, historic buildings, theaters, etc.

It is necessary to introduce bike rapid transit (BIRT). BIRT is a tube-shaped light structure, which requires relatively low cost of construction and maintenance. This bridge can be used all the time regardless of weather conditions. Because it can be constructed on the median part of roads or green roads, there is no need for separate land acquisition. Bicycle riders go faster on this transit system than on the existing bicycle road, and can save more travel time in commuting to bus rides.

The public bike system needs to be expanded for the various types of connection with bicycle and other modes of transport including walking. Public bike rental service, as a transport mode for short distance, is expected to address severe social problems such as traffic congestion, air pollution, oil price hikes, etc.

---

4 KOTI(2012b), pp.349-350.

Expansion of Public Transport Infrastructure and Service

Bus rapid transit (BRT) needs to operate and expand in GMC. It is essential to actively expand the BRT system as a low cost, high efficiency public transport modes to ease traffic difficulties. The BRT system in Gwangju can contribute to the improvement of bus speed.

It is necessary to establish multi-model transit centers (MTC's) in GMC. The MTC's should be constructed at major transport nodes such as railway stations, bus terminals, transfer stations, etc. to nurture green transport as a new growth engine for the urban economy, and high-density compact development to provide a variety of services to residents. The center is expected to reduce transfer distance and waiting time by 30%. The construction of MTC can create ripple effects such as the reduction of travel time, the decrease of transfer impedance, and the promotion of public transport use.

It is also important to expand urban railways to reduce the transport difficulties of new town residents and to reduce the private car use. The expansion would improve the urban railway modal share and ease the traffic congestion on major transport axes between the city center and its neighboring areas. GMC embarked on the expansion of Gwangju Metro Line 2 as soon as the Ministry of Land, Transport and Marine Affairs (MLTM) approved the revised plan in 2013. Construction will begin after the 2015 Universiade. It will proceed in three phases, and is expected to be completed by 2023. Specifics on the second line haven't been finalized yet. The newly revised plan aims to expand Line 2 from the initial 22.1 km to 41.7 km, connecting Gwanjgu City Hall, Baegungwangjang, Gwangju Station, Jeonnam University and the Cheomdan area. The city will form a task force team as soon as it gets approval and collect opinions to be gathered at public hearings.

The Honam HSR construction will make a contribution to the nation's balanced development through the establishment of the national transport network, and prepare for the increase of the traffic demand in Honam region, a south-western part of the Korean peninsula. Honam HSR is expected to reduce logistics costs by increasing transport capacity dramatically, enable a half-day living zone by reducing travel time from Seoul to Gwangju by 66 minutes, from 159 to 93 minutes, and help establish a transport network connected with the continental trains. It is also necessary to set up detailed action plans for the future project of high-speed construction on the major Gyeongjon Line to promote regional balanced development and improve railway modal share.

TDM Enhancement and Traffic Operation Efficiency

TDM is a wide range of policies, programs, services and products that influence how, why, when and where people travel to make travel behaviors more sustainable. Car sharing is defined by its environmental and social purpose, rather than business and financial objectives. Car sharing is primarily designed for shorter time and shorter distance trips as an extension of the transportation network, providing a public service designed to enhance mobility options. Car sharing is a membership based service available to all qualified drivers in a community. No separate written agreement is required each time a member reserves and uses a vehicle. CSOs help members save money over the cost of individual car ownership by encouraging members to drive less often, plan trips more, use other modes of transportation more, and share fuel efficient vehicles when a car is needed. Car sharing is designed for local users in support of community transit and environmental goals.

Intelligent Transport System (ITS) is a low cost, high efficiency smart transport system which, through the integrated application of advanced IT technology and transport information to the transport facilities, improves the efficiency and safety, and facilitates the automation and systematization of the urban transport operation and management. Urban ITS establishment is expected to decrease traffic congestion and accidents, and logistics costs. Eco-driving is an economical and environmentally friendly driving practice, which avoids sudden acceleration, deceleration, starting and braking. It leads to energy-saving and reduction of greenhouse gas emissions from cars. Eco-driving practise is expected to result in the decrease in fuel and maintenance costs, the capacity to proactively cope with a high oil price and energy crisis, and the decline of traffic accidents by 30-40%.

Table 9.11. Sustainable Urban Transport Strategies for GMC

Strategies	Detailed Tactics
Promotion of walking/cycling	• Pilot program of pedestrian zone preference zone • Establishment of urban walking trail • Introduction of bike rapid transit • Expansion of public bike systems
Expansion of public transport infrastructure and service	• Expansion of bus rapid transit operation • Expansion of urban railway service • Establishment of high-speed railway network
TDM enhancement and traffic operation efficiency	• Enhancement of car sharing system • Establishment of intelligent transport systems • Promotion of eco-driving in urban areas
City logistics improvements	• Neighborhood drop-off points • Centralized urban distribution and logistics centers • Construction logistics, Environmental zones

Source: KOTI(2012b)

City Logistics Improvements[5]

Urban freight traffic is growing fast in Korean metropolitan cities. E-commerce has facilitated the rapid growth of the small package delivery business in GMC. Increasing numbers of trucks on the road are below capacity or running empty, because of rapidly changing logistics and supply-chain pressures, such as just-in-time deliveries, as well as asymmetrical patterns of trade. Sustainable urban freight policy seeks to reduce empty truck

[5] Goldman and Gorham(2006), pp.268-269.

movements through neighborhoods and congested urban center, and improve the environmental and economic efficiency of urban freight operations.

Neighborhood drop-off points can significantly reduce trips associated with residential deliveries. They can be as simple as a dedicated counter in a local shop, or as high-tech as "Tower 24" in Dortmund, Germany, a fully automatic storage facility where neighbors can collect their packages 24 hours a day. Centralized urban distribution and logistics centers provide cooperative local delivery of goods, often using clean fuel vehicles. in the 1990s, several European cities experimented with coordinated goods distribution. Logistics coordination needs to be adapted as national and urban policy for major construction projects through GMC. GMC needs to restrict use of downtown loading zones (environmental zones) for trucks over a certain age, or that do not meet strict emissions standards. Use of the loading zones in the city center can require payment of a daily charge. Long-term, reduced-cost permits will be available for vehicles that can meet certain vehicle age, size and/or capacity utilization standards.

A self-portrait in the newspaper

Green Transport

Korea has voluntarily pledged to reduce its 2020 carbon dioxide emissions by 30 percent from the projected level. The self-imposed target is deemed very challenging in light of the fact that Korea's greenhouse gas emissions doubled between 1990 and 2005, the fastest rate of growth in the OECD.

One area where the Seoul government faces a tough challenge in cutting emissions is the transport sector. According to a recent survey, Korea ranks 22nd among the 23 polled OECD countries in terms of competitiveness in green transport. The low standing stems from Korea's heavy reliance on roads for passenger and freight transport. Until the 1980s, road transport accounted for less than 80 percent of the passenger and freight traffic. Now its share is more than 95 percent.

When you travel 1 kilometer by train, you produce 26 grams of carbon dioxide. If you drive a car, the emission surges to 151 grams. Suppose you have to travel from Seoul to Busan, a distance of about 420 km. If you use railroad, you will add 11 kg of carbon dioxide to your carbon footprint. Driving will add six times more.

To make the transport sector green and competitive, Korea needs to shift its focus in infrastructure construction from roads to railways. Between 2000 and 2009, the total length of expressways in Korea rose 77 percent from 2,131 km to 3,776 km. In contrast, railway network growth was minimal. The total length of the railroad system increased from 3,149 km in 1988 to 3,381 km in 2008, a mere 232 km extension. Few new railroad tracks were laid during this period except the bullet train line linking Seoul and Daegu.

On Wednesday, the Ministry of Land, Transport and Maritime Affairs unveiled a plan to review the current system of promoting road construction projects. It should have come up with such a move earlier. More than anything else, the new system should be able to prevent lawmakers from promoting pork-barrel projects in the process of deliberating on the administration's budget bills.

According to the ministry, 21 percent of the road projects that enter the construction or design stage this year are earmarks inserted by lawmakers. The amount of money set aside for them totals 3.9 trillion won. The nation already has many roads in provinces whose traffic volumes are so low as to make us wonder why they were built ahead of other more important projects.

Korea still needs more roads in cities where traffic congestion is serious. But we can hardly afford to throw taxpayers' money at ill-advised road projects. The government should ensure that more investment is made in expanding green transport facilities, including the railway system.

*** Source: The Korea Times (2012.1.15)**

References

Chang, Foun-Shea, "Sustainable Transportation Policies and Strategies for Urban Development", The Proceedings of the International Symposium on City Planning, Korea Planners Association, Kangnung, Korea, 1998.

City of Detroit (COD), Non-motorized Urban Transportation Master Plan, Traffic Engineering Division and Department of Public Works, June 2006.

Dalkmann, Holger and Charlotte Brannigan, Transport and Climate Change: Module 5e, Sustainable Transport: A Source book for Policy-makers in Developing Cities, Deutsche Gesellschaft fur Technische Zusammenarbeit (GTZ), October 2007.

EC (European Commission), Sustainable Urban Transport Plans, Annex, Technical Report-2007/018, September 2007.

ESCAP (Economics and Social Commission for Asia and the Pacific), Sustainable Urban Transportation Systems: An Overview, UN (United Nations), Citynet Publish Co., 2012.

Goldman, Todd and Roger Gorham, Sustainable Urban Transport: Four Innovation Directions, Technology in Society 28, 2006, pp.261-273.

Gwangju Metropolitan City (GMC), City Administration White Paper, 2000-2013 (in Korean).

GMC, Gwangju Transportation Improvement Midterm Plan, 1996 (in Korean).

GMC, City Administration White Paper, 2000-2011 (Each Year) (in Korean).

GMC, Gwangju Metropolitan Transportation Master Plan, Final Draft, August 2007 (in Korean).

GMC, Gwangju Metropolitan Public Transportation Plan, 1st Draft, December 2011 (in Korean).

GMC, The 2nd Transportation Safety Master Plan, November 2012 (in Korean).

GMC, Gwangju Statistical Yearbook, Each Year (2000-2011) (in Korean).

Hwang, Keeyeon, Linking ITS with TDM in Seoul, Lee, Gunyoung and Kyunghwan Park (edi.), Korea on the Move: Korea Current Transport Policy and Prospects for the Future, KOTI, 1997.

Hwang, Sangkyu, A Comprehensive Strategy for TDM Measures in Seoul, Lee, Gunyoung and Kyunghwan Park (edi.), Korea on the Move: Korea Current

Transport Policy and Prospects for the Future, KOTI, 1997.

Jeong, Bonghyun, Identification of Sustainable Transportation Strategies in Seoul, Korea, Journal of The Korean Regional Development Association, Vol.12 No.2, 2000, pp.187-204.

Jeong, Bonghyun, Development of Integrated Transport Planning Policies for Sustainable Urban Structure in Gwangju, Korea, Journal of The Korean Regional Development Association Vol.13 No.1, 2001a, pp.261-281.

Jeong, Bonghyun, Urban Transport Trends, Problems and Integrated Transport Policies for Sustainable Urban Structure in Gwangju, Korea, The Studies in Regional Development, The Center for Regional Development, CNU, Vol. 33 No.1, 2001b, pp.111-136.

Jeong, Bonghyun, New Transportation Policy in Regional Metropolitan City: Gwangju, Korea, CNU Press, 2005 (in Korean).

Jeong, Bonghyun, SOC and Regional Development: Standing Transportation Problems and Solutions in the Jeonlla Provinces, Korea, CNU Press, 2010 (in Korean).

Jun, Myungjin, Commuting Patterns in a Polycentric City: The Case of Seoul Metropolitan Area, The Journal of Korea Planners Association, Vol.30, No.2., Korea Planners Association, 1995. 4 (in Korean).

Kim, Jongsuk and Lee, Sungwon, Theory of Transportation and Environment, Korea Research Foundation for 21st Century, 1996.

Korea Environment Institute, A Study on the Strategies for Preventing Air Pollution in the 21st Century, KEI/1998/RE-20, December, 1998.

Korea Transport Institute (KOTI), Estimation of Road Traffic Accident Costs in Korea, 1998a (in Korean).

KOTI, Estimation of Traffic Congestion Costs in Korea, 1998b (in Korean).

KOTI, Toward an Integrated Green Transportation System in Korea (I), Convergence of Technologies and Policies, 2010.

KOTI, Toward an Integrated Green Transportation System in Korea (II), Global Green Convergence, 2011.

KOTI, Toward an Integrated Green Transportation System in Korea (III), Challenges for the Future, the World, and the People, 2012a.

KOTI, Economic Growth and Transport Models in Korea, KOTI Knowledge Sharing Report 2, Korea's Best Practices in the Transport Sector, 2012b.

Lee, Busong, Urban Transportation Economics and Policy, Bubmun Publishing Co., Seoul, 1998 (in Korean).

Lee, Gunyoung, Seoul of the 21st Century, Hankook Businesss Newspaper, 1995.

Ministry of Construction and Transportation (MOCT), Construction and Transportation White Paper, 1999 (in Korean).

Ministry of Environment (MOE), Environment White Paper, 1990-1999a (in Korean).

MOE, Estimation of Air Pollution Social Costs in Korea, 1999b (in Korean).

Newman, Peter, Cities, Transport and Greenhouse - Expectations and Practical Solutions, Transport and the Environment Moving People and Products in the 21st Century, Australian Academy of Technological and Engineering, Australia, 1990.

OECD (The Organization for Economic Co-operation and Development), Urban Travel and Sustainable Development, European Conference of Ministers of Transport, 1995.

OECD, Towards Sustainable Transportation, OECD Proceedings, The Vancouver Conference, 1996a.

OECD, Sustainable Transport in Central and Eastern European Cities, ECMT Publishing Co., 1996b.

OECD, OECD Guidelines towards Environmentally Sustainable Transport, 2002.

State of Jersey (SOJ), Jersey's Sustainable Transport Policy, Eco Active Travel, Transport and Technical Services, July 2010.

Tolley, Rodney, The Greening of Urban Transport: Planning for Walking and Cycling in Western Cities, 1990.

Chapter 10

Greenway Planning and Policy

1. Concept of Greenway Planning

1.1. Definition of Greenway

Numerous definitions have been proposed to reflect the variety of existing greenways. Charles Little (1990) described five greenway types based upon a combination of their purpose and scale: urban riverside, recreational trails, ecologically-significant natural corridors, scenic and historic routes, and comprehensive greenway networks. The definition proposed by Fabos (1995) of greenways as "corridors of various widths, linked together in a network" with his value characterization of "ecologically significant," "recreational," and "historical and cultural," has been widely referenced. Ahern (1995) defined greenways as "networks of land containing linear elements that are planned, designed and managed for multiple purposes." In general, greenways could serve to connect parks, nature reserves, cultural and historical sites and other protected lands.[1] Flink (2002) also encompassed man-made, natural, and social infrastructure in linear corridors, defining greenways as "multiple-use corridors that respect the inherent qualities of natural systems and accommodate manmade systems in a way that is compatible with nature." Jongman et al. (2004) emphasized the underlying ecological principles and processes in greenways, the interaction between social and ecological functions, and the potential of ecological networks to transcend international boundaries and administration.

Greenways in Korea's large cities are variable in size, type and function and have evolved through different landscape forms, the latest generation being "multi-objective" greenways. Greenway planning in Gwangju is largely focused on a green network only for pedestrians and non-motorized vehicles' mobility. It is regarded as a corridor of protected open space managed for conservation and recreation purposes. Greenways are the results of public·private partnerships, and are paths used for walking, bicycling, or other forms

[1] Arslan et al.(2001)

of recreation or transportation.

1.2. Sucess Factors for Implementing Greenways

The rapid progress in land acquisition, trail development, and landscape restoration of greenways warrants identification of the critical factors that contributed to their success. Several of these factors are discussed in literature on greenway planning.[2] In addition, literature in the field of ecosystem, watershed and resource management is relevant to the landscape-based greenway. While references for understanding greenways from ecological and spatial perspectives are commonly applied, the human actions and institutions required to enact protection, restoration and implementation have received less attention. Yaffee (1996) defended the importance of human institutions and processes to achieve ecological goals. Moote et al. (1996) identified principles of ecosystem management, all which encompass human factors. Therefore, literature from these fields, as well as from studies on organizational behavior, is useful to understand factors for planning and implementing landscape-based greenways.

1.3. Literature Review of Greenway Implementation

Most of the greenway research has concentrated either on technical aspects of the problem or on the visibility of policies for stimulating greenway development activities. Previous research also provided valuable knowledge about greenway design and planning, particularly focused on historic proceedings, and planning process.[3] Specific greenway planning issues have received close attention: planning process and organizational structure and cultural factors. Much has been written on the implementation of other public facilities.

---

[2] Fabos(1995)

[3] Taylor et. al.(1995); De Sousa(2003); Yang et al(2007)

The issue of greenway implementation has received no attention in the planning and economic development literature. Research on greening urban areas has explored both the benefits and barriers associated with greening. The existing literature from greenway planning has gone a long way towards identifying the features of successful greening projects and thus suggesting frameworks for their implementation. A set of implementation factors and techniques is required for this study in terms of organization and institutions. The proposed framework of greenway success factors derived from studying

Table 10.1. Literature Review of Greenway implementation Factors

Author	Title / Method	Relevant factors
Taylor et al. (1995)	■ From greenbelt to greenways ■ Canadian case studies	■ Form and function, development ■ Response to natural factors ■ Sustainability, public support and use
De Sousa (2003)	■ Turning brownfields into green space in the city of Toronto ■ Brownfield-to-green space redevelopment	■ Community and municipal involvement ■ Inventories, funding sources ■ Economic encouragement
Rottle (2006)	■ Factors in the landscape-based greenway ■ Case of Mountains to Sound Greenway	■ Planning process factors ■ Organizational structure and cultural factors ■ Implementation tools and strategies
Yang et al. (2007)	■ Planing system for urban greenway planning ■ International comparative case study	■ Networking methods, integrated greenway master plan ■ Partnership between public and private sectors
Jung et al. (2007)	■ Greenway Types for Integrative Planing of Pedestrian-friendly Space in Urban Area ■ Descriptive Case Study	■ Integrative planning for greenway master plan ■ Introduction of design techniques for integrative planning

Gwangju Greenway is as follow as[4]: form and function; development concept; response to natural systems and sustainability, public support, strengthening coalition (public support); funding; publicity; development of feasibility study; monitoring and management; cooperation with elected officials.

2. Characteristics of Toronto and Gwangju Greenway Projects

2.1. Survey Methodology

Two metropolitan cities, Toronto, Canada and Gwangju, Korea formed the basis of this study. These cities were chosen because they: (1) planned a network or system of linear open spaces; (2) focused on multiple functions and objectives; (3) represented projects implemented; and (4) served as often sited examples of greenway success stories.[5]

Because greenways have played a significant role in the development of both Toronto, Canada and Gwangju, Korea, comparative studies about the two case study cities were conducted in terms of context, planning approach, concepts and administration. The purpose of these studies was to discuss the outcomes of the implementation of each plan. Document analysis and a focus group interview process were used to gather comparative data for each case study.

A focus group interview (FGI) is an interview with a small group of people on a specific topic. The participants were typically a relatively homogeneous group of people who were asked to reflect on questions about successful factors of greenway planning implementation. A ten people group was selected, because they had certain and professional knowledge about the topic in common. They were working in the field of regional planning, landscape architecture and geography.

---

[4] Taylor et al.(1995); De Sousa (2003); Jeong(2009)

[5] MOE & KCLA(2002); Erickson(2004).

Table 10.2. Survey Plan of Focus Group Interview

Purpose	■ Produce highly qualitative data ■ Provide insights into their opinions on the topic
Sampling	■ Plan - Expert choice sampling ■ Unit - Experts in university and research institute ■ Size - Ten persons (5 in Korea and 5 in Canada)
Survey contents	■ Questions - Factors of greenway planning implementation ■ Response formats - Rating scale
Execution date	■ September and November, 2005

2.2. Context of Toronto Greenway Project

Project Context

This most recent Canadian greenway proposal was a broadly based strategy to develop a greenway system for the entire Greater Toronto Bioregion. The concept has grown out of the Royal Commission on the Future Toronto Waterfront. This commission was established by the federal government in cooperation with the Province of Ontario and Metropolitan Toronto. The mandate of the 3 year Royal Commission Study was to create a unique, world-class waterfront in Toronto by exploring means for greater cooperation among the various levels of government, conducting a full consultation with the interested public, exploring issues affecting the protection and renewal of the natural environment, and responding to other emerging issues.[6] The limit of the study was extended beyond the immediate Lake Ontario waterfront area to cover the entire Great Toronto Bioregion. Natural features of the region define this 10,000 km^2 area. The total area is approximately 200 km in length and includes all or parts of nine regional jurisdictions.

[6] Luymes & Tamminga(1995)

Figure 10.1. Greater Toronto Bioregion, Toronto, ON

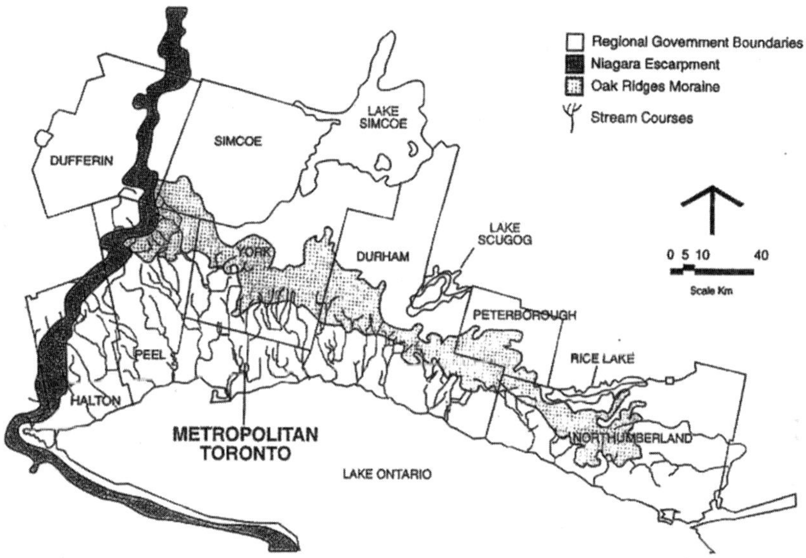

Source: Luymes & Tamminga(1995)

Planning Approach

The Royal Commission adopted an ecosystem approach that included examination of the lakeshore, associated with watersheds, and urban systems within the area municipalities. The commission employed the greenway concept as an important tool to meet the needs of a burgeoning human population and to protect a vulnerable ecosystem. The Greater Toronto greenway planning process recommended that an analysis of resources within each watershed unit should be undertaken to identify the following: significant green nodes and connecting corridors; existing and potential recreational attractions; available public lands and opportunities for securing other high-priority lands; visual corridors required to protect the scenic quality and appeal of proposed greenways, and to provide community separation where appropriate; significant heritage features.[7]

[7] Tayer et. al.(1995)

The greenway plans proposed to include guidelines for the safety and security of greenway users and adjacent landowners, strategies for enhancing ecological and recreational connecting links, and management guidelines for public lands and for compatible private land uses. Also included were the establishment of priorities necessary to create or complete greenways, and the identification of mechanisms and responsibilities for greenway implementation.

2.3. Development and Implementation

Development Concept and Implementation

The essence of the greenway concept was connections-not simply connecting recreational areas through trails, but connecting wildlife habitats to each other, human communities to other human communities, city to country, people to nature. The greater Toronto greenway concept proposed a two-tiered system with arterial greenways that established an interconnected framework across the region and local connectors within each community. The local connectors were to be developed according to priorities of municipalities and availability of existing land. Utilizing abandoned rail lines and utility corridors, these connectors were proposed to tie into community parks and tributary valleys, providing recreational trail loops.

In 1992, the Ontario government established a new agency, the Waterfront Regeneration Trust, to build on the strategic plan. A priority project of the Waterfront Regeneration Trust was to proceed with the implementation of the Lake Ontario Greenway Strategy (LOGS). A proposed first phase of the LOGS was the establishment of a continuous waterfront trail from Burlington at the southeast to the Trent River at the east of the Bioregion. The Trust provided an educational role to the public, conveying the benefits of ecosystem planning, and completed a strategy to address the management of shorelines, wildlife habitat, water quality, and cultural resources. An integrated approach to ecosystem-based environmental and land use planning was applied to the preparation of sub watershed plan.

Administrative Framework and Land Use Control

The Royal Commission viewed itself as a catalyst, working to achieve the greenway proposal. In implementing the plan, existing agencies, municipalities, landowners, and citizen groups were encouraged to cooperate in the planning and implementation of the greenway system. To administer the greenway plan at the local level, Community Greenway Alliance was proposed, which included broad-based representation and worked toward achieving various goals of greenway planning implementation. The work of the Alliances would be assisted by provincial policy support, technical advice, and financial assistance. Land use control was proposed to be exercised at the local level through normal planning and zoning, and through partnerships or agreements with public agencies and private landowners.

3. Greenway Planning in Gwangju Context

3.1. Project Context

A 10.8 km section of the railway crossing the urban center of Gwangju has resulted in road congestion, traffic noise and unbalanced urban development.[8] Before it was abandoned, around 40 trains served the section each day passing 28 crossings. Affected residents began to call for the relocation of the section of the tracks, and Gwangju City also felt the same way of the appeal. The Korean National Railroad accepted the city's appeal to close the tracks by 2000. The section was closed in August 2000 and the tracks removed, leaving 162,000 m^2 of land unoccupied.

---

[8] Jeong(2009)

It was widely held that the resulting space would be turned into an urban rail. The KFEM Gwangju and the Citizen Coalition for Rail-to-Greenway (CCRG) asked the city council to transform the space into a greenway, where only pedestrians and bicycle riders would have access. It took the CCRG two-years of countless demonstrations, signature-collecting campaigns, public hearings, seminars and petitions before the city officially abandoned the light rail construction plan in December 2001. Active participation by the general public was indispensible for the success of the greenway project. The making of Gwangju Greenway (GG) was heralded throughout Korea as one of the most successful cases of habitat rejuvenation.

Figure 10.2. Themes of Gwangju Greenway

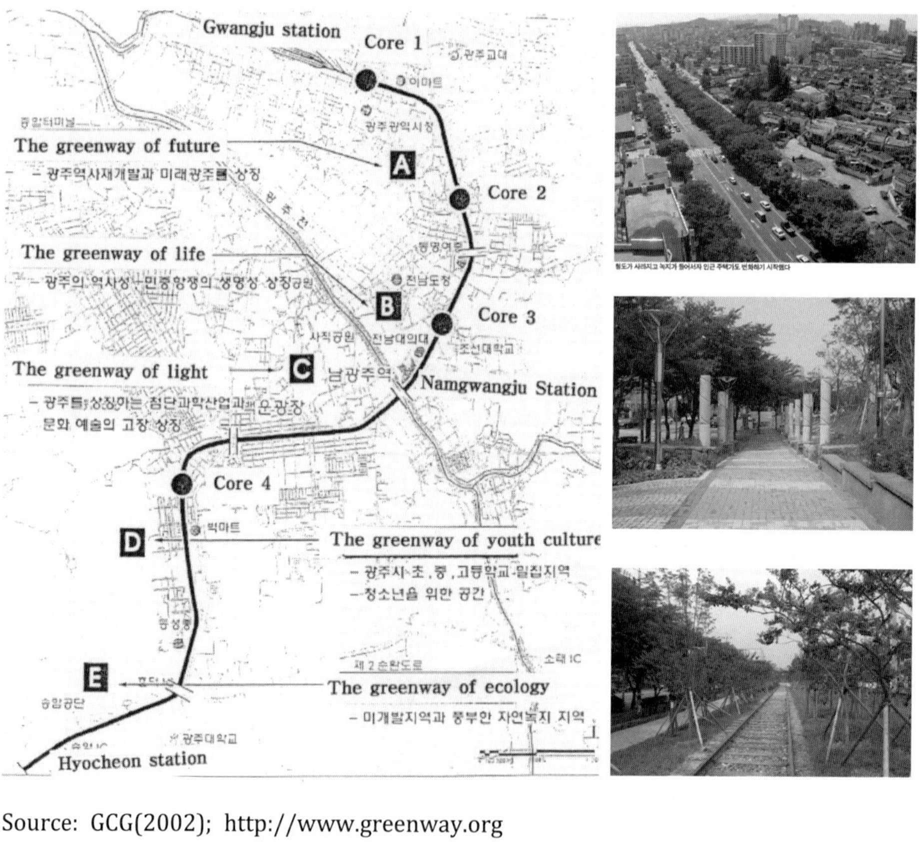

Source: GCG(2002); http://www.greenway.org

3.2. Planning Approach

Greenway planning and policy can make a major contribution to environmental quality and its enjoyment by the public. The greenway in Gwangju needed to provide routes for pedestrians, cyclists and natural process. It was identified as a green network only for pedestrians and bicycle mobility.[9] Gwangju City Government (GCG) organized a steering committee for the greenway planning, and completed a final draft of the greenway master plan, and explained the plan to Gwangju City Council (GCC). GCG designated the abandoned section as a city planning facility (neighborhood park) in 2002. It employed the urban design approach which was inclusive of inventory of natural and recreational resources, public consultation and participation in the planning process.

3.3. Development Concept and Implementation

The greenway could serve as a symbolic open space in the overcrowded city center of Gwangju from a standpoint of urban structure. It turned out to be a famous city' sight from a tourism perspective, and to create a new landscape value environmentally. Gwangju greenway was largely based upon pedestrian streets, bikeway, small parks or other linear features. The multi-purpose greenway changed lives and communities in Gwangju. Paths, wide enough to accommodate bikers and walkers would become public greenways connecting districts in the city center. There has been a still-growing desire to create new habitats and nature in Gwangju. The Gwangju greenway would assist Gwangju to realize its aims for cycling and encouraging walking: Greenway planning could contribute to environmental quality in Gwangju City.

The Urban Planning Department took the responsibility of planning the abandoned railway in Gwangju. The department commissioned a consulting

[9] GCGb(2002)

company to produce a Gwangju Greenway Master Plan in August 2000. Greenway Development Committee conducted advisory activities on Gwangju greenway's master plan. The fundamental notion of the plan was titled as "the greenway of light and life". The Gwangju Greenway land use plan established five broad themes for management of the greenway. Four locations in the railroad were created as development cores. The Park and Green Belt Department of GCG was responsible for implementation of the greenway master plan in 2002. GCG completed a 10.8 km greenway in 2010 with an investment of 12.3 million US $.

3.4. Administrative Framework and Land Use Control

City government was responsible for delivering services - like rail to greenway- to citizens. A partnership with a government agency started shortly after a citizen group was formed. The partnership evolved over the course of the rail-greenway project. Concerned and organized citizens instigated much beneficial government action after persistent efforts. Understanding the agency's mission was effective to receive the most help from a government agency. Another challenge was to find an agency both supportive of the rail to greenway conversion plan, and in the position to do something about it. The best agencies to work with were those with authority to plan and implement, such as the Park and Green Belt or Urban Planning Department. The government had the ability to fund for the rail-to-greenway plan. The agency created a rail-to-greenway advisory group consisting of a broad cross section of the community. A citizen group used the political process to help remove any restraints placed on the agency. It was desirable to publicly support the government agency and to arrange a public-private partnership for maintenance of the greenway.

The people implementing the greenway system should have a vision and criteria for creating and linking different segments of the greenway system, and consider how the system can be maintained over the long term. The greenway master plan needs to contain various components, such as context, inventory·analysis·synthesis, needs and desires, vision, plan development, and implementation strategies. However, Gwangju Greenway Master Plan didn't analyze detailed inventory data and provide how the plan would be implemented.

4. Comparison of Two Greenway's Planning

4.1. Form and Function

The physical forms of the two greenway systems have resulted from either an imposed urban design concept (Gwangju Greenway Planning: GGP) or the boundaries of natural systems (Greater Toronto Bioregion: GTB). Urban greenway has been used to provide a link to the rural areas (GTB) or to protect environmentally sensitive area and cultural landscape features and connect ecological systems (GGP). The functional use of greenways have varied with the times. The use of greenways as a land bank for institutional, agricultural, and other land uses is no longer feasible, owing to the high cost of land adjacent to urban areas. Common functions of greenway development include the protection of environmentally sensitive areas and cultural landscape features, and the connectivity of ecological systems and human use as supported by trail development.[10]

4.2. Development Concept

The GTB example is highly ecological in concept, and as a result closely follows natural shorelines, drainage courses and regional land units. This greenway evolves as local sub-watershed basin plans are completed, and local governments and action groups proceed with implementation. The Toronto ecosystems approach is commendable. The greenway planning for Gwangju

---

[10] Taylor et al.(1995)

City applied a highly structural link and node concept based on cultural resources and identifiable landscape units. The development nodes have proven to be successful in both dispersing human use and limiting the extent of human impacts within one trail-based corridor.

Table 10.3. Comparison of Two Case Study Cities

Items	Greater Toronto Bioregion, Toronto, ON	Greenway Planning, Gwangju
Date of Plan	1988-1991	2002-2010
Length	200 km (125 miles)	10.8 km
Area	1,000,000ha	16.2ha
Context	Lakefront, watershed systems and regional landform features	Abandoned rail-trail system
Response to natural and cultural factors	Sustaining ecological systems was basics of plan; comprehensive watershed planning approach to be used in implementation stage	Cultural factors were primary design determinant limited with consideration given to sensitive features and systems
Planning approach	Bioregion-based ecosystem approach; public consultation and participation in the planning process	Urban design approach; inventory of natural and recreational resources; public consultation and participation in the planning process
Concept	Connectors: arterial and local	Nodes and links, connector
Administrative framework	Multi-jurisdictional (federal, provincial, regional and municipal in cooperation with local interest groups)	Jurisdictional (Gwangju Metropolitan Government)
Land use controls	Proposed partnerships with landowners; local zoning and land use control	Local zoning, land use control
Current status	Planning and implementation in progress (Waterfront Regeneration Trust)	Development not completed as planned; planning and implementation in progress

Source: Taylor et al.(1995); GCGb(2002)

4.3. Response to Natural Systems and Substantiality

The Toronto greenway concept relies on the watershed as a primary framework and is based on an ecosystem approach to planning. The long-term viability of this greenway appears greater when considering public acceptance and use, ecological integrity and substantiality, and the feasibility of implementing and managing the area. It appears that success is more evident in the example that responds appropriately to the form and processes of the natural system.

Although the concept of sustainable development has recently gained popular acceptance, greenway planning in Canada has increasingly demonstrated principles of substantiality over the past 40 years. The GTG concept attempts to marry human needs and environmental substantiality, with the specific objective of supporting sustainable development within an eco-system. But, the planning approach for Gwangju greenway is not fully incorporated into the process of sustainable development.

4.4. Public Support and Use

As greenway planning has evolved in Canada, accommodation of public participation in the planning process has assumed a more important role. Public access, use, and the comprehension of form appear to be major considerations in building support for greenways. The GTG represents an approach that encourages full communication and cooperation among agencies and landowners. The implementation of the concept is proposed to be from the grass-roots level, with extensive involvement by local interest groups and local governments. Public consultation was a key element of the planning process for GGP and the concept was widely accepted. The GCG has assumed the role of catalyst in providing resources and expertise to facilitate the process of implementation at the local level.

The trends have been toward greater public participation in the planning process and in implementation of greenway plans at the local level. Increased public support is evidenced in greenway systems where conservation of significant ecological systems and cultural features was a primary goal.

4.5. Implementation Strategy

The Toronto greenway is broader in scope and proposes that implementation and management will be primarily assumed at the local level. The Waterfront Regeneration Trust has been established as a provincial agency to begin implementation of the work of the Royal Commission by working with all stakeholders. The Gwangju greenway has been developed based on a department exercising authority over greenway lands and their management. The Gwangju model builds on cooperation with existing departments of the GCG and agreements with private sector to achieve what will be the most effective greenway system in Korea.

5. Identification of Gwangju Greenway's Success Factors

5.1. Creating and Strengthening Coalition

The long-term success of a community's greenway project will be in the maintenance, advocacy and improvements made to it. Converting a railway into a greenway requires the help of a broad-based constituency. It is important to develop a diverse greenway coalition group, strong enough to overcome any hurdles along the railway.[11] Greenways appeal to a variety of groups and many different types of people. They include bicycling and walking clubs, environmental organizations, neighborhood associations, city council, landowners, and youth oriented organizations. Many residents and individuals were interested in working on a rail-to-greenway in Gwangju.

[11] CIGG(2008)

Citizen's Initiative for Gwangju Greenway (CIGG) and Gwangju Green Transport (GGT) have done much to launch a successful rail-greenway project.[12]

The single most important function of the organizations was to act as advocates of the greenway, defending it when necessary and promoting it at all times. A CIGG group was established by Gwangju Federation of Environmental Movements (GFEM), YMCA, YWCA, other NGOs, experts and lots of citizens in 2002. CIGG and GGT provided many important services to the greenway and often work in cooperation with the GCG to help maintain it. An open invitation meeting is needed for communicating with community organizations.

5.2. Quality Greenway Planning

Quality planning is a key component to a successful greenway system.

The people implementing the greenway system should have a vision, criteria for creating and linking different segments of the greenway system, and consider how the system may be sustained and maintained over the long term.[13] The initial presentation should be clear, concise and imaginative. The plan also should have the following components: context; inventory·analysis·synthesis; needs and desires; vision; plan development, implementation strategies. GCG established the Gwangju Greenway land use plan and the neighborhood unit plan of GG in 2002. However, the plan didn't analyze inventory data in detail and provide how the plan would be maintained and implemented. All greenway proposals should be based on a full appreciation of the local context.

---

12 Song(2001)

13 Jeong(2009)

5.3. Funding

There are many ways, such as government funding mechanisms, grants, private partnerships and other creative funding methods to fund greenways. The first key to funding is to identify, evaluate and document the transportation value of a rail-greenway proposal. Fundraising is a critical and crucial element of developing a greenway coalition. Funding can be obtained from community groups, private donors, companies and public bodies. A fund of US$ 330,000 was raised by citizens to make "a greenway by citizen's participation." About 132 species of trees were planted and maintained by more than 7000 people in this Greenway.[14] The most common sources of funds at the city level included budgetary allocations from specific bureaus, such as Environment and Afforestation Bureau and Urban Planning and Transportation Bureau in GCG.

5.4. Publicity

Few successful rail-greenway conversions have taken place without the awareness and involvement of active people in the community.[15] Publicity takes many forms, including brochures, mailings, posters, newsletters, and articles in the daily press, advertisements, public service announcements, speeches, rallies, and debates. GCG planned to construct a light-rail transit along the abandoned railway in September 1999, but local residents showed negative attitudes towards the city's plan for light-rail transit. Over 8000 people petitioned the GCG to discourage the light-rail transit plan and promote a greenway. It brought about considerable public and media attention in Gwangju city. Over 200 people marched through the streets to demonstrate against the light rail transit plan.

---

[14] CIGG(2008)

[15] MOE & KCLA(2002)

Kwangju Broadcasting Company (KBC), Gwangju Dream Newspaper, Jeonnam Ilbo (local newspaper company) and Gwangju Branch of Central Multi Broadcasting(CMB) have implemented advertising campaigns since the project started. These have attracted the attention and participation of citizens. It has been activated through the informing process of the greenway campaign and it encouraged fund raising participation through tree planting and greenway walking events. Public consultation took place through meetings, exhibitions, press articles, leaflet distribution, and the deposition of reports in libraries. Initial plans were modified, in response to the results of the public consultation.

5.5. Cooperation with Elected Officials

For a rail-greenway project to succeed we need to know how elected officials and government agencies make decisions about moving forward on the greenway project. We need to keep elected officials informed about the project and the development of the campaign. Officials have access to useful documents and official records, and can gain attention in numerous ways, such as legislation, public hearings, speeches, and articles. Elected officials know other politicians from different levels of government, and may be members of regional boards that could help a rail-greenway project. Local residents presented a petition to Gwangju City Council (GCC) for a greenway plan for the railroad in 1998. The Councils of Dongju and Seogu Districts memorialized the mayor of Gwangju City for the construction of new greenway along the abandoned railroad in 2000. The Mayor of Gwangju City held a press conference and declared that the abandoned railroad area would be used as a greenway according to the requirement of the GICC and citizens.

5.6. Monitoring and Management

If a greenway is well managed to lessen impacts, the greenway will remain successful. Therefore, maintenance and management should be addressed at the outset of a project to ensure: long-term success of the greenway; planning, design, and construction focuses on long-term maintenance issues; a greenway monitoring system is established so impacts are understood.[16]

Greenway construction and maintenance must be accomplished correctly. Volunteers who are constructing, maintaining, or monitoring a greenway can be extremely helpful and are critically important for public agencies so positive relationships can be established. The project is often initiated and carried out by a small, grassroots organization comprising a group of involved citizens. A greenway is generally managed and maintained through a variety of partnership arrangements.

Park maintenance should not be entrusted solely to government staff but it should also be supplemented by residents' participation to make it more vibrant. A system for volunteer organization is also considered for the continuous maintenance and sustainability of the project.

Establishing a greenway making network will be purposely compatible and beneficial in improving the everyday landscape and environmental conditions since Gwangju City is lacking of green sites. Open space was made in the train station with attached traditional market where continuous advertising and fund raising for the greenway project are possible for the activation and maintenance of the park, and it also enables the maintenance of a partnership with the local government.

---

[16] Cho(2007); Jeong(2009).

Table 10.4. Identification of Gwangju Greenway's Success Factors

Factors	Features of GG	Perceived effectiveness
Creating and strengthening coalition	■ Citizen Coalition for Greenway Construction ■ Gwangju Green Transport ■ Community Organization	+++++
Quality Greenway Planning	■ Land Use Planning of Abandoned Railway ■ Discussion and Forum Papers	+
Funding	■ Gwangju City Government Funding ■ Private Partnership and Company Grants	+++
Publicity	■ Brochures and Posters, News Letters ■ Public Announcement, Rallies, Debate ■ Petition, Media attention	++++
Cooperation with elected officials	■ Petition to Gwangju City Council ■ Donggu District Council ■ Seogu District Council	+++
Monitoring and management	■ Partnership Arrangement ■ Tree Donation from charitable organizations and companies	++

Note: GG refers to Gwangju Greenway; + to +++++ indicates the strength of the perceived effectiveness positively in focus group interview (FGI)

A self-portrait in the newspaper

Seoul to increase pedestrian access

As part of a 63 billion won year-long spending plan to improve public areas, Seoul City on Monday announced a plan to increase the number of pedestrian walkways in crowded parts of the city and restrict vehicle access to such districts.

Beginning in March, on every third Sunday of the month, a 550-meter-area spanning from the Gwanghwamun intersection in front of Gyeongbok Palace to the Sejongro junction will be designated as a pedestrian zone. If the trial operation is received positively, the city plans to increase the frequency of pedestrian-only access to once a week. The scheme is not just restricted to Gwanghwamun in central Seoul. Itaewon High Street, Gangnam-daero and Donhwamun-no in Jongno will be designated as pedestrian-only streets during weekends.

Other thoroughfares such as a street in Itaewon with a concentration of international restaurants, the 'fashion street' in Dongdaemun, and a street in Hongdae popular with young people will also become pedestrian access only areas throughout the year.

Streets only to be used by school children will also be created. During commuting hours, roads in front of schools will be restricted to vehicles. Ten streets in front of schools in the city will be designated as trial streets for evaluation. A "zone" for school children will also be on trial across seven regions in five districts until 2014.

More crossings will be created in major streets in Seoul and the length of time the green light is shown on pedestrian crossings will be extended from the current 1 second per 1 meter to 1 second per 0.8 meters. The city also plans to increase elevators and escalators in subway stations by 2,678 until 2014 and boost the number of bus stations with automated voice information service to 400. Three major historic or shopping tourist destinations in Seoul will be designated as "promenades" where visitors can enjoy walking.

*** Source: The Korea Times (2013.1.21)**

References

Ahern, Jack, Greenways in the USA: theory, trends and prospects, Ecological Networks and Greenways: Concept, Design and Implementation, Rob Jongman & Gloria Pungetti, (edi), Cambridge Studies in Landscape Ecology, Cambridge University Press, 2004, pp.34-55.

Banister, David (edit.), Transport and Urban Development, London: E&FN Spon, 1995.

Cho, Tong B., The present condition of Gwangju Disused Railway and Greenway Project. Environment and Landscape Architecture of Korea Vol. 169, 2000, pp.88-93 (in Korean).

Cho, Tong B., Landscapes of the Greenway and Old Town Along the Railroad; Narrative Drawings for Abandoned Railroad Park of Gwangju. Namudosi Publishing Co, 2007 (in Korean).

Choi, Dongho, The Need for Building Greenways from a Green Transport Perspective, Gwangju City Environments Research Report, 2001. The Institute for Environmental Protection in Gwangju (IEPG), Korea (in Korean).

Citizen's Initiative for Gwangju Greenway (CIGG), Gwangju Rail-to-Greenway Movement, 2008 Best Practices Data Base in improving in the Living Environment, UN-Habitat, 2008, (http://www.unhabitat.org/).

Cox, Norman D., and Vaughn, Coy, Southeast Livingston Greenways: Plan and Summary Report, The Greenway Collaborative, Inc. and Livingstone County Planning, November 2000.

De Sousa, Christophe A., Turning brownfields into green space in the City of Toronto, Landscape and Urban Planning 62, Elsevier Pub., 2003, pp.181-198.

Erickson, Donna L., Connecting Corridors: Implementing Metropolitan Greenway Networks in North America, Ecological Networks and Greenways: Concept, Design and Implementation, Rob Jongman & Gloria Pungetti, (edi), Cambridge Studies in Landscape Ecology, Cambridge University Press, 2004, pp.200-221.

Fabos, Julius Gy., Introduction and Overview: the Greenway Movement, Uses and Potentials of Greenways, Landscape and Urban Planning 33, Elsevier Pub., 1995, pp.1-13.

Gwangju City Government (GCGa), Light of Gwangju: Comprehensive Long-Term

Development Plan, 1998 (in Korean).
GCGb, Land use plan of Gwangju abandoned railroad, 2002 (in Korean).
GCGc, Environment & Afforestation Bureau's Policy Report, 2004 (in Korean).
Gwangju Greenway (GG), Dream of future while walking abandoned railroad. Design Daul Co., 2008 (in Korean).
Hoctor, Thomas S. et al., The Florida Statewide Greenway Project: its Realization and Political Context, Ecological Networks and Greenways: Concept, Design and Implementation, Rob Jongman & Gloria Pungetti, (edi), Cambridge Studies in Landscape Ecology, Cambridge University Press, 2004, pp.222-250.
Jeong, Bonghyun, Characteristics and Factors to Successful Greenway Planning for Sustainable Transportation: The Case of Toronto, Canada and Gwangju, Korea, Journal of the Korean Regional Development Association, Vol.21 No.1, The Korean Regional Development Association, 2009, pp.225-246.
Jeong, Hye-Jin et al., A Study on Greenway Types for Integrative Planning of Pedestrian-Friendly Space in Urban Area, Journal of the Architectural Institute of Korea, Vol.23, No.10, Architectural Institute of Korea, October 2007, pp.121-130 (in Korean).
Kim, He J. et. al., Sense of place, sense of community. Environment and Landscape Architecture of Korea. Vol. 169, 2002, pp.94-97 (in Korean).
Kim, Jung Y., Adriaan bridge. Environment and Landscape Architecture of Korea Vol. 169, 2002, pp.104-106 (in Korean).
Kim, Kiho and Mun, Gunhyun, Greenways: Living Power of City, Randomhouse Publishing Co, 2006 (in Korean).
Lee, Sangjun, Necessities and Benefits of Greenways, Gwangju City Environments Research Report, 2001. IEPG, Korea (in Korean).
Luymes, Don T. & Tamminga, Ken, Integrating Public Safety and Use into Urban Planning Greenways, Landscape and Urban Planning 33, Elsevier Pub., 1995, pp.391-400.
Ministry of Environment (MOE) and Korean Council for Local Agenda (KCLA) 21, Choice for Sustainable Development: Local Agenda 21 in Korea, 2002 (in Korean)
Morgan, David L., Focus Groups as Qualitative Research, Newbury Park CA: Sage, 1988.

Nam, Gi J. et. al., Gwangju Biennale Project4 Connection. Environment and Landscape Architecture of Korea. Vol. 169, 2002, pp.98-103 (in Korean).

Rails-To-Trails Conservancy (RTCa), Rail-Trails and Community Sentiment: A Study of Opposition To Rail-Trails and Strategies for Success, 2000, USA.

Rottle, Nancy D., Factors in the Landscape-based Greenway: a Mountains to Sound case study, Landscape and Urban Planning 76, Elsevier Pub., 2006, pp.134-171.

RTCb, Rail-Trails and Liability: A Primer on Trail-Related Liability Issues & Risk Management Techniques, September 2000, USA.

RTCc, Rail with Trails: Design, Management, and Operating Characteristics of 61 Trails along Active Rail Lines, November 2000, USA

Ryder, Barbara A., Greenway Planning and Growth Management: Partners in Conservation?, Landscape and Urban Planning 33, Elsevier Pub. 1995, pp.417-432.

Ryan, Karen-Lee and Winterish, Judle A. (edit.), Secrets of Successful Rail-Trails: An Acquisition and Organizing Manual for Converting Rails to Trails, Rails-To-Trails Conservancy, 2000, USA.

Shapins Associates, Innovative Non-motorized Trails Projects & Ideas, Colorado State Trails Committee, USA, August 2000.

Shin, Iksun, Values of Greenways from Urban Ecology and Landscape Standpoints, Gwangju City Environments Research Report, The Institute for Environmental Protection in Gwangju (IEPG), Korea, 2001, (in Korean)

Song, Insung, Approaches to Build Greenways through Citizen Participation, Gwangju City Environments Research Report, The Institute for Environmental Protection in Gwangju (IEPG), 2001, Korea (in Korean).

Tan, Kiat W., A Greenway Network for Singapore, Landscape and Urban Planning 76, Elsevier Pub., 2006, pp.45-66.

Taylor, James, Cecelia Paine, and John Fitz Gibbon, From Greenbelt to Greenway; four Canadian Case Studies, Landscape and Urban Planning 33, Elsevier Pub., 1995, pp.47-64.

The Greenway Collaborative, Inc., Red Cedar Greenway Master Plan, Michigan State University and City of East Lansing, Final Draft, May 2002.

The Government of the Republic of Korea (TGRK), Urban Planning Act, 2002 (in Korean).

Tom Turner, Greenway Planning, Design and Management, http://www.lih.gre.ac.uk/plan/greenways.htm/Greenway Planning, 2002.

Yang, Suk-Woo et al., A Study on the Planning System for Urban Greenway Networking, Journal of the Architectural Institute of Korea(planning and design), Vol.23, No.10, Architectural Institute of Korea, June 2007, pp.209-220 (in Korean).

Citizen Initiative for Greenway Construction (CIGC) (http://www.greenways.or.kr)

Gwangju City Government (http://www.gjcity.net)

Gwangju Federation for Environment Movement (http://kwangju.kfem.or.kr)

Rails-to-Trails (http://www.railstotrails.org)

The City of Toronto (http://www.toronto.ca)

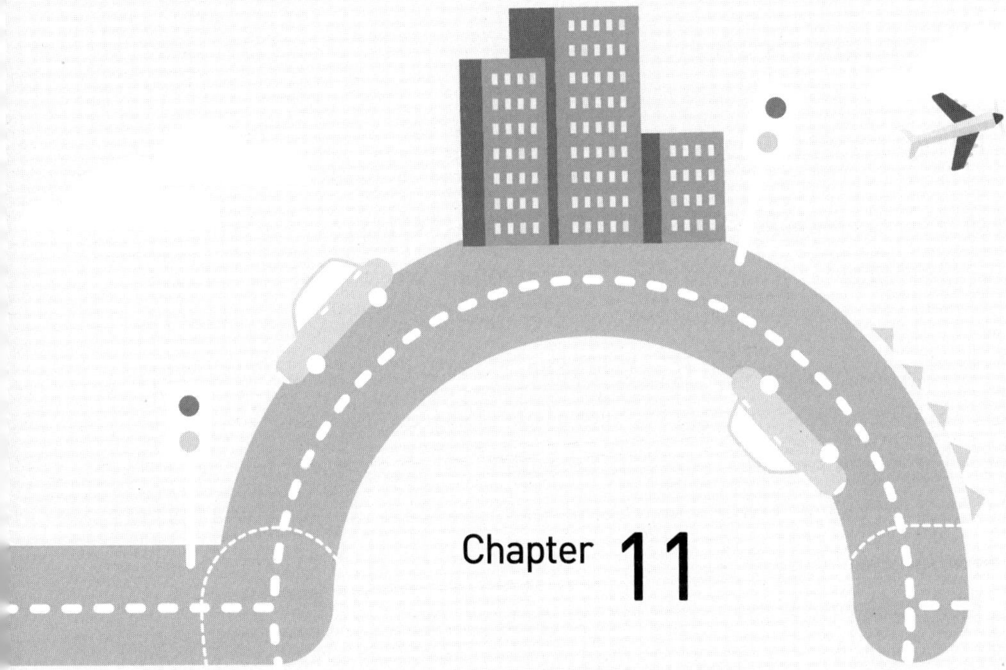

Chapter 11

High Speed Rail and Transport Policy

1. Introduction to High Speed Rail

1.1. Definition of High Speed Rail (HSR)[1]

HSR can be defined as trains operating at very high speed thanks to technical specificities from both tracks and rolling stock. HSR, according to this general acceptance, can be defined as a maximum speed of at least 250 km/h in Korea. Nevertheless, this definition doesn't allow for understanding of major differences in High Speed (HS) services related to variable commercial speed, or differences in operating with conventional rail.

Commercial speed on HS lines can be far lower than the maximum speed that can be reached on it according to several factors, such as conventional rail segments, safety reasons and the number of served stations. According to these elements, the functions and performances of HS lines can be completely different. A comprehensive definition was developed with the following requirements: HS means operations with maximum speed over 250 km/h; special trains that differ from conventional rolling stock by an increased power/weight ratio and several characteristics, such as aerodynamics, reliability, safety, etc.; special dedicated lines that enable operation of up to 220 km/h; upgraded conventional lines that enable operation of up to 220 km/h; a special in cab signalizing system, since traditional line side signals are inefficient over 200 km/h.

1.2. Benefits of HSR[2]

It is widely accepted that high-speed rail confers many benefits. HSR in Korea is nearly four times more efficient than highway travel. Comparing the three principal alternatives for increasing transit capacity on the Seoul-Busan corridor, HSR was deemed best in terms of transport efficiency. HSR

---

[1] Thomas Baron(2009), pp.11-12.

[2] Shin(2005), pp.6-7.

usually connects one city center to another, providing more convenience for travelers compared to airports, which are normally located on the outskirts of a city.

Table 11.1. Comparison of Alternatives for Capacity Increase on Kyungbu HSR

Items	HSR (A)	Highway (B)	Double-track rail (C)	A/B	A/C
Construction costs (bil. Won)	0.382	262	250	1.46	1.53
Transport capacity (persons/day)	520,000	25	27.5	2.08	1.89
Travel time	1h 56min.	5h 20min	3h 50min	△27	△1.98
Transport efficiency	3.93	1	1.60	-	-

Note: Transport efficiency = transport capacity / travel time x construction cost
Source: Shin(2005, 7)

The system, which relies on electricity, consumes less energy than the other alternatives (only 19% of the energy used by cars and aircraft). It also requires less land (29% of the land needed for a four-lane highway). It emits fewer pollutants like CO_2 and SO_2 (16%–18% of that from cars and aircraft). Moreover, HSR has an excellent record for safety and punctuality. It provides comfortable rides with less fatigue for passengers compared to other transportation modes. Finally, the introduction of HSR into a country facilitates the development of related technologies and industries, such as civil engineering, vehicle manufacture, industrial materials, and design. According to a survey, Japanese travelers take the Shinkansen mainly because of high speed, comfort, and punctuality of operation.

1.3. Issues and Effects of KTX Operation

Issues of KTX Stopping City

The introduction of high-speed services had the strongest effect on long-distance relations with a significant portion of the journey on the high-speed line, like Seoul-Busan. KTX service will have diversified effects on the city in which KTX stops in terms of transport demand, urban development, tourism and economics, etc. The city government needs to take proactive measures to deal with the issues faced by a KTX stopping city. The issues includes KTX station area development, establishment of regional transport network, and maximization of regional development effects.

Development projects related to the existing station area should reflect regional characteristics, and should be delivered to enhance the competitiveness of the inner city. Station area development should contribute to the growth of regional economics in the urban center. Members of the community need to participate in the station area development planning. It is important to build an integrated regional traffic network in the city. The interior traffic circulation system of the railroad station needs to be improved, and the KTX station should be connected with the region around the city by train and bus service. It is good to have pedestrian walkways in the KTX station area of influence.

A public transit center as well as park-and-ride facility should be established in the station's area. KTX service will contribute to the growth of the KTX stopping city, and will result in the influx of rural population to the city. An isolated region without KTX service can experience regional economic decline and population outflow. It is really important to develop the regional cities. KTX will thus trigger an exodus from areas not covered by its service and quickly trigger population booms in areas around major rail stations.

Table 11.2. Issues Faced in the City around KTX Station

Issues	Detailed information
Station area development	■ Existing station - reflect regional characteristics, enhance the competitiveness of the inner city ■ Contribute to the growth of urban center ■ Citizen participation in the development planning
Regional transport networks	■ Improve the circulation system of the station ■ Connected with region around city by transit service ■ Pedestrian walkway in the station, complex public transit center, park-and-ride facility
Regional development effects	■ City around KTX station - the influx of rural population to the city, catalyst for urban development ■ KTX unserviced area - decline in urban growth potential, local population drain, regional development concept

Source: Jeong(2005)

KTX Impacts on the National Territory

The operation of the KTX system will have various impacts on the national territory. Thanks to the development of KTX, one can now travel from one side of the country to the other within the same day. KTX will cause falling domestic airline and express bus passengers in the transport sector. There will be heavy traffic in the KTX station area of influence. It will have positive effects on regional industries and reduce logistic costs, in terms of regional economy. It will result in dispersing the population of the capital area gradually and activating the station area and urban development projects, with regard to regional development. The KTX will open new markets for the KTX serviced city and strengthen its tourism industry. It can bring about the expansion of academic events and performance in the city. On the other hand, residents of the local city can move into the Seoul metropolitan area, with the expansion of the capital area being a big socio-economic problem in Korea. It is called the "KTX straw effect".

Table 11.3. Impacts of KTX service on National Territory

Field	Detailed impacts	Type of effect	Period
Transport system	▪ Travel demand increase in KTX station	Good	S
	▪ Reduction in airline and express bus demand	Bad	S, L
	▪ Severe traffic congestion in station area	Bad	S, M
	▪ Regional transport improvement measures	Good	S, M
Regional economy	▪ Reduction in logistics cost, regional industry restructuring	Good	S, L
	▪ Development of regional special industry, attracting companies	Good	M
	▪ Sales growth in business district around station	Good	S, M
Regional development	▪ Capital area's population dispersion, local population inflow	Good	M, L
	▪ Activated station area and urban improvement projects	Good	M, L
	▪ High land use, station area development	Good	M, L
	▪ Expansion of the KTX serviced urban area	Good	M
Culture tour	▪ Increasing tourism in KTX serviced city	Good	S, M
	▪ Expanding academic events and performance	Good	S, M
	▪ Activation of culture and tourism business	Good	S, M
	▪ Increasing city tours in metropolitan area	Good	S
Negative impacts	▪ Outflow of local economy	Bad	S, M
	▪ Expansion of the capital area	Bad	S
	▪ Reduction in local branches of major companies	Bad	M, L

Source: Jeong(2005); Gwak, et al(2005); Chung(2010)
Notes: S means short-term; M midterm; L long-term

2. Development and Operation of HSR

2.1. Development of HSR Worldwide

Development of HSR[3]

Fast passenger trains have been around for many decades. They originally ran on conventional railway lines, limited by sharing track with slower passenger and freight trains. The modern era of fast train travel opened in the 1950s in Japan. The conventional, mixed use (passenger and freight) line between Tokyo and Osaka had become very congested. Japan built a new 515 kilometer-long, passenger-dedicated, electrified high-speed line on a new alignment. Construction began in 1959, so that the service could open in time for the 1964 Tokyo Olympics.

This Tokaido Shinkansen, or bullet-train, delivered a quantum improvement in travel time within a year through a maximum speed of 210 km/h and an average commercial speed of over 160 km/h. Significantly, it also offered a much higher frequency of service. The number of express trains between Tokyo and Osaka was increased on opening, from four each day to an hourly service. By 1970, with substantial traffic growth, the frequency had tripled to three trains per hour. This first route was a financial success. By 1967 revenue exceeded operating costs, including interest and depreciation.

The success of the Tokaido Shinkansen led to the adoption by the Japanese Government of the Shinkansen Development Law in 1970. The law set out a blueprint for a high-speed network of some 7,000 route-kms. The system was steadily extended, to Fukuoka in Kyushu (1975); to Morioka in northern Honshu (1982); and to Niigata on the west coast (1982). Subsequent extensions have seen the network reach its current size of nearly 2,200 route-kms. Speed has also increased: the Tokyo-Osaka service now has a commercial speed of 200 km/h (typically with four intermediate stops).

---

3 Paul Amos et al.(2010), pp.3-5.

These developments in Japan were watched closely in Europe. The next passenger services capable of operating at over 200 km/h were British Railways (BR) HS125 diesel-electric multiple unit trains that commenced operations on the mixed-use Great Western line from London to Bristol in 1976.

Across the Channel, the French National Railway (SNCF) was faced with the need to provide extra capacity on the busy main line between Paris and Lyon. But SNCF also wanted to be able to offer faster services and decided to adopt the Shinkansen approach of building a dedicated line on a new alignment. In 1981, the TGV Sud-Est opened between Paris and Lyon and was followed, between 1985 and 2007, by other lines: to south-western France (TGV Atlantique); to southern France and Switzerland (TGV Méditerranée and TGV Rhône-Alpes); to northern France, Belgium and Holland (TGV Nord); and to eastern France and Germany (TGV Est). France now has a high-speed network of nearly 1,700 route-kms.

Other European countries have since followed suit. New lines have opened in Spain, Germany, Italy, Belgium, the Netherlands and the United Kingdom. In 2010, the total length of dedicated high speed lines in Europe was 5,500 kms. With the benefit of both Japanese and European experience high speed lines have also been built in Taiwan, China (the THSR system) and in Korea. The THSR, between Taipei and Kaohsiung, opened in 2007. The total global length of high-speed line was estimated at nearly 12,500 km in 2010. In recent years, mainland China has taken its place on the international stage of high-speed rail, and is already dominant in terms of system length and utilization.

Figure 11.1. Route-km of High-speed Line by Country and Year

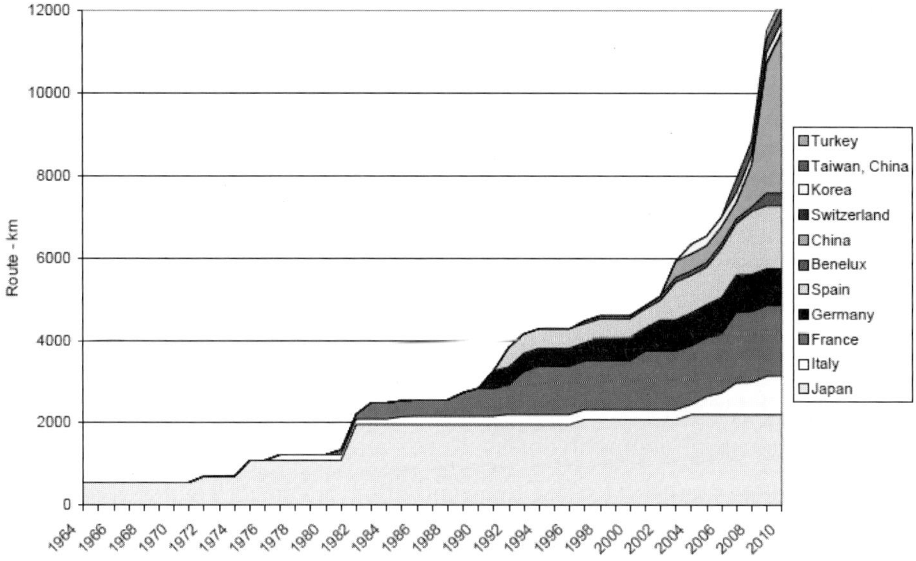

Source: Paul Amos et al.(2010), p.4.

Objectives of HSR[4]

The construction of high speed rail networks have complied with 4 main objectives[5]: first, it overcomes the limited capacity of conventional railways that were facing a growing demand. This is particularly true for the Shinkansen network but also the KTX network in South Korea and Taiwan. Second, it stimulates railway companies that were losing influence on transport markets or that had to prepare for concurrence. This is the case for the introduction of the TGV in France and the German Inter City Express (ICE). Third, it increases speeds on conventional lines whereas huge investments on infrastructure and use of "classic" material would not have allowed this to happen. This reason can mainly be advanced for the Inter City Express (ICE) German network. Fourth, it improves accessibility to

4 Paul Amos et al.(2010), pp.3-5.

5 Thomas Baron(2009), pp.12-13.

remote regions. This is the case for the Sanyo Shinkansen between Osaka and Fukuoka, but also for the AVE line Madrid Seville in Spain.

2.2. Background and Necessity of HSR in Korea

Background of HSR[6]

The background to the HSR initiative in Korea goes back to the 1980s when the country was suffering from serious road congestion caused by a surge in car ownership (17% average annual increase). Significant congestion in the Gyungbu(Seoul-Busan) corridor led to increased logistics costs and weakened industrial competitiveness. Korea already has a higher proportion of logistics costs to GDP (13.3%) than any other advanced countries, creating an urgent necessity to relieve the bottleneck on the Gyungbu rail corridor, which contains about 73.0% of the national population and carried 66% of the 7.3 million people riding railways in Korea each day in 1995. The government took the important decision to construct the Gyungbu HSR in May 1989, estimating that passenger and container freight traffic on the new line would increase 1.7 and 3.8 fold by 2011 compared to 1995.

In comparison to a 4-lane highway or conventional double-track railway, a HSR is most efficient for meeting the needs of long-distance, mass transport. In terms of transport efficiency, such as operation hours, construction costs, and line capacity, an HSR is two or three times better than a highway or conventional double-track railway.

Necessity of HSR

The HSR project was launched by constructing a test track between Cheonan and Daejeon in 1992. However, the economic crisis of 1997 forced the government to change its plan by constructing a new line between Seoul

[6] Kim(2005), pp.8-9.

and Busan using electrified and upgraded conventional lines between Daegu and Busan by 2004. This was to be followed by construction of an entirely new line between Daegu, Gyeongju, and Busan by 2010. Instead of building new tracks along the entire line, the amended plan adopted phased construction to make best use of the existing Daegu-Gyeongju-Busan tracks. To maximize the impact of the Gyeongbu HS line construction, the government decided to electrify the main Honam Line (Daejeon-Mokpo) with the two Gyeongbu and Honam main lines to be linked as a new system offering HS Korean Train Express(KTX) services.

The government looked at many possible funding sources for the project based upon its potential benefits and prevailing, financial circumstances. The total cost of the Gyeongbu HS lines was estimated to be about 18,4258 trillion Won with some 12,737 trillion Won needed for the first phase. Funds were raised from the government budget (45% and including loans of 10% of the total) and from the budget of the Korea Rail Network Authority (KR) (credits 29%; foreign loans 24%; private funding 2%). The difficult economic circumstances in Korea at that time required a number of measures to acquire foreign loans. Funding for electrification of the Honam line was provided entirely by the government.

To hold overall costs to reasonable levels, contracts were made with overseas contractors to provide only core rail systems, such as rolling stock, catenaries, train-controll system (ATC, CTC, SCADA). Other non-core systems such as civil engineering works, power supplies, tracks, and information systems were handled by Korean companies.

Thirty-four of the 46 TGV-style KTX high-speed train sets were built domestically in Korea based on a technology transfer from SNCF while the other 12 were built in France. Each of the 388-trains has 20 carriages, including two motorcars, two powered passenger carriages, and 16 passenger cars. Each train has 935 seats, including 127 in first class and 808 in economy. Operation safety is assured by an onboard computer system (OBCS), fire-detector system, and automatic sensors to detect any malfunctions.

The KTX stations have been designed as futuristic multi-purpose hubs to cater to customers' needs. KTX trains normally stop at Seoul, Gwangmyeong, Cheonan-Asan, Daejeon, Daegu, and Busan on the Gyeongbu Line, and also stop at Yongsan, Seodaejeon, Iksan, and Gwangju-Songjeong and Mokpo on the Honam Line. Seoul station is a five-story state-of-the-art building, with two floor underground; Yongsan Satation is eight-stories high with four floors underground. The other stations range in height from two to five stories, each with different numbers of underground floors. All stations are complete and equipped with fully automated systems using cutting-edge architectural technologies. Reservations, ticket purchases, and ticket issuing are fully automated. Each station has a travel information centre, providing comprehensive information on all transportation modes.

Figure 11.2. Korea Railroad Routes

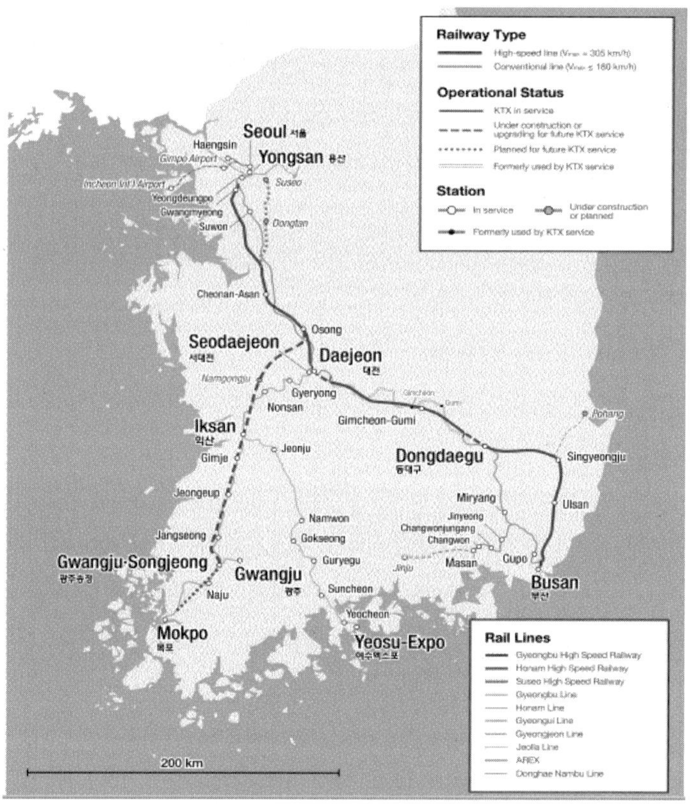

2.3. Operation of HSR in Korea[7]

There are three organizations related to Korea HSR (KTX). The MOLIT establishes policies and investment plans of railways. KR is responsible for building new lines and improving existing rail network. While Korail performs operation of railroad services, the private sector handles rolling stock design, manufacturing and construction.[8]

Gyeongbu high speed rail (HSR) started the commercial operation of the 1st phase in 2004, followed in 2010 by the 2nd phase, which runs 423.8 km at top speeds of 300 km/h from Seoul to Busan. Currently relevant construction is still under way in Daejeon and Daegu sections, and will be fully completed by 2014. The new HSR line is 406 km long and the section of 17.8 km from Seoul to Siheung is a conventional line. Travel time from Seoul to Busan without a stop takes 2 hours and 13 min. The fare is 43.20-46.30 USD and weekend fares are a bit higher than those of weekdays. The 1st phase (Osong-Gwangju, 182.3 km) was completed in 2014, and the 2nd phase (Gwangju-Mokpo, 48.7 km) will be completed in 2020. At present HSR in the Honam region runs on the existing tracks. The new line for Honam HSR opened on April 2, 2015.

A new corporation to be established under KORAIL will operate the new high-speed KTX routes expected to open in 2016. The line, which will connect to the nation's southern region, will depart from Suseo, southeastern Seoul. The existing KTX service starts from Yongsan, central Seoul. The new KTX section is expected to make access easier for people in eastern Seoul and Gyeonggi Province.

Even when the PPP (Purchasing Power Parity) is considered, HSR fare in Korea is relatively low compared to other countries. In case of other modes of transport, it is less expensive than that of airlines, but more expensive than those of express buses or private cars with more than two occupants.

---

[7] Lee et.al(2012), pp.38-41.

[8] Kim(2005), pp.9-10.

Table 11.4. Comparison of KTX Fares with Other Modes

Traffic mode / Week	Monday-Thursday	Friday-Sunday
Air	100%	100%
Low-cost air	87%	91%
HSR	65%	62%
Saemaeul	49%	46%
Express bus	41%	37%
Mugunghwa	33%	31%

Source: KOTI(2012)

Note: The above percentage refers to the comparison ratio of KTX fares with other traffic modes in Korea.

Figure 11.3. New KTX Routes in Korea

2.4. Impacts of Existing KTX Services[9]

The advantage of KTX is a positive effect to the nation's economy, but its role of connecting regions into "one-day zones" and contributing to local unity are equally important. The introduction of KTX in 2004 has resulted in a big drop in the number of passengers travelling with the other types of train. The KTX passenger numbers are on the rise continuously, but the overall rail passenger numbers show signs of only a slight increase.

Figure 11.4. Trends of Railway Passenger (Inter-regional)

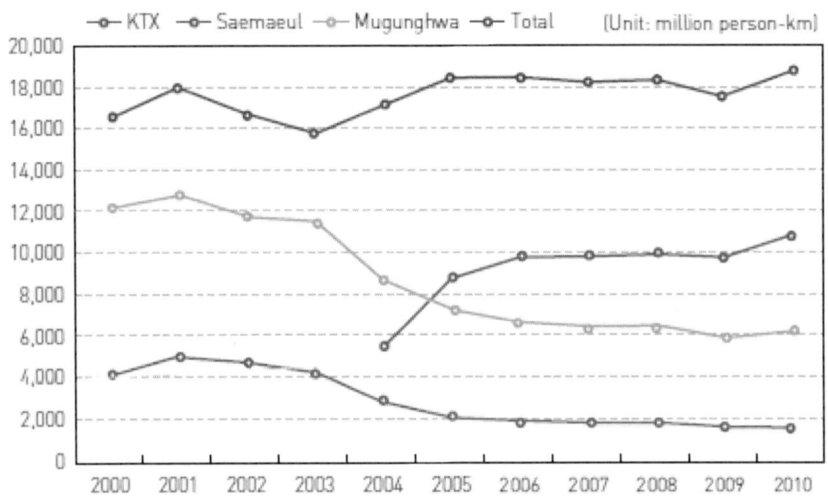

Source: Lee et.al(2012)

Since the opening of HSR in 2004, passenger number have showed a rising trend. Gyeongbu HSR had 107,000 passengerss a day in 2011, growing at an 8.5% annual rate. Honam HSR had 20,000 passengers a day in 2011, showing an average annual growth rate of 8.2%.

---

[9] Lee et.al(2012), pp.58-60.

Table 11.5. Changes in Ridership of KTX

(Unit: Thousand person/day)

Route	2004	2005	2006	2007	2008	2009	2010	2011
G-Line	60.7	73.6	82.7	84.9	86.2	85.0	94.5	107.2 (8.5%)
H-Line	11.6	15.1	17.3	17.3	17.7	17.7	18.8	20.1 (8.2%)
Total	72.3	88.7	100.0	102.2	103.9	102.7	113.1	136.7 (8.4%)

Source: Korail(each year)

Note: (%) indicates average annual growth rate during the 2004-2011 period.

HSR Gyeongbu line has shortened travel time among regions and improved railway mobility. For example, travel time between Seoul-Busan (424 km) has decreased from 250 min. to 138 min., and 118 min. Railway modal share between Seoul-Busan increased from 29.3% in 2003 to 66.0% in 2011, while airplane modal share decreased from 49.1% in 2003 to 19.1% in 2011, and express bus modal share decreased from 7.6% in 2003 to 6.7% in 2011. The opening of the HSR Gyeongbu shrunk greatly an area where travel time previously took more than three hours.

For the Seoul-Daegu(292 km) section, railway modal share jumped from 26.5% in 2003 to 59.7% in 2011, while modal shares of passenger cars and express bus dropped from 41.1% in 2003 to 27.0% in 2011, and from 13.7% in 2003 to 9.1% in 2011, respectively. The successful development of KTX has reduced demand for domestic air travel. There was a huge drop in air travel demand between Seoul and Daegu due to the HSR opening, which in the end brought about the cancellation of the relevant route in 2011.

Figure 11.5. Trends of Railway Passenger (Inter-regional)

	2003	2011	feature
Seoul - Daegu	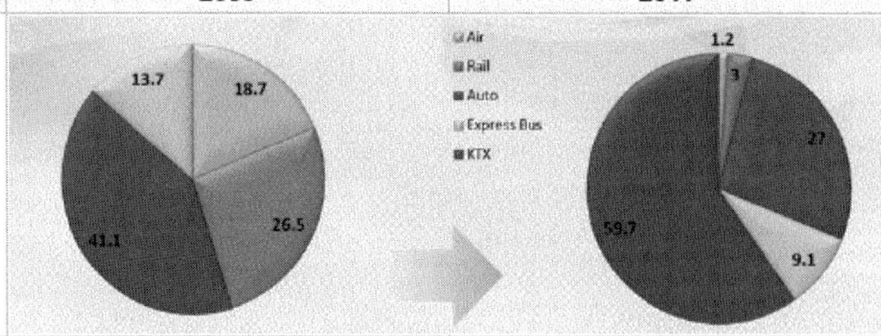		- Airplane: 19%→0% - KTX: 59.7%
Seoul - Busan	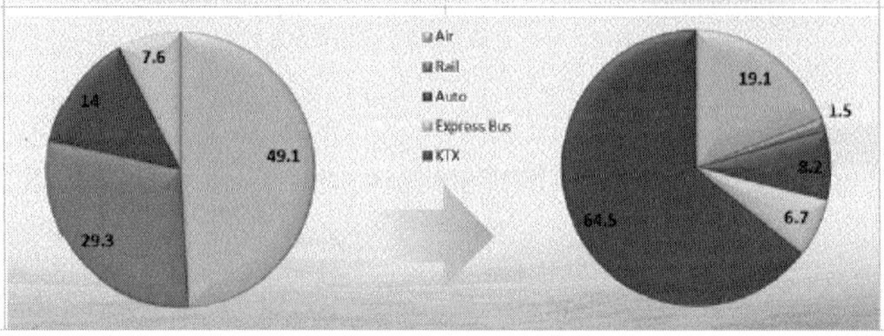		- Airplane: 49→19% - KTX: 64.5%

Data: Jinyoung Park(2013)

The benefit/cost ratios of HSR were 1.39 (Gyeongbu line) and 0.82 (Honam line), respectively, and those of the general services were 0.69 (Gyeongbu line) and 0.42 (Honam line), respectively, which suggested HSR had much better profitability compared to the conventional lines. HSR enabled long distance commuting due to shorter travel time, and brought about changes in various aspects such as business meetings, cultural activities, and medical services.

The construction of the HSR is expected to make a contribution to energy saving of 247 million USD a year, and environmental cost saving of 8 million USD a year due to CO_2 emission reduction. Also, it could increase the number of tourists, promote regional development through the improvement of stations' sphere of influence, and raise land prices around stations.

The opening of HSR increased the number of passengers by 14% between 2003 and 2009, and its positive effects raised investment in railways, which, in turn, strengthened the competitiveness of the railway industry. Also, railway technology has been improved in rolling stocks, signal/communication, etc, and KTX-II, domestically developed, has run on the tracks since 2010. At present a next generation HSR, High speed Electric Multiple Unit - 430 km/h experiment (HEMU-430X), is being developed.

Figure 11.6. Whole KTX Route Map

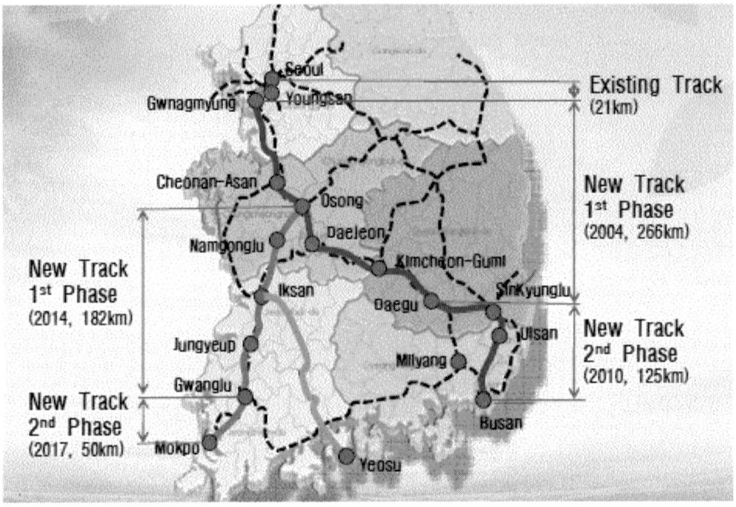

Source: KOTI(2012)

Figure 11.7. Comparison of Travel Time from Seoul Before and After Gyeongbu HSR

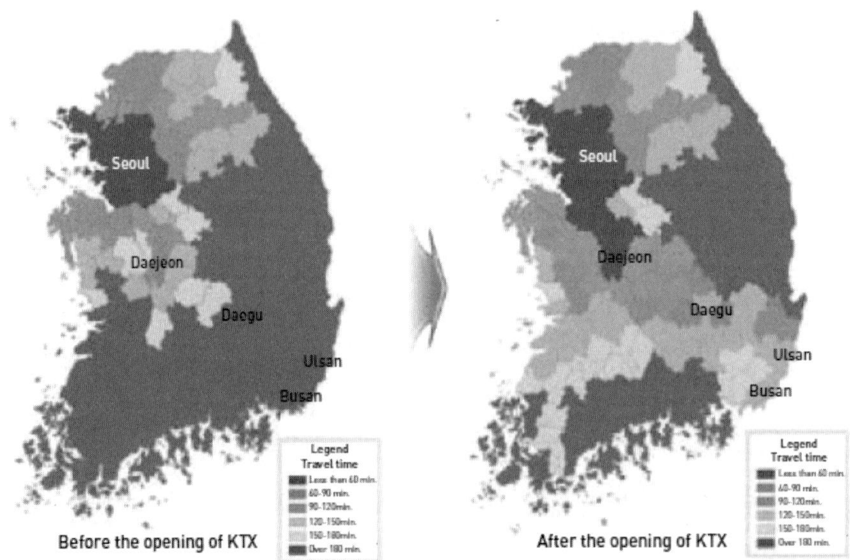

3. Construction of and Prospects for Honam HSR

3.1. National Railroad Policy for KTX Network[10]

The national rail network plan (2011-2020) includes HSR construction, speed upgrade, etc, seeking the improvement of inter-regional accessibility through added investment in railway infrastructure. In detail, the entire area where travel time is within 1 hour 30 minutes will be expanded to include population from 60% to 83%, and service area from 30% to 76%, and the area where travel time is within two hours will expand to include population from 74% to 96%, and service area from 55% to 90%.

According to the plan, road modal share will decrease from 81.4% in 2008 to 69.3% in 2020 and railway modal share will increase from 15.9% in 2008 to 27.3% in 2020. The length of HSR also will be extended from 406 km in 2010 to 743 km by 2020 including 45 km of Daejeon and Daegu sections, 231 km of Honam line, and 61 km of Suseo-Pyeongtaek line. HSR service will be extended into competitive sections. Conventional lines' speed improvement from 150 km/h to 230-250 km/h will be made in order to extend HSR services to broader areas and to strengthen the competitiveness of railways.

The government plans to build 40 intermodal transport centers by 2020 and to establish an efficient intermodal freight system. Major train stations will be transformed into the centers. Recently the government has been preparing strategies to nurture KTX stations as the center of regional economic development, in a way that prevents the 'straw effect' and promotes balanced regional development among local cities. The main work is to develop an economic model fit into relevant cities in connection with the development strategies for 5+2 mega economic zones. To this end the compact development and the establishment of a hub and spoke network are being carried out around KTX stations.

---

[10] MLTMA(2010), pp.109-114; MLTMA(2011), pp.55-67.

Figure 11.8. Master Plan for HSR Network

HSR Network Plan KTX Economic Zone Plan

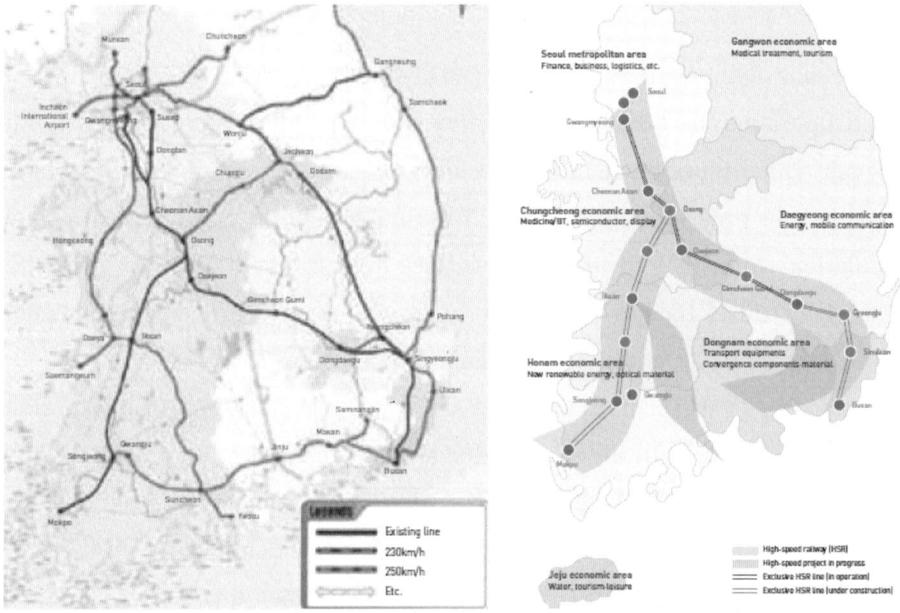

Source: MLTMA(2010, 2011)

3.2. Evolution of Honam HSR Project[11]

The most progressed plans for a second high-speed line were for the Honam High Speed Railway, a connection from Seoul to Mokpo in southwest Korea, accelerating the service on the existing route that was eventually established in KTX's first phase. The Honam High Speed Railway (Honam HSR) is a high-speed railway under-construction between Osong (on the existing Gyeongbu High Speed Railway) and Mokpo in Korea. The line will become part of Korail's Korea Train Express (KTX) system, accelerating Seoul-Mokpo and Seoul-Gwangju KTX high-speed services which presently use the existing conventional Honam Line.

11 http://en.wikipedia.org/wiki/Honam_High_Speed_Railway

The first feasibility study in 2003 came to the conclusion that the construction of a full line was not justified by demand, and proposed a two-stage construction. The first stage, to be realized by 2015, would involve a connection from a second Seoul terminus in the southeast part of the city to the Gyeongbu HSR, and a branch from the Gyeongbu HSR to Iksan, paralleling the existing Honam Line. The second phase would include the separate tracks on the section paralleling the Gyeongbu Line, and the extension from Iksan to Gwangju and Mokpo, paralleling the existing Honam Line. The cost of the entire project was estimated at 10,378.6 billion won. In 2005, the government decided to complete the project to Gwangju by 2015.

In plans made official in August 2006 in spite of a benefit-cost ratio below 1, the budget for the 182.75 km first stage (from the new Osong Station on the Gyeongbu HSR to Gwangju) was set at 8,569.5 billion won. The second stage, the 48.74 km remaining to Mokpo, will be finished by 2020 with a budget of 2,002.2 billion won. The altogether 230.99 km, 10,571.7 billion won project would enable Seoul-Mokpo travel times of 1 hour 46 minutes. The Osong-Iksan section of the first phase is intended for use as high-speed test track for rolling stock development, to be fitted with special catenary and instrumented track. The project is financed to 50% by direct government funds and 50% loans.

By December 2009, construction began on three sub-sections of the 182 km line from Osong to Gwangju, which shall enable Seoul-Gwangju travel times of 1 hour 33 minutes. The total project costs were estimated at 11.3 billion won (US$ 9.8 billion). The estimate for the entire line stood at 12,101.7 billion won. The entire line from Osong to Mokpo will include a total of 111.7 km of viaducts (48.35%) and 49.12 km of tunnels (21.26%).

Table 11.6. Introduction to Honam HSR

Item	Detailed contents
Route	First stage: Osong ↔ Gwangju, 182.3 km Second stage: Gwangju ↔ Mokpo, 48.6 km, Total: 230.9 km
Construction cost(won)	First stage: 8,69.5 billion, Second stage: 2,002.2 billion Total: 10,378.8 billion, Cost allocation: 50% by direct government funds, 50% loans.
Railroad station	Osong, Gongju, Iksan, Jeongeup, Gwangju-Songjeong, Mokpo
Travel time	Seoul-Gwangju section: 1 hour 30 minutes Seoul-Mokpo section: 1 hour 47 minutes
Completion year	First stage: 2014, Second stage: 2017(not fixed)
Daily travelling passenger	2015: 446 million persons per day 2017: 567 million persons per day

Source: Ministry of Land, Infrastructure and Transport http;//www.molit.go.kr

3.3. New KTX Service in Honam HSR

The KTX has become a competitive and reliable mode of medium-to-long distance intercity transportation. Investment in the KTX constituted a major change in government policy from the previous focus on road infrastructure, and has helped revitalize the railway industry and its competitiveness. The Honam KTX service launched on April, 2015. Top speed for KTX trains for regular service is currently 305 km/h, though the infrastructure is designed for 350 km/h. The domestically developed KTX Sancheon will be operated by Korail. The KTX business hours are six a.m. to ten p.m. Monday through Sunday. In 2015, the new KTX service with a route length of 304 km between Yongsan in Seoul and Gwangju will cut minimum travel time from 2 hours 49 minutes to 1 hour 33 minutes. In 2020, the minimum Seoul-Mokpo travel time will reduce to 1 hour 46 minutes over a travel distance of 352.7 km.

KTX offers two classes: First Class and Standard Class. Tickets also specify whether a seat is forward-facing or backward-facing according to the direction of travel. KTX fares are designed to be about halfway between those for conventional trains and airline tickets. The new KTX train runs at an interval of 22 minutes in the Yongsan-Gwangju section of the Honam Line in 2015. The KTX train frequency for the Yongsan-Gwangju section is 43 times per day in 2015, and 44 times per day in 2020 for the Yongsan-Mokpo section.

Table 11.7. KTX Services in Honam HSR

Item	Detailed contents
Business hours	Six a.m. to ten p.m. (16 hours per day)
Speed	Regular speed: 300 km/h, design speed: 350 km/h
Travel time	Yongsan-Gwangju: 1 hour 33 minutes Yongsan-Mokpo: 1 hour 46 minutes
Daily interval	Yongsan-Gwangju: 22 minutes 50 seconds Yongsan-Mokpo: 22 minutes
Daily frequency	Yongsan-Gwangju: 43 times, Yongsan-Mokpo: 44 times
Input train	Total: 360 cars (36 trains), 1 train-ten cars

Source: KRNA(2011), http://www.kr.or.kr

3.4. Travel Demand Forecasting of GS (Gwangju-Songjeong) KTX Station

The total amount of daily traffic volumes in GS KTX station is estimated at 13,370 trips in 2016, and 14,105 trips in 2020. Total traffic volume is estimated to be between 13,370 to 14,444 passengers during the 2016-2025 period. In 2025, the daily passenger traffic volume in the GS station is expected to be 14,444 passengers, including 13,586 passengers and 144 full-time employees.

The total volume of daily vehicular traffic in GS KTX station is estimated at 3,292 vehicles in 2016, and 2,854 in 2025. The traffic of vehicles during the 17:00-18:00 rush hour is forecasted to be 278 vehicles in 2016, and 241 vehicles in 2025, respectively. It is necessary to look at total traffic volume bound for Honam Area by travel purpose. The percentage share by travel purpose is as follows: going to work and school 6.4%; tour and vacation 12.9%; business trip 29.1%; family and relatives visitation 47.9%.

Table 11.8. Forecast of Daily Passenger Traffic in GS Station

Year	Passenger	Full-time employee	Total passenger traffics
2016	13,586	144	13,730
2020	13,961	144	14,105
2025	14,300	144	14,444

Source: KRNK(2008)

As of 2016, about 37.6% of the business trip total is expected to divert to KTX between Seoul and Gwangju, and about 49.5% between Seoul and Mokpo. In case of Gwangju, yearly diverted passenger traffic is estimated at 2,475,488 passengers in 2016, and daily diverted traffic is 6,782 persons in 2016. In particular, about 53.5% of the Seoul-Gwangju air passengers are expected to change to KTX for travelling in 2016. The yearly diverted air passengers are estimated at 284,515 persons, or 777 persons per day in 2016.

Table 11.9. Forecast of Daily Vehicular Traffic in GS Station

Division		Private car	Taxi	Bus	Total
Vehicular traffic in rush hour	2016	117	148	13	278
	2020	111	131	11	253
	2025	108	120	13	241
Daily total vehicular traffic	2016	1,384	1,755	153	3,292
	2020	1,319	1,549	142	3,010
	2025	1,282	1,420	152	2,854

Source: KRNK(2008)

4. Honam KTX and Urban Transport Policy

4.1. Construction of the GS Transit Center

Before the Gwangju-Songjeong Station (GS) Transit Center is built, there are serious vehicular circulation issues. The location is a suburban area subject to heavy traffic congestion from private cars, cyclists, taxis, and buses. Access to the GS station is not good throughout the city. In July 2014, an agreement was reached between the Gwangju Metropolitan Government and the developers. The developer of the project was the Seohee Construction Consortium, which includes Seohee Construction Co. (60%), Kyo Securities Co. (30%) and KT (10%). The transit center cost almost 230 billion won and will take nearly three years to finish from when the construction begins in 2014. It is being built on a 22,000 m^2 piece of land, providing eleven floors above ground and a gross floor area of 122,000 m^2.

The future transit center will have the station building, transfer facilities (bus terminal, parking lot) and supporting facilities equipped with culture, tourism, business, hotel, and commerce and logistics facilities. The center is a future transit center complex, under construction, which is located in the outskirts of the city. It should serve as a major connection terminal connecting all modes of bus, urban metro, and regional railway, and taxi as a transport interchange. The center will become a new landmark and hub, using the functional linkages among transportation, logistics, tourism and culture in the Honam Area. Additionally, Korea Rail Network Authority (KRNA) completed the GS station building in accordance with the 2015 opening of the Honam HSR. The GS project will provide 19,000 job for local workers yearly, and will be a boon to help the station area development gain momentum.

Table 11.10. Outline of the GS Transit Center

Item	Detailed contents
Location	Songjeong-Dong, Gwangsan District, Gwangju
Developer	Seohee Construction Consortium: Seohee Construction Co.(60%), Kyo Securities Co.(30%), KT(10%)
Area(m^2)	A 22,000 m^2 piece of land, A gross floor area of 122,000 m^2
Period	Begin in 2014, Complete in 2017, Construction cost: 230 billion won
Facilities	Station building, transfer facilities (bus terminal, parking lot) Supporting facilities equipped with culture, tourism, business, hotel, commerce and logistics facilities
Effects	19,000 job for local workers yearly, a new landmark and growth pole in Honam area
Aerial view	 

Source: Gwangju Metropolitan Government(GMC) (2010c)

4.2. Electrification and Double-track of the Gwangju-Suncheon Section in Gyeongjeon Line[12]

The Gyeongjeon Line is a major railway line serving South Gyeongsang and South Jeolla Provinces in Korea. It covers a total of 300.6 km, from Samnangjin Station in Miryang, South Gyeongsang, to Gwangju Songjeong Station in Gwangju. By the mid-2000s, alignment modifications shortened the line length to 300.6 km (186.8 mi). The line is being upgraded to an electrified and double-tracked line for 180 km/h in stages, to facilitate regional development. On September 1, 2010, the South Korean government

[12] http://en.wikipedia.org/wiki/Gyeongjeon_Line

announced a strategic plan to reduce travel times from Seoul to 95% of the country to under 2 hours by 2020. As part of the plan, the entire Gyeongjeon Line is to be further upgraded for 230 km/h. The upgraded section of Samnangjin-Masan-Jinju was implemented by a private-public partnership, and was completed in 2012.

The Jinju-Suncheon section of the line is being upgraded to an electrified and double-tracked line for 180 km/h in stages, to facilitate regional development, and its electrification is to reach Suncheon by 2014. KTX service from Seoul to Jinju was extended in 2012. The Suncheon-Gwangju section of the line is operated with a single pair of rails, and unelectrified as a winding railway line, because of cost. It reflects the regional rail investment disparity. With almost no money invested in upgrading the Gyeongjeon rail system in recent years, the quality of railroad equipment in South Jeolla has declined sharply.

It was mainly caused by backward regional development, insufficient rail transport capacity, logistics cost increase, deepening regional disparity, uneven regional development, local deprivation, and decrease in regional tourism. The rest of the Suncheon-Gwangju section should be upgraded to an electrified and double-tracked line for 180 km/h in stages, to facilitate balanced regional development, induce regional economic growth, and to decrease logistics costs. The government must implement the project to relay, double-track and electrify the Suncheon-Gwangju section quickly. This is compliant with upgrading in a new alignment under the government's 2010 plan for 2020.

4.3. Provision of Park-and-Ride Facilities (PRF)[13]

Park-and-ride facilities (PRF) provide a staging location for travelers to transfer between the auto mode and transit. They can serve a much wider

---

[13] Robert Spillar(1997), pp.9-10.

array of intermodal transfer, thereby increasing the activity at the PRF, and better integrating it with the surrounding community. Other modes supported by a PRF include: pedestrian, bicycle, paratransit, carpool, intercity bus transit, intercity rail, and other modes.

A transit center can play a vital role in both the transit and park-and-ride networks. Transit center park-and-ride lots have typically been built in higher demand locations than the typical suburban PRF. They often offer the patron a much higher degree of travel services. Although they typically require a greater investment on the part of the transit agency, they can portray a greater image of permanence on the part of the transit agency which, in turn, can generate opportunities for private investment in the center. Success of the GS PRF lies in its ability to connect the regional transport network and the selection of a site location within that network.

Hourly parked cars are estimated at 455 in 2015. The GS PRF is generally located in the right site of the station building, and will provide at least 1,000 PR spaces. Park-and-ride facilities serve the needs of commuters who live beyond practical walking distance from the railway station or bus stop which offers service to the city centre. Most facilities provide services such as passenger waiting areas, toilets, handicapped parking, and accommodation for the disabled. Transit, travel and parking information, such as leaflets, posters, parking map, and parking signs must be provided. The promotion of the PRF use has to be intensified, via a dedicated web-site, integrated into the regional traffic information centre. These are often encouraged by municipal operators to improve the attraction of using park and ride. GS KTX station needs to build a few large parking facilities at its commuter rail and metro stations near major highways and large arterial surface roads around the periphery of the city.

4.4. Establishment of Bus Terminal in the GS KTX Station

A bus terminus is a designated place where a bus or coach starts or ends its scheduled route. Termini can both start and stop at the same place, or may be in different locations for starting and finishing a route. U-Square Bus Terminal (also known as Gwangcheon Bus Terminal) is Gwangju's main terminus. From here one can take buses to the surrounding regions, or indeed almost any major town and city throughout Korea. Not just a bus terminal, U-Square houses art halls, galleries, IMAX theater, shopping malls, restaurants and a major book store. It also connects to Shinsaegae Dept Store, E-mart supermarket and nearby Keumho World Mall.

Buses from major cities throughout the country arrive and depart from Gwangju Bus Terminal, a large, fancy and recently renovated bus terminal near the geographic center of the city. The terminal building is the largest and fanciest in the country, and looks like an airport at a glance. Every taxi driver in Gwangju knows the bus terminal as "Busuh Teo-mee-nal". Seoul Gangnam to Gwangju prices are either 17,900 or 26,400 Won for the standard bus or the limousine bus respectively. Prices to other cities are comparable.

In 2015, bus passengers are estimated at 13,275 per day or 1,593 persons per hour respectively. Daily, 379 buses need to run at the station or hourly, 45 buses. The bus terminal is required for city, rural and long-distance services. For local and intercity service, bus stops are in any case desirable in order to give good access to passenger's destination, and permit cross-centre linking of services.[14] A layout is used for bus/rail interchanges, with a further aim of minimizing pedestrian conflict in access to the rail platforms. The end-on and sawtooth layout can be suitable at the GS station. All the facilities such as waiting rooms and inquiry offices are concentrated, with the front doors of buses adjoining the platform. The authority has to provide surface transportation on over 12 bus routes, including 2 express bus routes and 10 intercity bus routes. The bus terminal is being built on a 22,000 m^2 piece of land, providing two floors above ground and one underground and a gross floor area of 16,800 m^2.

[14] Peter White(1995), pp.59-60.

4.5. Opening of Direct Flights between Gwangju and Incheon Airport

Gwangju airport, especially with domestic routes only, has suffered from a drop in the number of air travelers whenever a new highway was built or the KTX bullet train expanded its railway network to nearby regions. Travelers prefer to travel by trains or wheeled vehicles since it cost less than air travel, while the travel time is catching up with that of flights. The government plans to boost the role of the railways and reduce dependence on roads and expand the KTX network so that it is possible to reach any part of the country within an hour and a half. Expansion of the KTX network will make it possible to reach any major city of the country within an hour and a half by 2020, in theory permitting workers to commute from any part of the country. About 83 % of the population will be able to travel to any part of the country within an hour and a half.

The travel time between Seoul and Gwangju will be shortened from the current two hours and 52 minutes to an hour and 11 minutes. The opening of KTX high-speed train services to connect major cities of the southwestern part of the country next year will deal a blow to airlines flying the route. Once the KTX bullet train network is completed and it connects to routes covering Jeolla Province, airlines may be faced with cutting their domestic services down to just a few routes. It is suggested that the government should create regular, direct flights between Gwangju and Incheon Int Airport, to promote regional development, and to attract more airline passengers.

4.6. KTX Expands to Incheon Airport[15]

The 20.4-kilometer section of railway, which cost 2.48 trillion won (US$ 2.15 billion), connects Seoul Train Station in the central part of the capital city with Gimpo Airport, and will effectively reduce travel time and costs

[15] Korea Times(2014.1.21.)

for travelers going to Incheon International Airport (IIA), the country's largest airport. The second phase follows the completion of the first leg of construction that connected Gimpo with IIA. That 37.6-kilometer-long railway was opened to the public in March 2007. Construction on the entire airport railway line started in January 2004 at a total cost of 4.22 trillion won.

The Airport Railroad and Gyeongui Line are connected in 2014, and passengers taking the KTX from Gwangju will have a new option in travel to Incheon International Airport. As the two lines are connected, KTX trains will be able to go directly to the airport without stopping at Seoul station. Passengers from Gwangju coming to the Seoul Station will not have to transfer to the airport train or limousine bus to get to the airport. This will reduce the travel time significantly. Once the KTX reaches to the airport, it will only take 2 hours and 9 minutes from Gwangju to the airport. Currently, it takes more than 4 to 5 hours to get to the airport from Gwangju via KTX or express bus. At the same time, Korea Rail Network Authority is working on the improvement of the train speed to 230 km/h. Meanwhile, the underground passageway connecting the Airport Railroad to Line 1 and 4 is currently under construction, and the accessibility will be enhanced once it is finished. The opening of the train service can greatly push up the number of travelers and can help the country cut back on energy use by getting people to ride on public transportation.

4.7. Upgrading of Public Transit Information System[16]

The Gwangju Metropolitan Government should upgrade the public transit information technology-based services to provide traffic information more accurately and quickly. The city government needs to merge its traffic control center and disaster response team into a new entity called the Gwangju Safety Control Center. They will share real-time digital videos and monitor traffic

---

[16] Korea Herald(2013.9.12.)

situations, disasters and public transit system at the same time. A total of 500 pieces of traffic information equipment including electronic traffic display boards, bus information guides and unmanned violation controllers will be shared with the disaster system in an emergency.

With a database with 10 years of information and the simulation technology, which the city adopted for the first time in the nation, the center will be able to accurately predict the traffic and provide the fastest route information when heavy traffic jams are expected. Gwangju will also export the city's intelligent transportation system and aid developing countries with advanced transport systems.

4.8. Reorganization of Bus Networks

A bus system has to provide the best possible service to the greatest number of people within the governing economic constraints. Bus services should be concentrated in heavy travel corridors, with the greatest service frequency and route coverage usually provided on approaches to the city centre. Representative guidelines for the bus routes are followed as routes and service, service area and route coverage, route structure, etc.

More than 80% of the residences in GMC should be within 500m of a bus stop and bus systems should serve major employment concentrations, schools and hospitals. Routes need to be fitted to major streets and land use patterns. Dispersed routing patterns are necessary in the activity centers of Gwangju because of dispersed outlying development areas or capacity limitations on the curb bus lanes. This will result in promoting the accessibility of residents in outlying areas. More than 80% of the total bus passengers can get to their destination in the city center in a single transfer, but one or two transfers will be necessary in unavoidable circumstances. Bus routes should also be direct and simple. But, irregular routes emerge due to topographic barriers or irregular street networks. Routes should be as short as possible to serve their markets, and excessively long routes should be avoided.

The bus routes reformation plan in Gwangju is designed to improve efficiency in bus services and to provide the best bus service to the greatest number of people. This planning is a short-range process that is usually done on a route-by-route basis. It is also important to establish clearly the steps to be addressed.

Publicly owned urban transport undertakings can think of charging different prices for different quality of services. Assuming that the shift of consumers between different quality of services is negligible, the availability of the range of services means that total potential consumer surplus will exceed that generated if only a single price and service package were available. The operator stands to gain as a result of this pricing strategy since costs of servicing each customer group are not drastically different.

Gwangju will have full-scale KTX service, the high speed rail to various places around the peninsula in 2015. We have to endure a quick and frequent bus ride or a relatively fast urban railway to go around Gwangju. The city government needs to create a few more pages of bus routes, primarily for the KTX GS Station. We will be on the fast track and get around to just about anywhere quickly. Many buses should be added to accommodate the GS station further. We can thus easily make our ways to the KTX for that lightening fast train ride.

A self-portrait in the newspaper

Railway reform

Time to build consensus on KTX privatization

The Lee Myung-bak administration is in discord with the ruling Grand National Party (GNP) over a plan to allow private companies to operate some KTX bullet train services from 2015. The discord showcases the absence of policy coordination between the government and the party. The public cannot but express concerns about the administration's unilateral decision-making process.

The Lee government has repeatedly made the mistake of poor communication not only with the people but also with the governing party. This has weakened the President's leadership and led to policy blunders. He had opportunities to improve his poor communication ability but regrettably failed to do so because he didn't listen to the voices of diverse interest groups.

No doubt the KTX row is not an isolated case. On Dec. 27, the Ministry of Land, Transportation and Maritime Affairs disclosed the plan to break down the state-run Korail's monopoly on the operation of high-speed trains. Before announcing this, the ministry should have held proper consultations with the GNP to iron out differences and reach an agreement. However, it did not undertake the due process, inviting opposition.

It is nonsense to push important policies such as the KTX privatization without discussion with party members. How can bureaucrats persuade opponents to accept the government's position? The situation is getting worse as both Korail management and its trade union are strongly against private firms' participation. Last week, the GNP's crisis management committee made clear its objections, adding fuel to the dispute and firming up the opponents' ground.

The poor policy-setting process might hinder the administration's efforts to initiate a much-needed railroad reform. Korail has maintained its monopoly in the railway sector for more than a century. It is tenaciously resisting privatization to keep its vested interests. However, it should realize that reform of the rail system can no longer be delayed because it is mired in huge debts and snowballing losses. It also lacks efficiency, transparency and accountability. It has long been blamed for frequent breakdowns, operational delays, and poor services.

Let's take a closer look at Korail's dire financial condition. Its debt is estimated at 9.7 trillion won. It is unable to make interest payments without government grants and suffers an annual loss of 500 billion won. Conventional rail lines have plunged deeper into trouble. Only KTX is making a profit. The state should not pour more money into the bottomless pit. Korail is deemed to fail unless it undergoes a drastic reform.

Of course, there are worries about privatization. Railroads are a key public infrastructure. It is not right to measure a railway operation only in terms of profitability. But it's urgent to boost its efficiency, provide better services and improve its financial health. So the government and the ruling party must work together with Korail to draw up a package to save the beleaguered railway system.

Unionized rail workers don't necessarily fear the private sector's participation. It is not intend to benefit any specific companies. And everyone knows it is hard to fully privatize Korail. The state operator will continue to control all rail networks. Private firms would only be allowed to provide some bullet train services. Introducing competition would result in higher efficiency, lower operational costs and cheaper fares.

This is not to say that the plan can solve all the problems. But private participation in KTX operations could be a starting point for change. We urge the government and ruling party to build a national consensus on this matter. They should map out wide-ranging railway reform before it's too late.

*** Source: The Korea Times (2012.1.15)**

References

Amos, P., Bullok, D. & Jitendra Sondhi, High Speed Rail: The Fast Track to Economic Development?, The World Bank, July 2010.

Baron, Thomas, Study on High Speed Rail Contribution to Sustainable Mobility, SYSTRA Conseil, Paris, September 2009.

Gwangju Metropolitan City (GMC), City Administration White Paper, 2000-2013 (in

Korean).

GMC, Gwangju Transportation Improvement Midterm Plan, 1996 (in Korean).

GMC, City Administration White Paper, 2000-2011 (Each Year) (in Korean).

GMC, Gwangju Metropolitan Transportation Master Plan, Final Draft, August 2007 (in Korean).

GMC, Gwangju Metropolitan Public Transportation Plan, 1st Draft, December 2011 (in Korean).

GMC, The 2nd Transportation Safety Master Plan, November 2012 (in Korean).

GMC, Gwangju Statistical Yearbook, Each Year (2000-2011) (in Korean).

Jeong, Bonghyun, New Transportation Policy in Regional Metropolitan City: Gwangju, Korea, CNU Press, 2005 (in Korean).

Jeong, Bonghyun, SOC and Regional Development: Standing Transportation Problems and Solutions in the Jeonlla Provinces, Korea, CNU Press, 2010 (in Korean).

Kim, Chun-Hwan, Transporation Revolution: The Korean Highway Speed Railway, 40 Years of High-speed Railways, Japan Railway & Transport Review 40, March 2005.

Lee, Dongmin et al., Economic Growth and Transport Models in Korea, KOTI Knowledge Sharing Report Issue 02, Korea Transport Institute (KOTI), 2012.

Lee, Yong-Sang, A Study of the Development and Issues concerning High Speed Rail, Working Paper N.1020, Transport Studies Unite, University of Oxford, January 2007.

Ministry of Land, Transport and Maritime Affairs (MLTMA), Plan for the Key National Traffic Network, 2nd Revised Plan(2001-2020), 2010 (in Korean).

Ministry of Land, Transport and Maritime Affairs (MLTMA), 2nd Master Plan for National Railroad Network (2011-2020), 2011 (in Korean).

Park, Jinyoung, Impact Assessment of High Speed Rail System in Korea, September 2013.

Shin, Dong-Chun, Recent Experience of and Prospects for High-speed Rail in Korea: Implication of a Transport System and Regional Development from a Global Perspective, Working Paper 2005-2, institute of Urban and Regional Development, University of California Berkeley, 2005.

Spillar, Robert J., Park-and-Ride Planning and Design Guidelines, Parsons Brinckerhoff Quade & Douglas, Inc, October 1997.

The Korea Transport Institute (KOTI), Construction of High Speed Rail in Korea, 2011 Modularization of Korea's Development Experience, 2012.
White, Peter, Public Transport, - Its Planning, Management and Operation, London: UCL Press, 1995.